PHILIPPIANS

THE NEW TESTAMENT DISCOURSE ANALYSIS COMMENTARIES SERIES

New Testament Discourse Analysis Commentaries (NTDAC) is a new and innovative commentary series on the Greek text of the New Testament. The volumes in the series pay close attention to the New Testament books as individual texts, based upon an explicit discourse analytic model articulated in the commentary and exemplified in the linguistic analysis.

Discourse analysis is an already proven productive method of textual interpretation for New Testament studies. It implies a theory of linguistic description that encompasses the smaller parts of language, such as words and even morphemes, but focuses upon the higher levels, such as the clause, the paragraph, and entire text as a meaningful unit. Discourse analysis—which may have a bottom up or a top down approach, or both—is not limited by traditional grammar but analyzes such linguistic features as the information structure, ideas and actions, and participant relations of a text, among other concerns. The interpretation provides both specific commentary supporting larger linguistic observations and broader commentary instantiated in textual particulars. The result is functional commentary useful to scholars for detailed knowledge of the Greek text and to practitioners for textually based information for preaching and teaching.

In the current landscape of commentary writing, in which commentaries have too often become simply comments on other commentaries, the NTDAC stands out by offering something different, compelling, and challenging. This is not to say that previous scholarship and reception history are irrelevant, but rather that the priority in the NTDAC is first and foremost a discourse analysis of the Greek text. In many ways, the series marks a return to what New Testament commentaries were originally designed to do, explicate the Greek text. However, the series seeks to do much more than that by introducing new observations on the Greek text that push interpretive boundaries and support previous findings by providing new linguistic insights.

The contributors to NTDAC approach the Greek text from a range of linguistic backgrounds. Nevertheless, they hold in common their desire to provide fresh interpretations of each book of the New Testament, based upon a specific discourse method.

STANLEY E. PORTER
MCMASTER DIVINITY COLLEGE
HAMILTON, ON, CANADA

PHILIPPIANS

JAE HYUN LEE

☙PICKWICK *Publications* · Eugene, Oregon

PHILIPPIANS

Copyright © 2025 Jae Hyun Lee. All rights reserved. Except for brief quotations in critical publications or reviews, no part of this book may be reproduced in any manner without prior written permission from the publisher. Write: Permissions, Wipf and Stock Publishers, 199 W. 8th Ave., Suite 3, Eugene, OR 97401.

Pickwick Publications
An Imprint of Wipf and Stock Publishers
199 W. 8th Ave., Suite 3
Eugene, OR 97401

www.wipfandstock.com

PAPERBACK ISBN: 978-1-5326-8650-4
HARDCOVER ISBN: 978-1-5326-8651-1
EBOOK ISBN: 978-1-5326-8652-8

Cataloguing-in-Publication data:

Names: Lee, Jae Hyun [author].

Title: Philippians / Jae Hyun Lee.

Description: Eugene, OR: Pickwick Publications, 2025 | New Testament Discourse Analysis Commentaries | Includes bibliographical references and index.

Identifiers: ISBN 978-1-5326-8650-4 (paperback) | ISBN 978-1-5326-8651-1 (hardcover) | ISBN 978-1-5326-8652-8 (ebook)

Subjects: LCSH: Bible.—Philippians—Commentaries. | Greek language, Biblical—Discourse analysis. | Bible.—New Testament—Language, style.

Classification: BS2705.53 L44 2025 (paperback) | BS2705.53 (ebook)

VERSION NUMBER 06/23/25

Unless otherwise specified, Scripture quotations are the author's own translation. Scripture quotations marked NASB are taken from the (NASB®) New American Standard Bible®, copyright © 1995 by The Lockman Foundation. Used by permission. All rights reserved. lockman.org

CONTENTS

Preface | vii

Abbreviations | ix

Introduction to the Letter to the Philippians | 1

    I. Historical Information | 2

    II. The Letter to the Philippians as a Text | 7

    III. The Contents of Philippians | 14

COMMENTARY ON PHILIPPIANS

1:1–2	**I. Letter Opening**	23
1:3–11	**II. Thanksgiving and Prayer**	30
1:3–8	A. Thanksgiving and intercessory prayer	32
1:9–11	B. The content of Paul's intercessory prayer	37
1:12—4:20	**III. The Body of the Letter**	42
1:12–26	A. About the situations caused by Paul's imprisonment	42
	1. 1:12–18A	43
	2. 1:18B–26	49
1:27—2:18	B. About the real problems of the church	56
	1. 1:27–30	57
	2. 2:1–4	63

	3. 2:5–11 | 68
	4. 2:12–18 | 78
2:19–30	C. Paul's plan to send Timothy and Epaphroditus | 87
	1. 2:19–24 | 87
	2. 2:25–30 | 91
3:1—4:1	D. About the potential problems of the church | 96
	1. 3:1–3 | 101
	2. 3:4–14 | 106
	3. 3:15—4:1 | 118
4:2–9	E. Final exhortations to the church | 130
	1. 4:2–3 | 131
	2. 4:4–9 | 134
4:10–20	F. A thank-you note for the gift from the church | 141
	1. 4:10–13 | 143
	2. 4:14–18 | 146
	3. 4:19–20 | 149
4:21–23	**IV. Letter Closing** | 151
4:21–22	A. Greetings | 151
4:23	B. Benediction | 153

Bibliography \| 155

Author Index \| 159

Subject Index \| 161

Scripture Index \| 165

PREFACE

WRITING A COMMENTARY ON PHILIPPIANS involves at least two challenging decisions. First, the author must decide how extensively to cite references. Philippians has been studied extensively throughout Christian history, resulting in a vast array of sermons, monographs, and journal articles. Should the author reference them all? Or to what extent should the author consider the references relevant and informative? This can be a challenge. Second, the author must decide how much detail to provide in their explication of the Philippians text. If every word is explained in detail, the commentary may become overwhelming for general readers, including ordinary Christians, to digest. However, if the explanation is too brief, readers may wonder why the author wrote the book in the first place. The answer to these questions ultimately depends on two factors: the intended audience and the author's goals for the commentary.

These two questions were no exception to the process of writing this commentary, but fortunately, they did not weigh heavily on my mind. This is due to the direction in which this commentary was written. The writing of this commentary began with a suggestion from Professor Stanley E. Porter, who was my supervisor. Porter made an offer with three conditions. The first was to utilize discourse analysis, a linguistic methodology I had previously employed in my dissertation. The second was to minimize references and provide explanations based on my understanding of the text. The third was not to write too long. His offer was so attractive that I had no choice but to accept it willingly, as it provided clear guidance on how to address the questions mentioned above.

However, the writing process was challenging. As this commentary is not a dissertation, using the same methodology as in my dissertation would have made it difficult for general readers. Therefore, I used a modified methodology to demonstrate my understanding of the text. Additionally, since the intended audience for this commentary includes ordinary believers and pastors who seek a clear understanding of the Bible's contents, I had to explain it without making it too complicated. In short, I had to write like a tightrope walker who kept the balance between being scholarly without being too academic and accessible to the layperson without losing insight into the text. It was not easy, but my role in connecting to students' real lives as a chaplain in a university environment was helpful. While writing this commentary, I aimed to bridge the gap between the academic realm and the practical life of the average Christian. I hope that readers of this commentary will see it from that perspective.

Writing a book is not a solitary endeavor. This book has benefited from the research and reflection of previous scholars and people of faith. I am grateful to all my seniors in the journey of faith. I am grateful to Professor Stanley E. Porter for suggesting that I write the commentary. He has always been a kind teacher and a reminder of God's grace. I am grateful to Sun Ah Jang for her help in writing and proofreading. I am also grateful to the students with whom I have studied through classes and Bible studies. They were another teacher who enriched my thinking. Finally, I would like to thank my wife and two daughters. They are the greatest gifts God has given me in my life.

JAE HYUN LEE
HANDONG GLOBAL UNIVERSITY
POHANG, SOUTH KOREA

ABBREVIATIONS

AYB	Anchor Yale Bible
BDAG	Danker, Frederick W., Walter Bauer, William F. Arndt, and F. Wilbur Gingrich. *Greek-English Lexicon of the New Testament and Other Early Christian Literature*. 3rd ed. Chicago: University of Chicago Press, 2000
BECNT	Baker Exegetical Commentary on the New Testament
BibInt	Biblical Interpretation Series
BLG	Biblical Languages: Greek
BNTC	Black's New Testament Commentaries
BZNW	Beihefte zur Zeitschrift für die neutestamentliche Wissenschaft
EDNT	*Exegetical Dictionary of the New Testament*. Edited by Horst Balz and Gerhard Schneider. ET. 3 vols. Grand Rapids: Eerdmans, 1990–93
EEC	Evangelical Exegetical Commentary
FN	*Filología neotestamentaria*
HThKNT	Herders Theologischer Kommentar zum Neuen Testament
JSNTSup	Journal for the Study of the New Testament Supplement Series
L&N	Louw, Johannes P., and Eugene A. Nida, eds. *Greek-English Lexicon of the New Testament: Based on Semantic Domains*. 2nd ed. New York: United Bible Societies, 1989
LBS	Linguistic Biblical Studies
LNTG	Library of New Testament Greek

LSJ	Liddell, Henry George, Robert Scott, Henry Stuart Jones. *A Greek-English Lexicon*. 9th ed. with revised supplement. Oxford: Clarendon, 1996
NTMon	New Testament Monographs
NAC	New American Commentary
NIBCNT	New International Biblical Commentary on the New Testament
NICNT	New International Commentary on the New Testament
NIGTC	New International Greek Testament Commentary
NTC	New Testament in Context
NovT	*Novum Testamentum*
PilNTC	Pillar New Testament Commentary
PSt	Pauline Studies
RevExp	*Review and Expositor*
SGBC	The Story of God Bible Commentary
SNTSMS	Society for New Testament Studies Monographs Series
SP	Sacra Pagina
TNTC	Tyndale New Testament Commentaries
WBC	Word Biblical Commentary

INTRODUCTION TO THE LETTER TO THE PHILIPPIANS

Philippians is one of the four Prison Letters, including Ephesians, Colossians, and Philemon, and it was sent to the church in the city of Philippi. Unlike Paul's other letters, this one does not contain any theological disputes or explicit doctrinal explanations. Even the passage about Jesus in 2:6–11 is not intended for a theological argumentation but serves as an example of exhortation on church issues that began in 2:1. In this regard, Philippians focuses entirely on the life of believers and the church, based on the relationship between Paul and his readers in the gospel. It offers many practical teachings, such as the proper life of believers, the relationship between the church and the ministers, working together in the gospel, the life of the church in the world, and the internal unity of the church.

How, then, should we approach and understand Philippians? While there are many ways, it is wise to begin by considering the two fundamental characteristics of this letter. The first is its historical context. The author and readers of this letter share a common point in time, the middle of the first century, and exist within their own space and circumstances in the actual stage of history. Thus, as a means of communication from the author to the readers, the letter is rooted in the reality of the circumstances of their lives. This contextual information can be found primarily in the text of the letter. However, for a proper understanding, it also needs to be reconstructed from other parts of the Bible and extra-biblical sources.

The second characteristic of Philippians is that it is a written text. Most of the letters in the New Testament, particularly those sent to churches, assume a situation where they are read aloud to the audience. However, the essence of a letter is that it is the product of an author's intention to communicate with the readers through the medium of text. This means that it shares the way people communicate through writing. Moreover, the letter is distinct in genre from poetry and the Gospels. Poetry often employs symbols and metaphors to convey the author's intent, while the Gospels primarily use narrative. Although the letter contains some narrative elements due to its historical context, its primary purpose is to communicate thematic information that reflects the author's intent. Therefore, it is essential to analyze the letter primarily by examining its logical progression in epistolary form and the methods used to convey information. This approach will help to uncover the author's themes and intentions.[1]

With these two characteristics in mind, this commentary will provide a detailed analysis and exposition of the Philippians. Before delving into the text, however, I will present some historical contextual information and outline the methodology I will use to approach it.

I. HISTORICAL INFORMATION

A. Author's situation

The author of Philippians is Paul (1:1). Although nineteenth-century scholar F. C. Baur questioned Paul's authorship, almost all modern scholars agree that Philippians is indeed the work of Paul. There are two primary pieces of historical information regarding the author. One is the place and time of writing, and the other is the situation of the author, both of which are interrelated. According to the text, the author is currently in prison (1:7, 12–14, 17). However, Paul does not specify the location of his imprisonment, which makes it difficult to estimate the place and time of writing. The book of Acts and other letters are crucial for tracing Paul's life and ministry. According to these sources, Paul was imprisoned for extended periods on two occasions, in addition to a brief imprisonment in Philippi.[2] One instance was his imprisonment in Caesarea. After completing his third missionary journey, Paul traveled to Jerusalem and was attacked by Jews. He was then imprisoned in Caesarea for two years while Roman officials dealt with his case (Acts 23:31—26:32). The other instance was his house arrest in Rome, where he awaited trial by the Roman emperor after being transported from Caesarea (Acts 28:30–31). If Philippians was written during Paul's

---

1. For more information about rhetorical devices in Pauline letters, see Porter, "Paul of Tarsus," 567–85.

2. During his second missionary journey, Paul might have also been imprisoned in Corinth for a trial by Gallio (Acts 19:12–17). However, this is not explicitly mentioned in Acts, and it is improbable that he wrote Philippians during this period.

imprisonment in Caesarea, it would date to around AD 57–59.³ Conversely, if it was written during his imprisonment in Rome, the time frame would be AD 60–62.⁴ However, there is another view. Although not mentioned in Acts, some scholars suggest that Paul was imprisoned in Ephesus during his third missionary journey (Acts 19:23–41) and wrote this letter then.⁵ If this is the case, Philippians was likely written between AD 52 and 55.⁶

Of the three views presented, Caesarea is the least likely. This is because both 1:18b–26 and 2:17 indicate that Paul anticipates his release but also has death in mind. During his imprisonment in Caesarea, however, Paul had appealed to the emperor following the Lord's revelation that he would go to Rome (Acts 23:11). Therefore, it is not appropriate to associate the Caesarea imprisonment with the prospect of death (Acts 25:21).

The case for Ephesus is also unconvincing because it is based on assumptions without biblical evidence. Despite these difficulties, the imprisonment in Ephesus has been postulated due to the long distance of over 1,900 km between Rome and Philippi.⁷ According to Philippians, there seems to be a sequence of events involving Epaphroditus: (1) news of Paul's imprisonment reached Philippi, (2) the Philippian church sent Epaphroditus, (3) the church received news of Epaphroditus's illness, and (4) Epaphroditus was distressed because the church had heard of his illness (2:25–26).⁸ If Paul had been imprisoned in Rome, the considerable travel time to Philippi would be inconsistent with the content and circumstances described in the letter. Therefore, Ephesus, which is relatively close, is suggested as the place of imprisonment instead of Rome.

However, if we consider the possibility of the temporal overlap in the processes related to Epaphroditus, the issue becomes easier to resolve. For example, in the process (3) mentioned above, if we assume that Epaphroditus became ill while traveling to Paul, and his companion(s) returned to the church to report the news, there is no need to establish a lengthy time

---

3. E.g., Hawthorne and Martin, *Philippians*, xxxix–l.

4. The chronology of Paul varies slightly among scholars. This timeline follows Schnabel, *Early Christian Mission*, 1:47–48; Riesner, "Chronology of Paul," 115.

5. E.g., Thielman, "Ephesus and Literary Setting"; Reumann, *Philippians*, 3; Hansen, *Philippians*, 19–25.

6. For the discussion of the issues regarding each viewpoint, see Keown, *Philippians 1:1—2:18*, 27–33.

7. Carson and Moo, *Introduction to New Testament*, 504.

8. In addition, Paul has several other plans related to his visit to Philippi. These include: (1) sending Epaphroditus to the Philippian church (2:25–30); (2) sending Timothy if the trial has a positive outcome (2:19, 23); (3) expecting Timothy to return with news about the church (2:19); and (4) planning to visit the Philippian church (2:24).

frame due to the long distance.⁹ In addition, in the process (4), it is possible that instead of assuming that someone from Philippi came to inform him of it, Epaphroditus anticipated the church's concern when sending someone in the middle.¹⁰ This explanation removes the need to establish a hypothetical imprisonment process based on the distance and time between Rome and Philippi.

What remains is the Roman imprisonment mentioned in Acts, which is the most likely explanation. Although not definitive, the internal evidence of the text supports this idea. One instance is the praetorian guard (πραιτώριον) (1:13). This term, a Latin transliteration, originally referred to the general's tent and its surroundings in the Roman army. Over time, it came to denote soldiers assigned to guard or accompany leaders and troops tasked with protecting the Roman emperor. In the context of Paul's imprisonment, it is more reasonable as referring to those guarding him or involved in his case. While the praetorian guard could have been deployed to other cities the emperor frequently visited, it seems more appropriate to associate them with Rome, where the emperor resided, rather than Ephesus or Caesarea. Another evidence is the mention of people from Caesar's household who sent greetings to the Philippian church with Paul in 4:22. These individuals likely refer to a small group of believers working within Caesar's household. It is far more plausible that they were based in Rome rather than in Ephesus or Caesarea.¹¹

In summary, Paul was imprisoned in Rome, awaiting the outcome of his trial by the emperor. Although he was later released and traveled to various places on a mission, he did not know the outcome when writing this letter. He expected to be released (1:25; 2:24), but if the outcome of his trial was unfavorable, he could face the death penalty. In this sense, Philippians might have been a kind of last testament to the readers.

---

9. Fee, *Philippians*, 277–78.

10. Holloway, *Philippians*, 24.

11. Traditionally, Rome has been recognized as the site of Paul's imprisonment, and many modern scholars support Roman imprisonment. O'Brien, *Philippians*, 16–26; Silva, *Philippians*, 5–7; Fee, *Philippians*, 34–37; Bockmuehl, *Philippians*, 25–32; Cohick, *Philippians*, 5–7; etc.

B. The situation of the readers

1. The city of Philippi

Philippi was a city in eastern Macedonia. Originally called Krenides, meaning "wells," it was conquered by Philip II, father of Alexander, in 356 BC and renamed after himself. In 168 BC, it became part of Rome and grew as a city on the Via Egnatia, a road that crosses the Greek peninsula from east to west.

An important feature of Philippi, relevant to the content of the letter, is that it was a Roman colony. This status was associated with two battles that followed the assassination of Julius Caesar. In 42 BC, the Brutus/Cassius faction, which had assassinated Caesar, fought against the Octavian/Antony faction near Philippi. After their victory, the Octavian/Antony faction relocated their veterans to Philippi and rebuilt the city. Later, in 31 BC, Octavian and Antony engaged in a battle at Actium for Roman supremacy. Following his victory, Octavian (later known as Augustus) relocated Antony's veterans to Philippi. He then granted Philippi *ius Italicum* (law of Italy), bestowing the same rights as Italy and making it a Roman colonial city with a new name, Colonia Augusta Iulia Philippensis, in honor of Augustus's daughter. The citizens of this city possessed Roman citizenship and enjoyed the corresponding privileges, which naturally fostered a strong loyalty to Rome. This loyalty can also be inferred from the widespread use of Latin in Philippi. Of the first-century inscriptions discovered so far, 85 percent are in Latin and approximately 15 percent are in Greek, which is a notable deviation from the general case in many Greco-Roman cities in Macedonia at that time.[12] This historical background and the atmosphere of Philippi created tension with Christians, who professed Jesus as their Lord instead of the Roman emperor. The citizens of Philippi, proud of their Roman citizenship, could not tolerate such a stance. As a result, Christians in Philippi likely faced physical, social, and economic hardships.

2. The church in Philippi

The Philippian church was established during Paul's second missionary journey (AD 49–51) as the first church in Macedonia. It appears that there were few Jews in Philippi and no synagogue, as Paul went outside the city to the river to pray on the Sabbath and met women there (Acts 16:13).[13] Lydia,

---

12. Porter, *Apostle Paul*, 330–31.
13. Keener, *Acts*, 3:2384.

a merchant of purple cloth, was the first person to be converted by Paul, and the jailer and his household were also among the first members. Later, Epaphroditus, Euodia, Syntyche, Clement, and others joined the church, but most were likely non-Jews.[14]

Paul visited the church at least two more times between its establishment and the writing of this letter (around AD 60–62 [Acts 20:1–2, 6]). The church continued to participate in missionary work through prayer and material support for about a decade after their first encounter with Paul (1:5; 4:15). They sent financial aid twice when Paul was in Thessalonica (4:16) and again when he was in Corinth (2 Cor 11:9; Acts 18:5). While in Corinth, Paul worked and ministered without the support of the Corinthian church because their support had intentions and purposes other than missions (1 Cor 1:12). However, he always welcomed and gratefully accepted the support of the Philippian church, knowing that their assistance was solely for participation in the work of the gospel. Furthermore, the Philippian church was a loving and serving community willing to give relief offerings to the Jerusalem church (Rom 15:26; 2 Cor 9:2). This time, when they heard that Paul was in prison, they sent necessary supplies through Epaphroditus (4:18).

The Philippian church faced various challenges. Externally, they were under pressure from citizens loyal to Rome (1:27–30; 2:14–15; 3:20–21; 4:5). While it is unclear whether this included the threat of martyrdom, they appeared to face severe physical, economic, and social hardships due to their confession of and service to Jesus the Messiah as Lord. This pressure was not solely a result of conflict with Rome but also arose from the clash between the church and the world of darkness, the rebellious realm opposing God. In the sense that Paul was also engaged in a struggle for truth in prison, confessing Jesus as the Lord against the authority of Rome, the Philippian church and Paul were in the same situation for the sake of the gospel (1:30).

Internally, the Philippian church faced a problem with division between two female leaders, Euodia and Syntyche. They were zealous for the gospel, but their rivalry and comparison seemed to have led to conflict (4:2). While the situation was not as severe as in the Corinthian church, if left unchecked, it could have hindered the church's ability to effectively spread the gospel amid the external pressures from the citizens of Philippi. Paul urged them to embrace each other with like-mindedness (2:1–12; 4:2) and encouraged others to assist in reconciling them (4:3).

Another issue in the Philippian church was the threat of false teachers (3:1—4:1). According to Paul's warning, they were Jewish Christians who

---

14. Keown, *Philippians 1:1—2:18*, 45.

emphasized circumcision, an identity marker of the old covenant. They insisted that non-Jewish believers must adopt Jewish practices to be considered true members of the new covenant. However, it does not appear that these false teachers had infiltrated the Philippian church or that the readers were directly under their influence. Unlike Galatians and 2 Corinthians, where false teachers directly impacted the church, there is no direct refutation of them or harsh criticism of the church for following them in this text. Instead, Paul offers a milder warning. Nevertheless, based on Paul's past experience, they were a potential threat that could shake the church with a predominantly non-Jewish membership. Recognizing that the Philippian church might become a target for their teachings, Paul issued a preemptive warning to his beloved congregation.

II. THE LETTER TO THE PHILIPPIANS AS A TEXT

A. How to approach the text: a linguistic methodology

As a use of language, the letter is a written mode of communication that transmits information from the author to the reader based on their respective histories and situations.[15] It contains at least three pieces of information centered around a core message: contextual, interpersonal, and textual. Contextual information relates to the history and situation and is divided into three levels in relation to the text: (1) the context of culture, (2) the context of situation, and (3) the context of text. The context of culture refers to the "large and complex knowledge system spread between the various members of a particular culture," which provides the institutional and ideological background for interpreting the text.[16] This context is the broadest of the three contexts. The context of situation is "the immediate historical situation in which a discourse occurs."[17] The context of the text, which is called the textual context, is further divided by M. A. K. Halliday into two categories: intertextual and intracontextual. The intertextual context involves assumptions that are drawn from other texts, while the intracontext, or "co-text," refers to the context within a text.[18] Of the three levels of con-

---

15. According to Teun A. van Dijk, the nature of a discourse has three aspects: (1) the use of language; (2) the communication of beliefs; and (3) the interaction in a social situation. In this sense, the letter has typical characteristics of a discourse ("Study of Discourse Analysis," 2).

16. Halliday and Hasan, *Language, Context, and Text*, 48–49.

17. Leckie-Tarry, *Language and Context*, 20.

18. Reed, *Discourse Analysis of Philippians*, 42.

text, the context of culture can be obtained from extratextual sources, such as archaeology or ancient literature, whereas the other two are primarily identified through the text itself.

Interpersonal information pertains to the relationship among the various participants in a given text. It includes information about the actual author and readers of the letter, as well as the various individuals and entities involved in the subject matter addressed by the author. Textual information is conveyed through the text itself and contains elements of both contextual and interpersonal information. Consequently, the letter can be understood as a text that conveys the elements of how (how) to deliver a topic (what) related to a person (who) in a specific environment (in what situation).[19] These elements provide valuable clues for analyzing the letter and understanding its content and the author's intention.

How, then, should we identify these three kinds of information in a text? With regard to contextual information, since this information is conveyed through words or expressions within various elements of a clause or sentence, it is important to observe the information corresponding to the who (subject), does (verb), what to whom (object), and in what situation (adjunct) elements in the clause. For instance, the situation of the author, Paul, in Philippians can be discerned from expressions such as "my chains" (1:7, 13, 14, 17), which refers to his imprisonment, and "death" in reference to him (1:20; 2:8), which indicates his uncertain future. On the other hand, one of the readers' situations can be inferred from expressions related to citizenship (πολιτεύεσθε [live as a citizen] [1:27]), which suggests that their situation is influenced by the atmosphere in the city of Philippi. To reconstruct the precise circumstances, however, it is necessary to consider the cultural context of the city of Philippi, known for its loyalty to Rome in matters of citizenship, with the help of sources beyond the text.

Interpersonal information can be identified primarily by examining personal pronouns and nouns used as subjects or objects and analyzing the gender, number, mood, and voice of the verb. For instance, in 1:12–26, the primary grammatical or logical subject is Paul, indicated by first-person references, which reveals that the text focuses on Paul's experiences. In this context, additional information about those around him, including their

---

19. This concept is related to what M. A. K. Halliday, a systemic functional linguist, insists. He proposes that the situational knowledge(context) consists of three components: field (the "what is taking place" part of a situation), tenor (the type of role interaction among participants), and mode (the function of the text in the event), and that each component is realized through three functional components of semantics in a text, such as ideational (content), interpersonal (participants), and textual components, respectively (*Language as Social Semiotic*, 123).

actions and intentions, can be inferred from the referents and verbs about the two groups preaching the gospel.

Regarding textual information, it is crucial to consider two inherent characteristics: sequentiality and hierarchy. Sequentiality refers to the progression of a text through a series of logical and semantic relations until the author has conveyed all the intended information. It involves combining and connecting each discourse unit, such as clauses, sentences, paragraphs, and sections, through lexico-grammatical cohesion and cognitive coherence to reach the intended end point of the information. Sequentiality is also related to the context of a text (co-text), in that the current text that the reader is reading is situated within the context of the author's ongoing themes and is narrated in a logical relationship with the previous and subsequent contents. To identify sequentiality, one should examine the continuity and discontinuity within the text through conjunctions, words, and expressions centered on paragraph-level units containing one topic. It is also important to examine the progression of the topic through logical relationships and connections within it.

Hierarchy is a method of structuring text through appropriate relationships between more important and less important information to help the reader discern the author's intent. This connection is commonly called a head-tail relationship, which can be observed within words and across clauses, sentences, paragraphs, and higher textual units. To identify hierarchical relationships, it is necessary to analyze the author's intent by examining various emphatic expressions at the level of clauses and sentences and beyond the sentence.

For actual analysis of the text to identify the author's intentions, the three types of information mentioned above should be examined in a three-step process.

(1) The first step is grouping, which involves analyzing the co-textual information and the sequence of the text to determine the extent to which a topic advances through its connections. This step requires identifying continuities and discontinuities at the beginning of a paragraph or section. In general, a paragraph or section of a letter begins by establishing a connection to the previous part before proceeding with its content. This connection is typically made through conjunctions, topical words, rhetorical devices, or information about the person and the temporal/spatial situation. The degree of continuity or discontinuity between the two parts provides clues to identify each paragraph or section's scope and locational function. For instance, a paragraph may be regarded as a new paragraph if it differs from the previous paragraph with respect to the information mentioned above. However, if there is a connection through causal or inferential

conjunctions, or if the same person or subject remains consistent, it is not a transition to a completely new topic. Instead, it may be seen as an additional explanation or another aspect of the same topic within the course of logical development. In cases where there is an apparent disconnection from the preceding text, however, the paragraph may be considered the beginning of a new section. Moreover, even clusters of paragraphs or sections may have logical relationships. Therefore, it is essential to determine whether they are entirely separate or part of a larger topic This can also be achieved by checking the degree of continuity of themes, characters, etc.

(2) The second step is to identify the topical elements. This process comprises three main tasks. The first task is to examine the structure of the paragraph. To do this, it is necessary to observe three different types of clauses. One is the primary clause. It is an independent clause that does not depend on or subordinate to any other clause. It serves to introduce new information or lead the message toward its intended goal. The primary clause is typically constituted by a finite or imperative verb, although it may also consist of a nonfinite verb other than an imperative or be verbless. Another type of clause is the secondary clause. It typically indicates a relationship of dependency or subordination to the primary clause through subordinating particles or conjunctions. Its primary role is to elucidate the primary clause in various ways. Rather than altering the content of the primary clause, the secondary clause provides additional information about the process described in the primary clause. This may include the projection of an idea, the presentation of a logical reason or consequence, or offering elaboration or enhancement, all of which are intended to keep the reader engaged with the message of the primary clause. The third type is the embedded clause. Unlike the secondary clause, which supports the process related to the verb in the primary clause, the embedded clause is inserted into the structure of another clause to explain a particular element. It often begins with a relative pronoun or a participle and serves to pause and focus on the message of the primary clause rather than moving or advancing it. In sum, it is crucial to analyze these three types of clauses and understand the structure and progression of the paragraph to identify the author's intent.

The second task in identifying the topical elements is to examine the characters. In general, the characters are presented within the context of the topic that the author intends to convey. However, since not all characters are relevant to the topic, it is necessary to observe the people who participate in the interaction centered on the process conveyed by the verbs. When examining the subject of a verb, it is important to consider both the grammatical and logical subject, as well as the voice of the verb. The grammatical subject is the entity designated as the subject by the nominative in Greek.

Depending on the voice of the verb, the subject of a passive verb focuses on the recipient of the process, while that of an active verb focuses on the doer of the process. In contrast, the logical subject refers to the actual entity who actually performs the process indicated by the verb, regardless of the voice of the verb. By distinguishing between these types of subjects and examining their roles in the process, the relationships between the characters and the topic can be clarified.

The third task in identifying topical elements is to analyze the words and expressions in the text. This involves examining the frequency of words and expressions, as those that appear more frequently are more relevant to the topic the author intends to convey. However, when analyzing word frequency, it is crucial not only to consider repeated occurrences of the same word but also to account for words that belong to the same semantic domain or have semantic relationships, such as antonyms, hyponyms (e.g., color and blue), or meronyms (e.g., body and hand). This is because the author may use diverse vocabulary to communicate the topic. In addition, when identifying topics through words and expressions in the text, it is important to consider their position and the amount of information they convey. For example, a word or expression in the primary clause is more likely to serve as a topical element than one located in the embedded clause. Furthermore, words or expressions that are repeated in the primary clause or supported by relatively much information through the subordinate or the embedded clauses are more likely to be a topic element.

(3) The third step is to determine the significance of the information. It involves analyzing the hierarchy of textual information in the paragraph to identify the author's intent. One effective method is to examine prominence features at the within-sentence level. As a way the author conveys the relative importance of specific information, prominence can be defined as "semantic and grammatical elements of discourse that serve to set aside certain subjects, ideas, or motifs of the text as more or less semantically and pragmatically significant than others."[20] Prominence is expressed through various grammatical and semantic forms and syntagmatic orders, including particles, verbal aspect, word order, clause relationships, clause ordering, and more.[21] Moreover, it is essential to assess the significance of the infor-

---

20. Reed and Reese, "Verbal Aspect," 186. David I. Yoon defines prominence as "a semantic description of a linguistic element based on observable deviations of normal patterns of marked/unmarked elements in relation to a particular discourse" ("Prominence in NT Discourse," 5–6).

21. For detailed explanations and examples of the prominence features, see Porter, "Prominence"; Porter and O'Donnell, *Discourse Analysis*, 128–89; Lee, *Paul's Gospel in Romans*, 68–79.

mation at levels beyond the sentence. This process involves examining the logical progression, using conjunctions, the quantity of information provided, and the form of emphasis achieved through rhetorical expressions.[22]

The point to keep in mind here is to maintain awareness of the interconnectedness between the relatively important information identified through observation and the structure and topical elements of the paragraph. When composing a letter, the author typically employs a top-down approach, starting with a comprehensive understanding of the topic they wish to convey and then elaborating on it through constructing individual clauses and sentences. In this context, the use of individual emphases serves to convey the intended topic rather than as an end in itself. For instance, in a head-tail relationship, the secondary or embedded clause is the tail, while the primary clause is the head. Accordingly, the emphasis or lengthy information provided in the secondary and embedded clauses functions to underscore the importance of the message in the primary clause, which is the head. Furthermore, since there is a logical head-tail relationship among the primary clauses, the emphatic expressions in the tail can be understood as reinforcing the content of the head clause.

In the end, to discern the author's intent in a text, it is essential to (1) identify the paragraphs and sections using grouping methods, (2) analyze the structure, characters, and words within each paragraph to identify the topical elements, and (3) determine the significance of the conveyed information through various emphatic expressions and connect it to the topical elements. Each step involves examining individual elements of the text, organizing and synthesizing them, and considering their relationships to one another.

In addition to these ways of analyzing a text, it is also important to consider the characteristics of the letter format since Philippians is a letter. The typical letter format of the time followed a tripartite structure: an introduction with information about the sender and recipient, including a greeting; a body containing the author's main message; and a closing. However, Paul's letters often include a section of prayer for the readers and thanksgiving before the body or ethical exhortations between the body and closing.[23] In many cases, Paul uses a four- or five-part format based on the three-part structure. More importantly, he uses the format as a means to convey his intentions to the readers. Therefore, to understand Paul's intent in Philippians, it is necessary to compare its format and content with his other letters.

---

22. Lee, *Paul's Gospel in Romans*, 80–84.
23. McDonald and Porter, *Early Christianity*, 380–86.

INTRODUCTION TO THE LETTER TO THE PHILIPPIANS

In this commentary on Philippians, I will apply the three-step methodology mentioned above to analyze and approach the text while considering the format of the letter. However, I will not analyze each process separately as I have done in other works. Instead, I will divide paragraphs and explain each content in logical progression units, as is typical of other general commentaries. Nevertheless, all descriptions will be guided by the three steps, with observations integrated throughout. In other words, I will present the results of the discourse analysis in the format of a general commentary.

B. Unity of the text

Before analyzing the text of Philippians using the discourse analysis method briefly mentioned above, it is necessary to address one issue: the unity of the text. Although Philippians is a relatively short letter, modern scholars continue to debate its unity due to perceived traces of disunity within the text.[24] For instance, some scholars view the sudden mention of external problems of the church in 1:27–28 or the thanksgiving for the gift of the Philippian church in 4:10–20 as out of place and not aligned with the proper flow of the letter. Additionally, the expression τὸ λοιπόν (finally) in 3:1 and 4:8 is a frequent point of contention. Since this phrase is commonly used at the end of a letter (e.g., 2 Cor 13:11), some argue that 3:1 marks the end of a separate letter. Scholars have questioned the unity of Philippians based on internal and external evidence, with some suggesting that it may be a combination of two or three letters.[25]

What is certain, however, is that the existing manuscripts provide no evidence to support the composition theory. Consequently, those who doubt the unity of Philippians must first answer several questions related to external textual evidence before asserting their hypothesis. If Philippians is a composite of several letters, who compiled it and when? Why were the original letters divided to create a new one? What happened to the original letters that were separated and to those that were not included?[26]

Furthermore, the lack of external evidence means that arguments for doubting the unity of the text are based solely on textual interpretation. However, before arguing for the hypothesis of a composite letter, proponents must address several questions from a hermeneutical perspective. For instance, why should changes in tone or atmosphere necessarily be

---

24. Including a recent commentary of J. Reumann (*Philippians*, 8–13).

25. Stanley E. Porter addresses nine cases that are presented as evidence of disunity and offers a rebuttal (*Apostle Paul*, 334–42).

26. Porter, *Apostle Paul*, 39–42; Hansen, *Philippians*, 18.

interpreted as insertions from another letter? Does this not impose an arbitrary standard of what scholars consider a consistent flow on Paul? Since a letter is intended to communicate with the reader according to the situation of both the author and the reader, is it not possible for the author to write in varying tones or styles depending on the circumstances or the author's intention to emphasize a specific topic? For example, after discussing his circumstances in 1:12–26, Paul might have shifted his tone in 1:27 to focus on the issues of the church. Such a shift does not inherently present any problems. Similarly, expressing gratitude for the church's gift later in the text is entirely acceptable because there is no rule dictating that it must appear at the beginning. It is ultimately up to the author to use any method to articulate his intentions. In the case of τὸ λοιπόν in 3:1, it also functions as a topic introducer in Paul's other letters (1 Thess 4:1; 2 Thess 3:1), as well as 4:8 of Philippians itself. Therefore, it can reasonably be interpreted as a shift in the topic rather than an indication of a separate letter.[27] Moreover, Philippians demonstrates overall integrity through both verbal and thematic parallels, which makes it difficult to view it as merely a compilation of separate letters.[28] Notably, the letter presents the inside-out pattern that inward discernment is expressed through outward actions, which Paul introduces in his intercessory prayer, as an overarching principle that runs through it.[29]

In conclusion, the changes in the flow of the letter that scholars have identified should not be automatically interpreted as interpolations or combinations of other letters. If the question of the unity of Philippians is solely a matter of textual interpretation, it is more appropriate to tentatively recognize it as a single letter with multiple intentions for the readers. Additionally, different hermeneutical approaches can be employed within its analysis until definitive external evidence from the manuscripts emerges.

III. THE CONTENTS OF PHILIPPIANS

A. Major topics

Based on the content of the letter, there are four main topics that Paul addresses. The first is an introduction to his current status. Paul seeks to comfort the Philippian church, which is concerned about his imprisonment, by informing them of his situation. This topic appears in 1:12–26, the first part of the body of the letter.

---

27. Keown, *Philippians 1:1—2:18*, 18–21.
28. As for this, see Holloway, *Philippians*, 18–19.
29. Lee, "'Think' and 'Do.'"

The second topic is Paul's gratitude to the Philippians for their service, specifically for the gift sent through Epaphroditus (4:10-20; 2:25). However, Paul's appreciation extends beyond the material gift itself. He values their love and commitment because the gift reflects the heart of the Philippian church, which has supported his ministry of the gospel for nearly a decade. Paul's sincere appreciation is also evident in 1:3-11.

The third topic is Paul's admonition concerning the situation of the church. The church faced external pressure from the city of Philippi and internal conflict among its members. These situations serve as the background for the exhortations in 1:27—2:18 and 4:2-3. Additionally, Paul includes a warning to beware of the Judaizers (3:1—4:1). Although this is not an actual situation in the Philippian church, Paul, based on his past experiences with other churches, preemptively warns them that false teachers could pose a future threat.

The fourth topic is Paul's recommendation of Timothy and Epaphroditus (2:19-30). Paul plans to send Epaphroditus back to the church since he has recovered from his illness. Epaphroditus is likely the one carrying this letter to the Philippian church. Timothy, on the other hand, is the person Paul intends to send later to inform the church of the positive outcome of his trial. Both Timothy and Epaphroditus are familiar to the church, as Timothy was present when Paul founded it, and the church sent Epaphroditus to Paul. Nevertheless, Paul introduces them as valuable ministers who have sacrificed themselves for the sake of the gospel. This is to encourage the church to view them as models of faith to follow and to show hospitality to them.

B. Bridging the Letter to the Philippians to the modern Christians

1. How to live as a Christian in the world?

Despite their faith in Jesus, believers continue to live in this sinful world. The question arises: How should they live in it? In what could be seen as a testament, Paul offers a guiding principle to his beloved readers through the content of his intercessory prayer (1:9-11). This principle is a life of love with discernment through the knowledge of God and the wisdom of the Holy Spirit.

This principle largely encompasses two processes. The first is the process of discernment, which involves two key steps for believers. The first step is to have a standard for discernment. This standard should not be based on worldly principles or personal or church needs but on the knowledge of God, including his will and what he expects. The second step is to actively discern according to this standard. It requires wisdom, especially the wisdom imparted by the Holy Spirit. The second process in the principle of the believer's life is to follow the outcome of the proper discernment and live a life of love in truth until the Lord returns. These two processes have a thorough "inside-out" pattern, beginning with transforming inner thought and expressing it in outer attitudes and actions.

Throughout the letter, Paul consistently presents this principle by placing words of thought before words of action, and he summarizes it in his final exhortation to the readers in 4:8–9. If this is the principle of the believer's life that the aged apostle in prison tries to convey in his letter to the Philippian church, whom he loves and who loves him, then all believers should listen to it, take it to heart, and live their lives accordingly. This principle is essential for all believers who must live as God's people in this world.

2. Models of faith

Philippians presents several individuals as models of the believer's life. The ultimate example is Jesus (2:6–11), who perfectly embodies a life of love with discernment, following the elements of thought and action mentioned above. Paul also offers himself as a model (3:17), not because his life is perfect but because he continually strives to pursue Jesus. Other examples are those who pursue Jesus by following Paul's example (3:17), including Timothy (2:19–24) and Epaphroditus (2:25–30). Paul mentions these individuals to encourage the members of the Philippian church to observe them and imitate their way of life.

Living as a believer in the world means creating one's own history of faith before God. However, this is not an isolated journey but part of a long procession of numerous predecessors and successors of faith. The apostle Paul teaches his readers that the history of faith, which involves walking in the right way before God, must continue by following role models of faith. Today's churches are the successors of a faith that dates back two thousand years, and they also serve as the predecessors of the faith for future generations. It is essential to leave behind the footsteps of the right faith.

3. The church in the world and the witness of the gospel

The church in Philippi faced both internal and external challenges. Internally, there was conflict arising from competition and comparison among its members. In response, Paul calls for unity. However, he does not propose that they should be united merely because they belong to the same church. Instead, he emphasizes the role of the church as a conduit for revealing the Lord's gospel (1:4-7). This relates to the external pressure from the citizens loyal to Rome. Paul urges the Philippian church to maintain internal unity and solidarity, to stand firm in the gospel, and to reveal God's truth and love to a world that rejects him (1:27—2:18). After all, one of the primary reasons for the existence of the church on earth is to serve as a channel of life through which the light of God's gospel flows to a broken world. For this, the church must be united internally in the truth and love; externally, it must reveal truth through love. The letter to the Philippians illustrates the position and role of the church in the world well.

4. Faith expecting the end-time

The church and its members persevere in the world for the sake of the gospel, relying on the promise of complete salvation in the future. At that time, the world, which threatens the church with its power and authority, will be judged and destroyed. In contrast, those who endure the pressure and suffering of the world will experience future salvation (1:28). Furthermore, believers will enjoy a perfect relationship with God and Jesus through a new body in the resurrection (3:20-21). Throughout Philippians, Paul encourages his readers to maintain this perspective and to continue living in the gospel despite any difficulties they may face. Today's believers and churches should follow Paul's teaching and example and anticipate the consummation of future salvation while enduring in the gospel. This is one of the appropriate applications of Philippians.

C. Outline

I. Letter Opening (1:1-2)

    A. Senders and recipients (1:1)

    B. Greeting (1:2)

II. Thanksgiving and Prayer (1:3-11)

    A. Thanksgiving and intercessory prayer (1:3-8)

        1. Thanksgiving and intercessory prayer (1:3-4)

        2. The reason for intercessory prayer (1:5-8)

    B. The content of Paul's intercessory prayer (1:9-11)

III. The Body of the Letter (1:12—4:20)
   A. About the situations caused by Paul's imprisonment (1:12–26)
      1. Two external situations (1:12–18a)
         a. A report on Paul's situation (1:12–14)
         b. Two kinds of proclaimers (1:15–17)
         c. Paul's response (1:18a)
      2. Paul's internal situation (1:18b–26)
         a. Another report on Paul's situation (1:18b–20)
         b. Paul's dilemma (1:21–24)
         c. Paul's confidence and reason/purpose (1:25–26)
   B. About the real problems of the church (1:27—2:18)
      1. About the external problem of the church (1:27–30)
         a. Paul's command (1:27a)
         b. The purpose of the command and additional explanations (1:27b–30)
      2. About the internal problems of the church (2:1–4)
         a. Paul's command on the internal problem of the church (2:1–2)
         b. Additional commands (2:3–4)
      3. Jesus Christ, the supreme model for the church (2:5–11)
         a. Introductory command (2:5)
         b. The example of Jesus (2:6–11)
      4. Concluding exhortations on the problems of the church (2:12–18)
         a. Command 1: On the internal problem (2:12–13)
         b. Command 2: On the external problem (2:14–16)
         c. The rejoicings of Paul and the readers (2:17–18)
   C. Paul's plan to send Timothy and Epaphroditus (2:19–30)
      1. Paul's plan to send Timothy (2:19–24)
         a. Paul's plan to send Timothy (2:19)
         b. A reason to choose Timothy (2:20–22)
         c. Reiteration of Paul's plans (2:23–24)
      2. Paul's plan to send Epaphroditus (2:25–30)
         a. Paul's plan to send Epaphroditus (2:25–28)

INTRODUCTION TO THE LETTER TO THE PHILIPPIANS

        b. Paul's command regarding Epaphroditus (2:29–30)

    D. About the potential problems of the church (3:1—4:1)

        1. A warning against the Judaizers (3:1–3)

            a. Introduction (3:1)

            b. A warning against the Judaizers (3:2–3)

        2. The example of Paul's past and present (3:4–14)

            a. Paul's situation before being saved (3:4–6)

            b. Paul's situation after being saved 1 (3:7–11)

            c. Paul's situation after being saved 2 (3:12–14)

        3. Application to the readers and Paul's command (3:15—4:1)

            a. Concluding exhortations (3:15–16)

            b. Concluding commands 1 (3:17–21)

            c. Concluding command 2 (4:1)

    E. Final exhortations to the church (4:2–9)

        1. Toward a unity of the church (4:2–3)

            a. Appeal to Euodia and Syntyche (4:2)

            b. Appeal to another person (4:3)

        2. Toward a proper Christian life (4:4–9)

            a. General command (4:4)

            b. To the outsiders (4:5)

            c. About prayer (4:6–7)

            d. Concluding commands (4:8–9)

    F. A thank-you note for the gift from the church (4:10–20)

        1. Paul's joy (4:10–13)

            a. Paul's joy over the gift from the readers (4:10)

            b. Additional comment (4:11–13)

        2. Paul's commendation (4:14–18)

            a. Paul's commendation of the readers (4:14–16)

            b. Additional comment (4:17–18)

        3. Paul's wish and doxology (4:19–20)

IV. Letter Closing (4:21–23)

    A. Greetings (4:21–22)

    B. Benediction (4:23)

COMMENTARY ON
PHILIPPIANS

PHILIPPIANS 1:1–2

OUTLINE:

I. Letter Opening (1:1–2)

II. Thanksgiving and Prayer (1:3–11)

    A. Thanksgiving and intercessory prayer (1:3–8)

    B. The content of Paul's intercessory prayer (1:9–11)

I. LETTER OPENING (1:1–2)

IN LINE WITH THE LETTER-WRITING customs of his era, Paul begins his letter by identifying the senders and recipients and offering a greeting. This opening contains two distinct groups of participants. The first group is the human participants, including Paul and Timothy as the senders and the saints in Philippi as the recipients. The second group is the divine participants, namely God and Jesus, who are introduced as the source of identity for the human participants since both the senders and the recipients belong to Jesus. Moreover, the divine group is presented as those who maintain the relationship between Paul and the readers. In essence, this introduction of each participant group and the salutation serves as a boundary indicator, signaling the start of the letter. The structure of this unit is as follows.

1. Senders and recipients (1:1)
    1) Senders: Paul and Timothy
    2) Recipients: The saints, including overseers and deacons in Philippi
2. Greeting: Grace and peace to you from God and Jesus Christ (1:2)

A) 1:1

In the opening of his letter, Paul introduces himself and Timothy as servants of Christ Jesus. There are three notable features in this introduction. The first feature is its brevity. Philippians provides the shortest elaboration on the senders among Paul's letters, except for 1 and 2 Thessalonians, which do not elaborate on the senders. The second feature is that Paul does not mention his apostleship but designates himself as a servant of Christ Jesus. While in some of his letters Paul does not mention "apostle" in the opening part (1 and 2 Thessalonians, Philippians, and Philemon) or calls himself both an apostle and a servant of Christ (Romans and Titus), Philippians is the only letter in which he introduces himself as a servant of Christ without mentioning "apostle." The third feature is the use of the plural form δοῦλοι (servants) to introduce Timothy as a co-sender, implying that Timothy has the same status as Paul as a servant of Christ. However, this does not mean that Timothy cowrote the letter. The predominant use of first-person singular references (fifty-seven pronouns and sixty-six verbs) indicates that Paul is the author.[1] In other Pauline letters, Timothy is mentioned as a co-sender in six instances, although he is not the author. Notably, except in 1 and 2 Thessalonians, Timothy is never introduced on an equal footing with Paul. Thus, the phrasing used in this introduction is quite distinctive.

Why, then, does Paul begin his letter with such an introduction? A clue to the answer can be gleaned in Paul's other letters, where he does not mention his apostleship. In nine of his thirteen letters, Paul introduces himself as an apostle, regardless of whether he founded the church. The exceptions are 1 and 2 Thessalonians and Philemon, including Philippians. In 1 and 2 Thessalonians, Paul does not elaborate on the senders but simply lists the church's founders. Commentators suggest that the situation of the church is the main reason for Paul's omission of apostleship in these letters.[2] However,

---

[1]. Reed, *Discourse Analysis of Philippians*, 184–85.

[2]. For example, Charles A. Wanamaker explains that Paul does not mention his apostleship because his apostleship is not an issue in the church in Thessalonica

it is more significant that Paul explicitly states in the body of the letters that he does not want to exercise his apostleship over the Thessalonian church (1 Thess 2:7; 2 Thess 3:9). Similarly, in Philemon, Paul expresses that he is not using apostolic authority in the matter of Onesimus (Phlm 8–9). These examples demonstrate that the way Paul introduces himself in the introduction part is connected to the content of the body of the letter, which he presents later. This pattern is also evident in Philippians.

Paul does not present himself as an apostle. Instead, he uses the term "apostle" only to describe Epaphroditus, who was sent by the church, in accordance with the original meaning of the word "apostle" (ἀπόστολος) as a "sent one" (2:25). Moreover, in the letter, Paul addresses his readers as coworkers in the ministry of the gospel (1:5–7; 4:15–16), beloved with the heart of Jesus (1:8; 2:12), brothers and sisters (1:12; 3:1, 13, 17; 4:1, 8), and his joy and crown (4:1). This shows that although Paul is an apostle and the founder of the Philippian church, he is not writing the letter from a position of authority as an apostle. Instead, he writes as a coworker in the ministry of the gospel in Christ, emphasizing the importance of giving and receiving love. Therefore, the decision to omit to mention his apostleship in the introduction part can be seen as a strategic choice that sets the tone for the letter in a more intimate and relational sense. It reflects how he intends to unfold the content of the body of the letter.

Could this strategic intent be present in other elements of information about the sender? It is very likely. Let us examine them one by one. The first thing to consider is the brevity of the introduction to the sender. While we can only speculate why Paul wrote it so concisely, there are likely two reasons.

One possibility is that, as in the case of 1 and 2 Thessalonians, the readers already knew Paul well, obviating the need for a long and elaborate introduction. The opposite case is found in Romans, where he wrote a letter to the church he had not established himself. In that case, Paul might have felt the need to introduce himself more extensively. In Philippians, however, the situation may not have required a lengthy self-introduction from Paul.

Another reason could be that the subsequent content of the letter primarily focuses on matters other than Paul himself. The entire content of this letter is actually intended for the readers. Although Paul provides the information on his current condition in 1:12–26, it is to reassure concerned readers about his imprisonment, so the focus of this section is also on the readers. Additionally, Paul's explanation of his past and present situation in 3:5–14 is meant to provide a counterexample in relation to the potential

---

(*Epistles to the Thessalonians*, 68).

threat of false teachers. In conclusion, Paul seems to have omitted a lengthy introduction about himself in order to focus more on the situation of his readers who knew him well.

Paul's strategic choice is also reflected in the second feature of the presentation of the sender, where he identifies himself as a servant of Christ. At first glance, this expression may appear ordinary, as it also appears in the other letters of Paul. However, considering its connection to the subsequent content of the letter, at least three thematic links can be discerned.

The first theme is related to belonging and affiliation. The genitive case Χριστοῦ Ἰησοῦ (of Christ Jesus) implies that Paul belongs to Christ and should therefore be loyal to him alone. Loyalty to Christ is presented as both the core issue behind the church's external problem and the primary means of overcoming it in 1:27–30. The members of the Philippian church are facing pressure from the citizens of Philippi because of their loyalty to Jesus rather than the Roman emperor. In response, Paul urges them to remain steadfast in their loyalty to Jesus and not succumb to this pressure.

The second theme is the attitude of servanthood. During that time, the term "servant" (δοῦλος) was associated with a lowly position and humble obedience to one's master. Interestingly, in addressing the internal conflicts of the church, Paul uses the same word to present Jesus as an example for them to imitate (2:7). He urges the readers to treat one another with humble service, just as Jesus, the Lord of all believers, became a servant and demonstrated such an attitude.

The third theme is being a model for the believer's life. Several times in the body of the letter, Paul presents himself as an example for his readers to follow. When dealing with the external problem of the church, he introduces himself as a model for his readers to emulate and endure by stating that he, too, is under pressure from Rome because of his loyalty to Christ (1:30). Furthermore, in 3:17 and 4:9, he directly commands them to imitate his pursuit of Christ and to strive to be like him. In summary, Paul's self-identification as a servant of Christ foreshadows one of the keys to understanding the content he later presents to the church in the body of the letter.

Paul's strategic choice regarding the introduction of the senders is also reflected in the portrayal of Timothy as a fellow servant of Jesus. In 2:19–24, when Paul presents his plan to send Timothy to the church, he uses ἐδούλευσεν, the cognate verb of δοῦλος (servant) to describe Timothy as one who served with him (σὺν ἐμοὶ ἐδούλευσεν) in the ministry of the gospel. According to this link, Paul's intention in introducing Timothy at the beginning of the letter is twofold. First, he wants to provide a preliminary recommendation of Timothy, whom Paul will mention in the body of the letter.

Second, he seeks to present Timothy as a model of loyalty and humility in the service of Jesus, encouraging the readers to hold him in high esteem.

After introducing the senders, Paul addresses his recipients using the dative case. His expressions have both common elements with other letters and unique aspects specific to this letter. The phrase "to all the saints in Christ Jesus who are in Philippi" is a common expression that reflects two aspects of the readers' reality.

The first aspect is their relationship with God. The term "saints" is used to refer to the members of the church. Paul draws from the Old Testament, where God consecrated Israel as a holy nation and the covenant people for his service (Exod 19:6; Lev 11:44; 19:2; etc.). However, this does not mean that the readers are or should be the Israel of the old covenant. By adding "in Christ Jesus" (ἐν Χριστῷ Ἰησοῦ), Paul makes it clear that the identity of his readers is based solely on Jesus. Through Jesus, they have become participants in the fulfillment of the promised new covenant, entering into the kingdom of God and establishing a new covenant relationship with God.

The second reality for the readers is their relationship with the world. Paul describes this situation with the phrase "to those who are in Philippi" (τοῖς οὖσιν ἐν Φιλίπποις), which contrasts with the expression "to the saints in Christ Jesus" (τοῖς ἁγίοις ἐν Χριστῷ Ἰησοῦ). While Philippi refers to the geographical location of the readers, it also signifies the space in which they encounter various environments. These include the difficulties they experience as they live in the region of Philippi on a local level and the hardship they face from the fallen dark world that rejects God on a universal level.

This twofold reality of the readers represents the dual identity of believers. In other words, believers belong to the kingdom of God and have an intimate "father-child" relationship with him. However, they still live in a world that opposes God. This dual identity is linked to the twofold obligation of the new covenant people. One obligation is to be faithful to their relationship with God by obeying his will, which is to love God and love people, as revealed in the law (Matt 22:37–40; Deut 6:25). The other obligation is to serve as priests, connecting the world to God by revealing God to the world (1 Pet 2:9; Exod. 19:5–6). Fulfilling these roles, however, can expose believers to persecution from the world that rejects God because it is hostile to those who do not conform to its ways.

Paul's reference to the readers in this way is related to the rest of the letter. It serves to provide them a context for understanding their current situation and the solution to their problems that Paul suggests. The reason for the church's external problem (1:27–30) is that the readers have become God's new covenant people through faith in Jesus, but they still live in the city of Philippi, which is loyal to the Roman emperor. Paul's exhortation to his readers to exercise discernment and pursue what is good for God (1:9–10; 4:8–9) is also related to the fact that they are still in the world with a dual identity. Furthermore, the issue of false teachers is relevant to the dual identity of believers. Christians, as the new covenant people, must be wary of both the potential threat of false teachers (3:1–17) and the life of worldly pursuits (3:18–19) because their identity is rooted in the correct understanding of Jesus. In conclusion, as in the opening of his other letters, Paul addresses his readers as those with a dual identity, which includes a strategy that helps them understand the content of this letter.

On the other hand, the inclusion of overseers (ἐπισκόποις) and deacons (διακόνοις) as recipients is unique compared to Paul's other letters. The term ἐπισκόποις appears as a reference to the church office only in controversial letters such as 1 Tim 3:2 and Titus 1:7, but not in the opening parts. This uniqueness has led some scholars to question its authenticity, suggesting it may be a later addition.[3] However, the absence of this term in other letters of Paul does not necessarily mean that there was no church order or that the idea of church leadership developed later. For instance, in 1 Thess 5:12–13, one of Paul's earliest letters, there are implications of a kind of church order and leadership in the early stages of Paul's mission.[4] It is probable that this leadership does not imply an official hierarchical status but instead focuses on its function within the church community. This function includes guiding and caring for the church members through the teachings of God and the apostle. In the case of the Philippian church, these leaders are called overseers and deacons.

The more important question, however, is why Paul includes these leadership groups among his recipients. The use of σὺν (with) with the dative in the opening part is an uncommon pattern (compare to 1 Cor 1:2; 2 Cor 1:1). However, the connection between the introduction of the senders and the body of the letter suggests that the mention of the leadership group is intended to inform the readers that the body of the letter may contain messages relevant to them. Several explanations have been suggested for this. One is that Paul mentions the leadership group to establish their authority in the face of challenges within the church.[5] However, the letter does not show any apparent tension between the leadership group and the rest of the church members. Another suggestion is that since the overseers and deacons are responsible for the gift sent to Paul, he acknowledges them

---

3. E.g., Schenk, *Philipperbriefe*, 78–82.

4. Considering that Paul stayed there for only a few weeks (Acts 17:2), the existence of a particular church order in a relatively short period also shows that establishing a church order in a local church was not unusual in the Pauline churches.

5. Silva, *Philippians*, 42, 144.

in the opening to show recognition.⁶ While this is plausible, its weakness is that Paul never distinguishes the leadership group from the rest of the church when addressing their gift in the body of the letter (4:10–20). A more likely explanation is that the mention of the leadership group is related to their active role in resolving the disunity situation in the Philippian church, particularly in 4:2–3, as it is the only part of the letter that mentions the leadership group.⁷ It is not easy to pinpoint the specific message that Paul wants the leadership group to hear. In reality, it is all the church members (πᾶσιν) who should be listening to Paul's letter. Nevertheless, it is evident that the mention of the leadership group serves to call their special attention to the letter.

B) 1:2

Paul greets his readers according to the letter format of his day, known as the "A to B greeting" form. His greeting consists of the noun form of his wish (χάρις [grace] and εἰρήνη [peace]) and a modifying prepositional phrase that conveys the source of the recipients' well-being (ἀπὸ θεοῦ πατρὸς ἡμῶν καὶ κυρίου Ἰησοῦ Χριστοῦ [from God our Father and the Lord Jesus Christ]). This pattern remains consistent throughout Paul's letters, although it differs from what was common among his contemporaries. Along with the information about the senders and recipients, this greeting aims to foster a sense of intimacy and connection with the readers, preparing them to receive the content of the body of the letter effectively.⁸ In particular, the use of the first-person plural reference (ἡμῶν) creates an "in-group" relationship between Paul and his readers.

---

6. Lightfoot, *Philippians*, 82; Witherington, *Friendship and Finances*, 31; etc.

7. Collange, *Philippians*, 41; Hawthorne and Martin, *Philippians*, 10; Fee, *Philippians*, 69; Reumann, *Philippians*, 89; etc.

8. J. L. White describes the opening (and ending) as "the keeping-in-touch aspect of letter writing (maintenance of contact), which reveals the general character of the correspondents' relationship toward each other" (*Light from Ancient Letters*, 219).

PHILIPPIANS 1:3–11

OUTLINE:

I. Letter Opening (1:1–2)
II. Thanksgiving and Prayer (1:3–11)
    A. Thanksgiving and intercessory prayer (1:3–8)
    B. The content of Paul's intercessory prayer (1:9–11)
III. The Body of the Letter (1:12—4:20)
    A. About the situations caused by Paul's imprisonment (1:12–26)

II. THANKSGIVING AND PRAYER (1:3–11)

As with his other letters (Rom 1:8; 1 Cor 1:4; Col 1:3; 1 Thess 1:2; 2 Thess 1:3; Phlm 4), Paul mentions thanksgiving and prayer for his readers after the greeting. The epistolary convention of thanksgiving and the use of the first-person reference (εὐχαριστῶ [I thank]) signal 1:3–11 as the beginning of a new discourse unit. In addition, the mention of God at the beginning and ending points (1:3, 11) also functions as an *inclusio*, marking the boundary of this unit.

Phil 1:3–11 consists of three primary clauses (1:3, 8, 9) and several dependent secondary clauses. Two finite verbs in 1:3 and 9 indicate that thanksgiving (εὐχαριστῶ [I thank]) and prayer (προσεύχομαι [I pray]) are the main themes of 1:3–11. Although thanksgiving and prayer are often combined in a prayer context, Paul seems to focus more on prayer for two reasons. First, he does not mention the content or reason for thanksgiving, which is typically introduced by ὅτι (because: Rom 1:8; 1 Cor 1:5; 2 Thess 1:3). Second, Paul spends more space (1:4–11) describing his intercessory prayer. The participial clause with ποιούμενος (doing, pray) in 1:4 is subordinate to εὐχαριστῶ in 1:3. However, it does not refer to his thanksgiving but rather to his subsequent or simultaneous intercessory prayer (τὴν δέησιν).[1] Furthermore, Paul's extensive explanation of the reason for his prayer in 1:5–8 emphasizes its sincerity and importance to the readers. Consequently, even though Paul provides his readers with his prayer situation, his primary intention is to deliver his intercessory prayer for them. In terms of the process of prayer, 1:3–11 consists of the introduction of Paul's thanksgiving and intercessory prayer (1:3–8) and the actual content of his prayer (1:9–11).

In his thanksgiving and prayer, Paul identifies four participants and describes their interrelationships. The first and most significant participant is Paul himself, introduced through first-person references. He is a prisoner for the sake of the gospel (1:7) and has a deep affection for the Philippian church in Christ (1:7–8). Out of this love, he thanks and prays to God on behalf of the readers (1:3, 9). The second participant is the members of the Philippian church, referred to with second-person references. As the objects of Paul's love and concern, they are presented as actively engaged in the ministry of the gospel that Paul has carried on (1:5, 7). Their growth in maturity is a particular focus of his prayer. The third participant is God, to whom Paul expresses gratitude (1:3) and whose glory is the ultimate goal of Christian maturity (1:11). God has begun the good work in the Philippian church and will bring it to completion at the eschaton (1:6). In addition, God appears in 1:8 as a witness to Paul's love for the readers. The final participant is Jesus, who is mentioned as the agent of the final consummation ("the day of Christ Jesus" [1:6, 10]) and the source and role model of Paul's affection for his readers (1:9). Jesus is also the means by which believers can bear the fruit of righteousness (1:11).

In summary, Paul seeks to demonstrate the close relationship between himself and his readers through thanksgiving and prayer. He conveys his intention in three ways. First, he emphasizes the centrality of his love for them and their shared partnership in the ministry of the gospel, along with the significant role of God and Jesus in shaping their relationship and ministry over time, including the past, present, and future. Second, by openly sharing his intercessory prayer with them, Paul communicates the importance of the content of the prayer and his hope that the readers will live accordingly (1:9–11). Last, Paul shows his sincere desire to effectively communicate this

---

1. Fee, *Philippians*, 76. According to Stanley E. Porter, "If a participle occurs after the finite (or other) verb on which it depends, it tends to refer to concurrent (simultaneous) or subsequent (following) action" (*Idioms*, 188).

message through the extensive and complex explanation of the reason for his prayer (1:5–8). The structure of this paragraph is as follows.

1. Thanksgiving and intercessory prayer (1:3–8)
    1) Thanksgiving (1:3)
    2) Intercessory prayer for the readers (1:4)
    3) The reason for Paul's intercessory prayer (1:5–6)
        a. The reason: Because of the participation of the readers in the gospel (1:5)
        b. Paul's confidence in God's work among the readers (1:6)
    4) Elaboration on the reason for the prayer (1:7–8)
        a. Paul's love for the readers participating in the gospel (1:7)
        b. Affirmation of Paul's love for the readers (1:8)
2. The content of Paul's intercessory prayer (1:9–11)
    1) Paul's prayer (1:9a)
    2) Content 1: Paul prays that the love of his readers may be enriched through discernment with wisdom and understanding (1:9b–10a)
    3) Content 2: The resultant state of the readers' discerning love (1:10b–11)

A. Thanksgiving and intercessory prayer (1:3–8)

Thanksgiving and prayer demonstrate the mutual relationship between Paul and his readers and his affection for them. In the thanksgiving part (1:3), Paul establishes this relationship in two ways. First, he uses first-person singular references (εὐχαριστῶ [I thank] and μου [my]) to signify his personal relationship with God. While the first-person plural (θεοῦ πατρὸς ἡμῶν [God our Father]) in the greeting implies an "in-group" association, the first-person singular in the thanksgiving indicates Paul's intimacy with God. Thus, Paul solidifies his relationship with the readers by including them in his relationship with God. Second, Paul shows his interest in his readers by using the ἐπὶ plus dative construction (ἐπὶ πάσῃ τῇ μνείᾳ ὑμῶν [because of all my remembrance of you]). In particular, the use of πάσῃ (all) emphasizes the depth of their intimacy.

The meaning of Paul's expression in 1:3 has been a subject of debate, and there are three different interpretations concerning the words ἐπί and ὑμῶν. The first view suggests that ὑμῶν is the subject of μνείᾳ, giving the phrase a causal meaning: "for all your [the readers'] remembrance of me [Paul]."[2] Proponents of this view associate it with a recent gift from the Philippian church. The second interpretation suggests that the phrase is temporal, meaning "every time I remember you."[3] This view appears more likely because it is consistent with the pattern in Paul's other letters, where the modifying genitive about "remembering" always refers to the object being remembered.[4] Moreover, there is no semantic evidence to support that the financial gift is the central issue in thanksgiving and prayer. It seems improbable that the participation (κοινωνία, συγκοινωνός) in the gospel (1:5, 7) refers only to financial support.

However, the second interpretation's understanding of ἐπί is not without difficulty. As J. T. Reed aptly points out, there is no need to link a causal interpretation of ἐπί with the subjective genitive view of ὑμῶν.[5] In Pauline thanksgiving, the temporal sense of the ἐπί phrase always takes the genitive (1 Thess 1:2; Phlm 4), while the ἐπί plus dative construction typically denotes a causal sense (1 Cor 1:4). Moreover, since the construction of ἐπί plus dative in 1:5 has a causal sense, it is more natural to understand the same structure in 1:3 as having a similar function. Therefore, the third option, which combines the causal sense of ἐπί with an objective understanding of the genitive, is preferable: "because of all my remembrance of you."[6] In summary, Paul invites the readers into his intimate relationship with God and reveals his affection for them through thanksgiving.

As in many of his letters, Paul's expression of thanksgiving leads to his intercessory prayer in 1:4. He introduces his prayer with a complex structure that includes elements such as the frequency of the prayer (πάντοτε ἐν πάσῃ δεήσει μου [always in every prayer of mine]), the beneficiary (ὑπὲρ πάντων

---

2. Schubert, *Form and Function*, 74; Jewett, "Epistolary Thanksgiving," 53; Garland, "Defense and Confirmation," 329–30; O'Brien, *Philippians*, 56–60; Peterman, *Paul's Gift from Philippi*, 93–99; Reumann, *Philippians*, 101; etc.

3. Gnilka, *Philipperbrief*, 42–43; Hawthorne and Martin, *Philippians*, 15–17; Silva, *Philippians*, 48; Fee, *Philippians*, 78–80; Bockmuehl, *Philippians*, 58; Holloway, *Consolation in Philippians*, 88–89; etc.

4. (1) μνεία: Rom 1:9; 1 Thess 3:6; Phlm 4; see also Ps 110:4; Job 13:13; Zech 13:2; Isa 23:16; Ezek 21:37; 25:10; (2) μνημονεύω: Col 4:18; 1 Thess 1:3; see also Ps 6:6; 62:7; Luke 17:32; John 15:20; 16:4, 21; Acts 15:35; Heb 13:7. Fee, *Philippians*, 78; Reed, *Discourse Analysis of Philippians*, 200.

5. Reed, *Discourse Analysis of Philippians*, 199–200.

6. Reed, *Discourse Analysis of Philippians*, 201; followed by Fowl, *Philippians*, 22–23.

ὑμῶν [for all of you]), and his emotional attitude (μετὰ χαρᾶς [with joy]). This complexity shows his intention to express affection toward the readers in several ways. First, the three adverbial elements describe Paul's prayer situation and indicate that his prayer stems from his genuine concern for his readers. Second, since the more leftward position in a Greek clause or sentence usually receives more emphasis than other positions, the placement of the elements before Paul's prayer (τὴν δέησιν ποιούμενος) emphasizes the sincerity of his prayer. Third, the repetitive use of πᾶς also intensifies the degree of his love for them: every time (πάντοτε), every (πάσῃ) prayer, and for all (πάντων) of them.

In 1:5–6, Paul justifies his intercession with complex explanations. At the outset, he cites the readers' long-term partnership (κοινωνία) in the gospel as the basis for his prayer in 1:5. Although Paul does not provide details about their partnership in this verse, his language implies two things about their involvement in the gospel. First, Paul's reference to their involvement as the rationale for his prayer reflects the importance of their koinonia in his relationship with the readers. Second, the phrase ἀπὸ τῆς πρώτης ἡμέρας ἄχρι τοῦ νῦν (from the first day until now) suggests that the readers have been actively and faithfully engaged in the ministry of the gospel for a long time, beginning with their initial acceptance of Paul's teachings and continuing to the present. It also indicates that their commitment to the gospel has been profoundly meaningful to them.

In connection to 1:5, Paul elaborates on the reasoning behind his intercessory prayer by expressing his confidence in the importance of participating in the gospel in 1:6. In contrast to 1:5, Paul's assurance has two key aspects. The first aspect is that the time frame for the readers' involvement in the ministry of the gospel is extended from the past and present (ἀπὸ τῆς πρώτης ἡμέρας ἄχρι τοῦ νῦν) to the future (ἄχρι ἡμέρας Χριστοῦ Ἰησοῦ [until the day of Christ Jesus]). The second aspect is that the agent in the process of participation shifts from the people who have participated in the gospel (1:5) to God, who has initiated a good work (i.e., to bring about their participation in the gospel) and will carry it on to completion until the day of Christ (1:6).[7] These two aspects highlight the significance of participating in the

---

7. Some scholars understand "good work" as referring to a recent gift or God's work for the conversion of the Philippian congregation (e.g., Martin, *Philippians*, 61; O'Brien, *Philippians*, 64; Bockmuehl, *Philippians*, 61). However, the focus of the temporal sequence in v. 5 is not on the so-called salvation process itself but on their participation in the gospel from their conversion to the present time. Thus, the expansion of temporal sequence from the past to the future in v. 6 is also relevant to their participation in the gospel. In this sense, "good work" refers to God's work that led the Philippian Christians participate in the gospel (Hawthorne and Martin, *Philippians*, 21; Hansen, *Philippians*, 52; etc.).

gospel for both the readers and God, and this participation should continue until the end of time. Paul conveys his conviction that God will complete this critical task in the readers (ἐν ὑμῖν) through three emphatic markers: (1) the stative aspect of πεποιθὼς (being confident), (2) the emphatic expression of αὐτό,[8] and (3) the cataphoric reference of τοῦτο.[9] Through the use of these markers and the content of his conviction, Paul explains the rationale for his intercessory prayer: "I (Paul) intercede for you because you (the Philippians) are engaged in such an important work concerning God."

In 1:7a, Paul further reinforces his conviction and rationale for intercessory prayer by adding more comments. He supports his positive attitude toward his readers with a causal sense of καθώς (because), stating that "[because] it is right for me to think this way about all of you" (1:7a). This statement, which reflects Paul's self-assurance regarding the cognitive and attitudinal dimension (φρονεῖν [to think])[10] toward the readers, conveys that his conviction for the readers in 1:6 is sound and that his prayer is sincere.

Paul continues to support his thoughts to the readers with two additional statements in 1:7b–8. First, using a participle (ὄντας [being]), he describes all the readers as fellow participants (συγκοινωνούς) in his imprisonment, defense, and confirmation of the gospel. The readers already know that Paul's imprisonment is for the sake of the gospel, and even though they cannot be physically present with him, they participate in his ministry by sending him the support he needs. The phrase "all of you" implies that all the readers are involved in supporting Paul. As a repetition of 1:5, this comment emphasizes that the readers have been with Paul in his ministry of the gospel from the beginning until now.

Second, Paul expresses his love for the readers. Unlike 1:5–6, where he focuses on the participation of the readers in the gospel and God's work, he uses emotional and relational language to emphasize his relationship with the readers in 1:7b–8. Paul refers to his readers as "partakers with me" who share his situation of being in "my chain," emphasizing their participation in

---

8. With τοῦτο, NASB renders it as "this very thing."

9. The co-referential link within a text, endophoric reference, consists of anaphoric and cataphoric references. Anaphoric reference refers to the referential connection between one element in a text and the preceding part, e.g., "I bought a watch. That watch was expensive." Cataphoric reference is the referential relationship between one element and a subsequent element, e.g., "As she entered the room, Carroll noticed that the window was open." Since anaphoric reference is more common, cataphoric reference can be considered an emphatic element (Lee, *Paul's Gospel in Romans*, 44; Levinsohn, *Discourse Features*, 55–57).

10. Basically, this term denotes a cognitive process, such as judging, thinking, careful consideration, etc., but it also includes the attitude derived from the cognitive process ("φρονεῖν," BDAG 1065–66).

Paul's ministry of the gospel. In addition, he establishes a personal relationship between himself and the readers by using the first-person "I" and the second-person "you," saying, "I have you in my heart" (1:7b). In 1:8, he even declares his love for them with the affection of Christ Jesus (ἐν σπλάγχνοις Χριστοῦ Ἰησοῦ), with God as his witness. The term σπλάγχνον refers to the intestines in a person's body and symbolizes deep-seated love, mercy, or compassion that comes from the innermost being. Although Paul's love cannot be compared to the love of Christ, he claims to have the same intense love for the readers. Furthermore, Paul's use of God as a witness to his love in 1:8 is an unusual expression compared to his other letters. This reflects his strong desire to convey the genuineness of his love and affection for the readers. After all, Paul's love for his readers and their participation in his ministry are interconnected. He loves them in Christ Jesus, and his love for them deepens as they participate with him in his ministry. This love, in turn, motivates Paul to intercede for them in prayer.

In Paul's language in 1:7b, there is another interesting observation. He portrays the readers who have actively participated in his ministry of the gospel as participants in "grace" (χάριτος). Despite using the phrase "my chain" to symbolize his present imprisonment, which might seem to distance this situation from a state of grace or blessing from God, he focuses more on the implications and consequences of his situation than on the physical circumstances themselves. Paul's imprisonment was due to his ministry of the gospel rather than any offense against Rome, so his current situation is a testament to his faithfulness to the gospel. Moreover, since Paul's suffering is in the name of Jesus, he is entitled to one of the eight beatitudes of the Sermon on the Mount: Blessed are those who are persecuted for Jesus's sake (Matt 5:10–12). As a result, his suffering is not in vain. Furthermore, his imprisonment has a positive outcome. Personally, it allowed Paul to defend and affirm the gospel before the Roman authorities (1:7, 12–13). Ecclesiastically, it enabled other brethren to boldly proclaim the gospel through Paul (1:14). In this light, Paul's imprisonment, which seems humanly unfortunate, is actually a favorable circumstance, a grace from God. As such, the readers who have joined Paul in his ministry of the gospel have also partaken in this divine grace.

Paul uses this language to demonstrate his understanding of his situation and to provide a model of how to approach and respond to readers facing similar issues. This intention is further developed in the body of the letter, where Paul urges his readers, who are under pressure from Philippian citizens loyal to Rome, not to give in to external persecution but to continue living a life worthy of the gospel (1:27–30). He even goes so far as to say in 1:29 that the readers have received salvation in order to suffer for Christ.

Paul teaches the readers not only to view their situation of being pressured by Rome for the gospel's sake as a natural part of the Christian experience in a world that rebels against God but also to interpret it as a sign of their strong relationship with God. Furthermore, he encourages them to see this situation as a gracious opportunity to bear witness to the truth by living righteously in accordance with the gospel. In this regard, Paul's reference to the readers as "partakers of grace" in 1:7b can also be understood, like other expressions in the introduction of the letter, as a foreshadowing of the exhortation to the readers in the body of the letter.

B. The content of Paul's intercessory prayer (1:9–11)

With the expression "I pray [προσεύχομαι] this," Paul introduces the content of his intercessory prayer in 1:9–11, focusing on the love of the readers who have consistently participated in his ministry of the gospel. His prayer is that their lives of love would: (1) be more abundant through inward discernment with truth and understanding, (2) be filled with the fruits of righteousness appropriate to their relationship with God, (3) glorify and praise God, and (4) remain sincere and blameless before God and people until the day of Christ. The style and content of Paul's expression contain several noteworthy aspects.

In terms of style, Paul employs an unusual method by mentioning the pronoun "this" first and then introducing its content afterward through the dependent conjunction ἵνα, rather than using the more typical conjunction ὅτι (that) to create an objective clause for the verb προσεύχομαι. Generally, a pronoun functions as an anaphoric reference, referring back to a previous noun or noun group, and typically follows its antecedent. In this text, however, the order is reversed, creating a cataphoric reference that emphasizes the content of the prayer and intentionally draws the readers' attention to it.

There are also several observations about the content of the prayer. The first one is that Paul does not use the imperative to command them to love. The subject of the ἵνα clause, which contains the content of the prayer, is the love of the readers (ἡ ἀγάπη ὑμῶν [your love]), and the main verb is "may abound" (περισσεύῃ). Paul's request is not that the readers should begin to love one another but rather that their lives should become even more abundant, assuming they already live a life of love. In fact, they were already living a life of love as believers, and Paul knew it. They had willingly collected relief offerings for the church in Jerusalem (Rom 15:26; 2 Cor 8:1–2), supported Paul financially during his ministry (4:15–16; 2 Cor 11:9; Acts 18:5), and even sent what was necessary for Paul through Epaphroditus

(4:18). Nevertheless, Paul prays for their love, expecting it to continue to flourish. This desire is clearly reflected in the addition of the expression "still more and more" (ἔτι μᾶλλον καὶ μᾶλλον) in the process of abounding.

The second observation is the sequence of processes in the life of love. Paul presents the believer's life of love as a combination of two kinds of processes. The first is an inside-out pattern that begins with inner cognitive discernment and expresses its result in the actual life of love. Regarding the beginning of this process, Paul uses the preposition ἐν (in) and presents two elements necessary to enrich the life of love. One is knowledge (ἐπίγνωσις), which refers to the dimension of truth and includes the teachings of God and Jesus. This knowledge can be understood to encompass cognitive and experiential knowledge derived from relationships. The other element is the capacity for understanding (αἴσθησις), which is the ability to comprehend the believer's situation and God's will. These two elements are necessary for the next step, which is to discern (δοκιμάζειν) what is best. To discern well requires both standards and actual processes of discernment. Knowledge corresponds to the standard for discernment, and understanding corresponds to wisdom, which is the discernment process. In this sense, the life of love that Paul prays for his readers begins with an inner cognitive process that involves a discernment based on knowledge and understanding.

The next step in the inside-out pattern is to express inner discernment in the outer way of life. In the second ἵνα clause (purpose clause) in 1:10, Paul describes the outward state of a life of love characterized by discernment as sincerity (εἰλικρινής) and blamelessness (ἀπρόσκοποι). The word εἰλικρινής refers to pure motivation without hidden agendas, which is the integrity of life in both personal and church contexts. Ἀπρόσκοποι means not receiving negative evaluations from God and the world in ethical contexts. These two qualities imply the maturity of a believer's life that God approves. Furthermore, Paul describes this state of maturity with a participle clause using πεπληρωμένοι (having been fulfilled) as being full of the fruit of righteousness (δικαιοσύνης) through Jesus Christ (1:10). Righteousness is related to the Old Testament concept of צְדָקָה (tzedaqah), which means faithfulness to one's identity and relationships. It can be applied to both God and man. On God's part, it refers to being worthy of his identity and role as Creator (Gen 18:25; Deut 32:4; Ps 33:5; etc.) and being faithful to the covenant relationship with his people (Hos 2:19). On the human side, righteousness refers to one's uprightness as a creature who responds worthily to the Creator, on the one hand, and the faithful state to the covenant relationship with God by living according to his will, on the other hand (Deut 6:25). The expression in the text refers to the righteousness of people, signifying a way of life that is worthy of a relationship with God as those who have experienced the new creation and entered into a new covenant relationship through the work of Jesus's cross and resurrection. Since God's will, as expressed through the law, is to love God and to love people (Matt 22:37–40), the life of love that Paul prays for his readers can also be understood as living according to God's pleasing will, as a new covenant people. In summary, the life of love in the inside-out process that Paul presents involves three steps: (1) cultivating internal discernment through knowledge centered on God's will and understanding through the Holy Spirit, (2) expressing this discernment through external attitudes and actions, and ultimately, (3) leading a life as believers that is appropriate and faithful in their relationship with God.

The second kind of process that Paul presents regarding the believer's life of love is the progression of time from the present to the future. He prays for his readers' present situation of living a life of love and anticipates that their life of love will become more abundant through expressions of love via the inside-out process. The culmination of this journey is the day of Christ Jesus (εἰς ἡμέραν Χριστοῦ). This is the same point mentioned in 1:6, where he expresses his hope that God will complete the good work of laboring together for the gospel until the day of Jesus. Just as he hopes that his readers' commitment to the gospel will persist until the end of time, whether that be their personal end or the end of history, so too does he pray that their life of love will endure, aligning with God's will and remaining faithful in their relationship with him. In this sense, the life of love that Paul envisions, characterized by discernment through the inside-out process, is not a one-time success or failure but rather a continuous journey that will continue until the day of Christ's return.

The third observation about the content of prayer is the focus of Paul's proposed life of love (1:10). He does not explicitly mention the objects of the readers' love. However, since the essence of God's law is to love God and people, it can be inferred that the love Paul prays for is also directed toward both groups. What deserves more attention is the objective of the life of love that Paul proposes. He uses the purpose preposition εἰς to indicate that it is for the glory and praise of God (εἰς δόξαν καὶ ἔπαινον θεοῦ). Love is inherently relationship centered and, therefore, impure when there is a purpose other than the object of the relationship. However, the purpose of the life of love that Paul speaks of is not problematic because it is centered on God, who is both the origin and the object of love. Since true love is based on a vertical relationship with God and extends horizontally to people, aligning the beginning and end of a life of love with God provides the proper perspective to express inside-out love adequately. Conversely, seeking self-satisfaction or simply trying to satisfy people in the name of love is the real problem. Such love is another expression of sin that rejects the Creator and seeks to live for selfish desires.

The fourth observation is why Paul introduces the content of his intercessory prayer. Since intercessory prayer is private, there is no need to introduce it to others, nor is there any reason to mention it in the letter. Nevertheless, Paul deliberately includes his intercessory prayer in the letter, with its emphatic structure and content, for two reasons. One reason is that he wants to teach his readers about how their lives should be. Paul wrote this letter while in prison, and his release was uncertain. If he is not released, this letter could be the last thing he writes to the Philippian church and possibly his last testament. Therefore, Paul's intercessory prayer for his readers reflects what he hopes they will be like before he dies, and his introduction can be seen as an indirect exhortation to share with them essential principles of the Christian life. Based on the observations above, Paul's expectations for the readers can be summarized as a life of love that (1) discerns what is best in the new covenant relationship with God through Jesus, (2) takes a comprehensive view of the believer's life that includes both the present and the future, and (3) remains steadfast in the gospel without losing sight of the ultimate focus of God's glory and praise. Paul's prayers to God for the readers to live such a life indicate that while he anticipates God's assistance in their lives, the readers themselves should also rely on God and live accordingly.

Another reason Paul mentions intercessory prayer is to set the stage for the rest of the letter. Three clues support this idea. The first clue is the context. The intercessory prayer mentioned in this passage is about the readers' lives of love, but Paul goes on to explain at length that the reason for this prayer is that they are partners in the ministry of the gospel. By combining these two elements, the content of the prayer and its reason, we can understand that Paul envisions a life for the readers that integrates the gospel and love. This concept reappears in the body of the letter, where Paul exhorts the readers about their situation. Regarding the gospel, he urges them to remain committed despite pressure from fellow citizens who hold Roman citizenship (1:27–30). Concerning the life of love, Paul acknowledges the internal conflict centered around Euodia and Syntyche and commands the church to be united in love (2:1–4; 4:2–3). Thus, the gospel and love form the foundation of Paul's exhortation to the readers.

The second clue is the inside-out principle, which presents inward discernment as an outward expression of life. Paul employs this principle when he introduces his situation (1:12–26) and when he admonishes the readers about their internal problems (2:1–4, 12–13), using Jesus as an example (2:5–11). Furthermore, the principle of discernment is applied in his teaching about false teachers who could influence the readers' church (3:15–16). The final exhortation to the readers is also an expression of right thinking through action, guided by the application of the inside-out process (4:8–9). Thus, the inside-out pattern is a recurring theme throughout this letter, and Paul's prayer serves as its starting point.[11]

The third clue is the language used to describe the resulting state of the life of love. The Greek words for sincerity (εἰλικρινής) and blameless (ἀπρόσκοποι) in 1:10 reappear in the body of the letter through a semantic domain connection. As for εἰλικρινής, Paul uses the term ἁγνῶς (purely) in 1:17, which belongs to the same semantic domain of honesty and sincerity,[12] to describe those who preach the gospel in response to his imprisonment. Specifically, it depicts individuals who approach preaching the gospel with impure motives, driven by competition and comparison. This situation is later connected to the internal conflict within the readers' church caused by Euodia and Syntyche (2:1–4; 4:2–3). Similarly, in 2:15, the concept of ἀπρόσκοποι is conveyed as an instruction for dealing with external pressure through the terms ἄμεμπτοι (blameless) and ἀκέραιοι (pure), which belong to the same semantic domain related to sin, wrongdoing, and guilt.[13] Here, Paul urges the readers not to be blamed by the world but rather to be like lights.

From these three clues, it can be understood that Paul's intercessory prayer forms the foundation for the exhortations to the readers that will be presented in the body of the letter. Specifically, it contains the theme of (1) continuing to live faithfully to the gospel with a life of truth and love, applying the inside-out principle to internal and external problems of the church, and (2) maintaining a life of love rather than competition among church members.

In conclusion, although it is not in the form of a direct exhortation with an imperative, Paul introduces his intercessory prayer to teach the readers what kind of Christian life they should lead in both internal and external problematic situations. While this passage was originally intended for the believers in Philippi, the Christian lifestyle that Paul presents through his intercessory prayer serves as a principle for all believers living in a world hostile to God. It provides a framework for prayer, a way of life, and hope for believers across all generations.

---

11. Lee, "'Think' and 'Do.'"
12. "Εἰλικρινής, ἁγνῶς," L&N 746.
13. "Ἀπρόσκοπος, ἄμεμπτος," L&N 776; "ἀκέραιος," L&N 745.

PHILIPPIANS 1:12—4:20

OUTLINE:

II. Thanksgiving and Prayer (1:3–11)

    A. Thanksgiving and intercessory prayer (1:3–8)

    B. The content of Paul's intercessory prayer (1:9–11)

III. The Body of the Letter (1:12—4:20)

    A. About the situations caused by Paul's imprisonment (1:12–26)

    B. About the real problems of the church (1:27—2:18)

III. THE BODY OF THE LETTER (1:12—4:20)

A. About the situations caused by Paul's imprisonment (1:12–26)

THIS SECTION CONTAINS BOTH continuity and discontinuity with the previous part. Regarding discontinuity, 1:12-26 departs from the theme of thanksgiving and prayer in 1:3-11. Since the content of the prayer ends in 1:11, it is evident that 1:12 marks the beginning of a new topic. Moreover, the phrase "brothers and sisters" also signals this discontinuity. It draws the readers' attention and introduces a new theme in this context. Therefore, we can consider that the main body of the letter begins in 1:12.

On the other hand, 1:12–26 also contains elements of continuity with 1:3–11. The crucial link is the reference to the "gospel" in 1:12, which has been mentioned as a connecting factor between Paul and the readers. It suggests that Paul intends to use the gospel as a guiding theme to advance the body of the letter. Therefore, even though the entire content of the letter has not yet been fully unfolded, Paul presents the overarching message, which relates to his and the readers' situation, through the framework of the gospel.

The first section of the letter's main body extends to 1:26. The reason for this division is the first appearance of the imperative mood in 1:27, which marks the beginning of Paul's specific exhortation to the readers and demonstrates his focus on their situation. In 1:12–26, however, Paul begins by detailing his circumstances with the phrase "what has happened to me" (τὰ κατ' ἐμὲ). Although he is still mindful of the readers, this indicates that the primary focus in this section is on his own situation.

1. Two external situations (1:12–18a)

The section of 1:12–26 can be divided into two units, 1:12–18a and 18b–26, based on three factors. The first factor is character information. In 1:12–18a, there is no mention of second-person plural references except for 1:12, where Paul begins this section by addressing the readers as "you." In contrast, 1:18b–26 contains five occurrences of the second-person references (1:19, 24, 25 [x2], 26). This implies that the main focus of 1:18b–26 is the interaction between Paul and the readers. The second factor relates to the content of the gospel. While 1:12–18a contains references to the gospel as a noun (εὐαγγέλιον [1:12, 16]) and verbs related to preaching (λαλέω [to speak] [1:14], κηρύσσω [to preach] [1:15], καταγγέλλω [to proclaim] [1:17, 18a]), 1:18b–26 does not explicitly mention the gospel. Last, the third factor is the use of tense forms. There is no future form in 1:12–18a, but it appears seven times in 1:18b–26 (1:18b, 19, 20 [x2], 22, 25 [x2]). In 1:18, Paul even changes the form of the verb "rejoice" from present to future with the conjunction ἀλλά (but). Moreover, most of these future forms are accompanied by expressions of Paul's expectation, hope, confidence, and knowledge. This indicates that while 1:12–18a focuses on past and present situations related to Paul, 1:18b–26 addresses situations that he anticipates or hopes for in the future.

The structure of 1:12–18a can be divided into three parts based on the use of the main verb and conjunctions. The first part is 1:12–14, where Paul informs the readers of his situation in prison using first-person verbs (1:12).

Two infinitives present the specific results of his situation: one indicates that the gospel has spread to those around him (1:13) and the other that many believers have gained confidence in the Lord to speak the word (1:14). The second part is 1:15–17, where Paul contrasts two groups who boldly proclaim the gospel, using third-person plural references and two correlative conjunctions (μὲν ... δὲ). It further explains those who preach the gospel in relation to Paul. The third part is 1:18a, where Paul provides his assessment of the situation using a first-person verb (χαίρω [I rejoice]).

In this structure, there are at least four groups of characters. The first group is Paul and the readers. Paul presents his situation in the letter, and the readers hear his story. The second group includes the entire praetorian guard, who have been given the opportunity to hear the gospel, as well as everyone who proclaims the gospel courageously. These individuals participate in the outcomes resulting from Paul's imprisonment. Among those who proclaim the gospel, some do so with pure intentions, while others do not. The third group is Christ, who, in this text, is presented more as the content of the gospel than as the agent of action. Based on these observations, we can outline the structure of 1:12–18a as follows.

1. A report on Paul's situation (1:12–14) 　1) Introduction: I want you to know that my circumstances have turned out for the greater progress of the gospel (1:12) 　2) Twofold consequence (1:13–14) 　　a. It has become known throughout the whole praetorian guard and to all the rest that my imprisonment is for Christ (1:13) 　　b. Most of the brothers *and sisters*, trusting in the Lord because of my imprisonment, have far more courage to speak the word of God without fear (1:14)	The first-person verb (Paul)

2. Two kinds of proclaimers (1:15–17) 　1) Comparison 1: Two proclaiming groups (1:15) 　　a. Some are preaching Christ from envy and strife (A) 　　b. Some are preaching Christ from goodwill (B) 　2) Comparison 2: Elaboration of the two groups (1:16–17) 　　a. They do it out of love, knowing that I am appointed for the defense of the gospel (1:16) (B) 　　b. They proclaim Christ out of selfish ambition rather than from pure motives, thinking that they are causing me distress in my imprisonment (1:17) (A)	* The third-person references * Correlative conjunction (an explanation of those in 1:14)
3. Paul's response (1:18a) 　1) Comment: What then? 　2) Paul's evaluation of the situation of the two proclaiming groups: I rejoice over the one thing, that Christ is proclaimed	A first-person verb (Paul)

A) 1:12–14

This is the opening of the body of the letter. Paul shows an intimacy with the readers by addressing them as "brothers and sisters" (ἀδελφοί) and provides information about his situation (τὰ κατ' ἐμὲ) in relation to the gospel by stating, "I want you to know" (1:12). The news he shares is that his imprisonment has actually helped spread of the gospel. He then presents two specific outcomes using infinitive clauses. The first is that his imprisonment has given unbelievers, including the entire praetorian guard (πραιτώριον) and others (1:13), the opportunity to hear the gospel. The term πραιτώριον is a Latin transliteration that originally referred to the general's tent and its surroundings in the Roman army. Later, it came to refer to soldiers who guarded or accompanied leaders and a group of troops assigned to protect the Roman emperor. In this context, it is better to understand this term as referring to the people who guarded Paul in prison or were involved in his case. This situation might have arisen because Paul explained that his imprisonment was for Christ's sake or because he directly preached the gospel to them. The use of "all" (ὅλῳ and πᾶσιν) is an exaggeration, but it emphasizes that a significant number of people have heard the gospel. The second outcome of Paul's imprisonment is that many fellow believers were encouraged by his situation to proclaim the gospel (1:14).

There are several noteworthy points in Paul's description. The first point is how Paul acknowledges his circumstances. He refers to his imprisonment as "my chain," which is why his readers are concerned about him and why they sent Epaphroditus to support him. However, Paul goes beyond this simple description and repeatedly adds the phrase "in Christ" to his explanation (1:13-14). This key phrase demonstrates how Paul understands both his situation and his life. Regarding his situation, Paul recognizes that he is not merely in prison but, as stated in 1:7, engaged in defending and confirming the gospel. Regarding his life, the phrase "in Christ" implies that his life is deeply rooted in his relationship with Christ and that he lives as an instrument for the gospel of Christ.

The second point to note is Paul's intention in sharing this information. He wants to comfort his readers, who are concerned about his condition. However, he also has a deeper purpose to remind them of the importance of a gospel-centered life. At first glance, it may appear that Paul is suffering under Roman authority because of the gospel, but the profound reality reveals a different perspective. Since his life is devoted to the gospel of Jesus, his tribulations are not meaningless. Moreover, his circumstances not only facilitate the spread of the gospel but also serve as evidence of his dedication to it. This idea is echoed in 1:28-29, where Paul refers to the difficulties the readers experience caused by the Philippian citizens who are loyal to Rome. He encourages them to remain faithful to the gospel, assuring them that their endurance will yield valuable outcomes, just as his suffering has advanced the gospel. In this sense, Paul's account of his circumstances in 1:12-14 can be seen as an indirect exhortation for the readers to persevere in living according to the gospel and as a presentation of a good model of such living.

The last point to note is that God is at work. The situations arising from Paul's imprisonment are not of his own making. Although the text does not explicitly attribute these events to God's intervention, it is evident that Paul views his circumstances as being shaped by divine action. As a result, this description of the situation can also be understood as offering readers further evidence that God, who began the good work in relation to the gospel, will bring it to completion (1:6). In other words, Paul's other intention is to reassure the readers that just as God has worked in his life, God will also work in his own ways in their lives. Therefore, they should endure their difficulties with the expectation of God's work. In this sense, while his primary purpose is to comfort the readers who are worried about him, he also seeks to guide them on how to approach their problematic circumstances.

B) 1:15–17

Paul explains the people who courageously preach the gospel because of his imprisonment. He uses correlative conjunctions to compare those with negative and positive motivations, using an inverted parallelism to clarify the contrast between the two groups. This contrasting structure consists of A (those with negative motivation)—B (those with positive motivation)—B (a description of those with positive motivation)—A (a description of those with negative motivation). These two groups share three characteristics: (1) they are Christians who live near the place of Paul's imprisonment; (2) they all recognize that Paul is imprisoned because of his faith in Christ and dedication to the gospel; and (3) they are all motivated by Paul's imprisonment to witness to Christ.

However, the two groups have distinct motivations and goals in proclaiming the gospel. One group preaches Christ out of envy, strife (1:15), and selfish ambition (1:17). According to Paul, they preach the gospel to cause him emotional pain while he is in prison. In other words, they intended to provoke Paul's competitive spirit and make him feel inferior by demonstrating that they were more successful in their ministry than Paul could be while imprisoned and unable to preach the gospel freely. They seek the vainglory of being recognized as better evangelists than Paul. It is unclear how Paul became aware of their motives. Perhaps drawing on his experience with the language and signs of competition in the Corinthian church a few years earlier, Paul might have characterized their motives as impure (οὐχ ἁγνῶς in 1:17) and pretentious (προφάσει in 1:18). In contrast, the other group preaches Christ with goodwill. They acknowledge that Paul is imprisoned for defending and affirming Christ and the gospel (1:7, 14) and testify to Christ out of love for Paul and to join him in the ministry of the gospel (1:16).

Questions may arise about the identity of the two groups Paul describes and how he became aware of their activities. However, the more significant question is why Paul includes this description. He could have introduced his situation by simply mentioning the positive outcomes of his imprisonment in 1:12–14 without further elaboration. Yet, he chooses to include it, likely because it relates to the second problem faced by the readers, the internal conflict within the church. The language used to describe those who preach with negative motives overlaps with the vocabulary used to address internal strife within the church (e.g., ἐριθεία [selfishness] [1:17; 2:3]). Additionally, their lack of the same mindset as those with good intentions (2:2; 4:2–3) is also similar. Thus, it appears that Paul's additional explanation here is intended to help the readers understand and accept his instructions regarding the church problem by sharing his own similar experience. In summary, while 1:15–17 appears to address Paul's circumstances on the surface, it can be understood as a foreshadowing of his upcoming solution to the problem of the readers.

C) 1:18A

Paul responds to the two groups of gospel preachers mentioned in 1:14–17 by stating that he rejoices in the fact that Christ is preached in every way, whether from false motives or true. This response may seem surprising, as one would expect Paul to prefer those who preach with good intentions. However, Paul's perspective is quite different. He is not concerned with how he is personally affected but rather with the fact that the gospel is being spread. His sole focus is on the proclamation of Christ and those who come to faith through the gospel. This is where his true joy lies. Paul's attitude exemplifies a life of love that discerns what truly matters, guided by a standard of proper knowledge and wisdom, as he prayed for the readers in 1:10. He evaluates situations based on the surpassing value of Christ and his gospel, remaining unswayed by comparisons, competition, or selfish interests. As a result, he experiences peace and joy.

Paul expresses his thoughts in three ways. First, he uses the expression "What then?" This phrase indicates that Paul is about to evaluate the two groups mentioned above and give an appropriate response. Second, he employs a cataphoric construction. In the Greek structure, Paul first states the ὅτι (that) clause, which serves as the object of the verb χαίρω (rejoice) and receives its content in the phrase ἐν τούτῳ (in this) before the main verb. This structure highlights the importance of Christ being preached by reversing the usual order, where the subordinate clause typically follows the main verb, emphasizing its content. Third, Paul uses the verb "I rejoice," which appears for the first time in this letter and ten times afterward (1:18b; 2:17, 18, 28; 3:1; 4:4 [x2], 10; συγχαίρω in 2:17, 18; see also four occurrences in the noun form [1:4, 25; 2:2, 29; 4:1]). This expression underscores where Paul's focus lies. Furthermore, given the positive relationship between Paul and the readers, this statement also suggests that Paul wants the readers to find joy in the same things that bring joy to Paul.

Based on these elements, Paul's explanation of the two groups involved in preaching the gospel seems to serve three purposes: (1) to provide the readers with an example of discernment guided by knowledge and wisdom; (2) to convey that Christ and the gospel are the central principles of evaluation and discernment; and (3) to encourage the readers to abandon the spirit of competition and division and instead focus on more important values by following Paul's example. Overall, Paul's presentation of his situation reflects his love for Christ and his heart for the readers, aiming to comfort them and offer guidance in dealing with their difficulties, both from external pressures and internal conflict within the church.

2. Paul's internal situation (1:18b–26)

This is the second paragraph of the first section in the body of the letter, where Paul provides additional information about his imprisonment. In 1:12–18a, he addresses the reactions of outsiders to his situation, but in 1:18b–26, he shifts the focus to his own understanding and expectations. This paragraph consists of three subunits. The first subunit (1:18b–20) presents a possible outcome of Paul's situation using a future verb (1:18b) and explains it with the verb οἶδα (I know) (1:19–20). The second subunit is 1:21–24. It is connected to the previous subunit with the conjunction γὰρ (because), but a series of infinitives distinguish it. These infinitives describe Paul's two options: to live (τὸ ζῆν [to live] [1:21, 22]) and to die (τὸ ἀποθανεῖν in 1:21). These options refer to remaining alive in the flesh (τὸ ἐπιμένειν [ἐν] τῇ σαρκί [1:24]) or departing to be with Christ (τὸ ἀναλῦσαι and σὺν Χριστῷ εἶναι [1:23]), respectively. The structure of 1:21–24 centers on Paul's dilemma between choosing death and life, with the consequences of each decision structured as follows: (A) Option 1: To die and its result (1:21)—(B) Option 2: To live and its result (1:22a)—(C) Paul's dilemma (1:22b)—(A´) Option 1: To die and its result (1:23)—(B´) Option 2: To live and its result (1:24). The third subunit is 1:25–26, where Paul shifts away from the use of infinitives and instead conveys his conviction using the verb οἶδα (I know). Here, he expresses his confidence that he will be released and come to the readers.

There are three characters in this structure. The first character is Paul, the first-person narrator who experiences both joy and inner conflict and can make choices. The second character is Christ, who sent the Holy Spirit and is the ultimate goal and primary focus of Paul's hope. Christ is also a significant factor in Paul's internal conflict about whether to live or die because Paul desires to deepen his relationship with Christ. The third character is the readers, who love Paul and pray for him (1:19). They also contribute to

Paul's struggle in choosing between life and death, as he expresses his affection for them as well. The structure of 1:18b–20 is as follows.

1. Another report on Paul's situation (1:18b–20)
 	
   1) Introduction: I will also rejoice in my situation (1:18b)
 	
   2) The reason for his joy: I know that this will lead to the state of salvation (1:19–20)
	Paul's fundamental attitude toward his future situation

2. Paul's dilemma (1:21–24)
 	
   1) Premise: Whether to live or die, both are profitable to Paul (1:21–22a)
 	
      a. Personal profit: For to me, to live is Christ, and to die is gain (1:21)
 	
      b. Profit related to the ministry: To live in the flesh is a fruit of his work (1:22a)
 	
   2) Paul's dilemma: I do not know which to choose (1:22b)
 	
   3) Two kinds of options (1:23–24)
 	
      a. Option 1: To die and be with Christ (1:23)
 	
      b. Option 2: To live and stay with you (1:24)
	The use of infinitives, Paul's dilemma

3. Paul's confidence and reason/purpose (1:25–26)
 	
   1) Paul's confidence: I am convinced and know that I will remain with you (1:25)
 	
   2) Reason/purpose: For your progress and joy in the faith, so that your boast in Christ Jesus may abound on account of me through my coming to you again (1:25–26)
	Paul's confidence

A) 1:18B–20

Paul begins to introduce another result of his imprisonment in 1:18b with the expression χαρήσομαι (I will rejoice). This expression carries two implications. First, the future form of the verb indicates that the information Paul is about to share has not yet occurred and, therefore, belongs to the realm of anticipation and hope. It contrasts with 1:12–18a, which focuses on his past and present situation. Second, the use of the verb "rejoice" reveals what

Paul considers important. Just as he demonstrates what he values through the verb "rejoice" in 1:18a, his repetition of the same verb here is intended to communicate to the readers what he regards as significant, even in the face of uncertainty about his future.

Paul's reason for rejoicing is that he knows the outcome of his situation. He declares that he knows that this (τοῦτό) will lead to salvation (σωτηρία) (1:19). Despite its simplicity, this statement has sparked considerable debate regarding its meaning. The first issue concerns the meaning of "this." Since there is no specific reference to it, it is better to view "this" as referring to the preceding context, that is, what has happened to him, including his imprisonment. The second issue is the meaning of "salvation," which is more complex. Generally, this term denotes the transition from a negative state to a positive one, with its specific meaning varying depending on the context.[1] In this passage, some interpret it as Paul's release from prison,[2] while others see it as future vindication or praise from God, drawing parallels to a phrase in Job 3:16.[3] However, it is more appropriate to understand this expression as referring to the salvation process and something experienced in that process. Specifically, it points to the state in which Christ is exalted through Paul's body.[4] Several reasons support this interpretation.

First, interpreting "salvation" as a release from imprisonment does not align with Paul's later statements. Although he expresses confidence in his release in 1:26, his personal preference in 1:21–24 is to die and be with Christ rather than to be released. Furthermore, since Paul uses the term "rejoice" to indicate the values he considers essential, it would be inconsistent for him to express joy over his release as though it were his highest priority.

Second, it is questionable why this expression should be understood in connection with the book of Job.[5] Even if Job is referenced, it is not necessary to analyze the present context of Philippians based on the content of Job. Instead, it is more appropriate to prioritize the way and content that Paul expresses in the text.

Third, the passage offers little evidence to interpret its content as a projection of Paul's eventual vindication. Vindication suggests that, although Paul is currently in prison, God will confirm his innocence and righteousness in the future. The key to this interpretation lies in the assumption that

---

1. "Σωτηρία," BDAG 985–86.
2. Thurston and Ryan, *Philippians & Philemon*, 62; Hawthorne and Martin, *Philippians*, 49–50; etc.
3. Melick, *Philippians, Colossians, Philemon*; Fee, *Philippians*, 130–31; Bockmuehl, *Philippians*, 82–83; etc.
4. Hansen, *Philippians*, 80; Reumann, *Philippians*, 244; Silva, *Philippians*, 72; etc.
5. Contra Hays, *Echoes of Scripture*, 21–24.

Paul is concerned with whether he will be rewarded. In this passage, however, Paul is not preoccupied with his situation. In 1:18a, what brings Paul joy is not his own situation but the fact that Christ is being proclaimed. In 1:20, he does not mention dying or living as the core of his hope. When Paul expresses confidence in his release in 1:25–26, he does not focus on himself. Therefore, the interpretation of vindication that centers on Paul's condition does not align with the passage's content.

Fourth, Paul presents the state that leads to salvation as the fulfillment of his hope. The core of his hope is the exaltation of Christ through his body (1:20), and he emphasizes this hope in several ways. Regarding the hope itself, Paul underscores it by repeating ἀποκαραδοκίαν (eager expectation) and ἐλπίδα (hope). Regarding the importance of Christ's exaltation, he emphasizes this aspect using three comparative expressions: (1) "I will in no way be ashamed" vs. "with all boldness," (2) now and as always, and (3) by life and death. In this context, being unashamed and bold means that he will not miss the mark regardless of the situation. The temporal comparison shows his determination to live according to this hope, and the contrast between life and death emphasizes the importance of Christ over Paul himself. These elements help effectively communicate where Paul's joy and primary focus lie to the reader. In this regard, it is appropriate to understand that what Paul anticipates and rejoices in regarding his future is not his release or vindication but rather the exaltation of Christ through his life and death. Therefore, in this passage, salvation can be understood as the salvation process in which Paul participates by the grace of Christ. He regards the exaltation of Christ through his life and death as the ultimate of this process.

Paul mentions two means to accomplish this process. The first is the prayers of the readers. While their prayers may include requests for Paul's release, they more broadly intercede on his behalf, asking that he faithfully fulfill his apostolic mission to the end. The second is the help of the Holy Spirit. This aid is not only a response from the Holy Trinity to the prayers of believers (see God's help in 1:7) but also the support that empowers Paul to carry out his ministry faithfully.

In summary, Paul's main message in 1:18b–20 is centered on his ultimate hope. Regardless of what may happen in his near future, his sole purpose in life and death is for the glory of Christ, which he sees as his joy and the purpose of his existence and ministry. This passage serves as a reminder to readers who are concerned about Paul of what to pray for and how to live. It also provides a foundation and starting point for Paul to introduce his decision and conviction.

B) 1:21–24

Paul articulates his internal conflict and decision-making process regarding his current situation. He begins by providing a basic overview of his circumstances (1:21–22a) and views both potential outcomes, whether he is executed and dies or released and continues to live, as advantageous to him (ἐμοί and μοι [to me]). Since he is living with Christ in the flesh, he believes it would be even more beneficial for him to die because he would be with Christ. However, if he is set free and remains alive, this also would benefit him because it would result in the fruit of his labor. In this context, "the fruit of labor" refers to the positive outcomes he experiences while witnessing the gospel. It seems that Paul has two specific scenarios in mind. If he is released, it would signify that Rome recognizes both his innocence and the truthfulness of his testimony about the gospel of Christ. Overall, Paul considers his imprisonment beneficial, regardless of the outcome. This perspective aligns with the message in 1:19–20, where Paul emphasizes that the exaltation of Christ is more important than his own life and death.

Paul faces the dilemma of choosing between life and death. He admits uncertainty about which option to choose (1:22b). Ultimately, whether Paul lives or dies is not within his control, as the decision lies with the Roman authorities and, ultimately, with God. However, Paul shares his thoughts on both scenarios, offering them to comfort and strengthen the readers.

In the first scenario, Paul contemplates receiving a death sentence and being executed. He expresses a preference for this outcome, not because he has given up on life but because he longs to be with Christ forever (1:23). Paul's ultimate hope is to be transformed into the likeness of Christ's glorious body through the resurrection (3:20–21) so that he can have full fellowship with Christ. In his current physical state, Paul is unable to see Christ face-to-face or fully respond to his love (1 Cor 13:12). Therefore, Paul believes that the only way to fully know and have fellowship with Christ, except in the case of Christ's second coming, is through death. This is why he desires death more than life.

The alternative scenario Paul considers is being set free and continuing his life in the flesh. This would be beneficial to him because it would bear the fruit of his labor (1:22a). However, Paul shifts his focus to the readers, stating that it would be more necessary for them (1:24). If he had to choose between these two scenarios, what would Paul decide? Interestingly, in both cases, Paul uses the comparative form to weigh each scenario's relative importance or necessity. While the first option is better for himself (κρεῖσσον [better]), the second is more necessary for the readers (ἀναγκαιότερον [more necessary]). The use of the comparative form suggests that he considers both scenarios significant. However, Paul describes the first as relatively more important by adding the phrase πολλῷ μᾶλλον (much more). If so, would he opt for his death between the two?

C) 1:25–26

Paul's choice is to be released from prison for the sake of advancing the faith and bringing joy to his readers. They will rejoice and thank God when Paul is released and reunited with them. There are several notable observations in Paul's statement.

The first observation is the use of various elements of emphasis, including the use of τοῦτο (this) as a cataphoric reference at the beginning of the sentence. While its general use is to refer back to preceding information, in this case, it acts as a demonstrative pronoun to emphasize what follows. This technique serves to capture the readers' attention. Another element is repetition. Paul emphasizes his decision by using the participle τοῦτο πεποιθὼς (being convinced) and the main verb οἶδα (I know). He also repeats the idea of his release with the verbs μενῶ (I remain) and παραμενῶ (I remain with). Moreover, Paul adds a purpose clause with ἵνα (so that) to clarify the intended purpose of his release: the advancement of their faith and joy. The change in word order also appears to be another way for Paul to emphasize his point. In Greek, the genitive case usually functions as a modifier after a noun, but it gains emphasis when the word order is altered.[6] There are two instances in this passage. The first occurs when Paul explains the purpose of his release from prison, he breaks the closeness between the article and the noun, placing the genitive case ὑμῶν (your) before the nouns 'progress and joy.' This structure highlights Paul's focus on the benefit of the readers. The second instance is when he places the genitive case ἐμῆς (my) before the noun παρουσίας (presence) (1:28) to emphasize his return and its impact on the joy of the readers. In conclusion, Paul seeks to convey the conviction that he will be with the readers for the progress of their faith and joy.

The second observation is how Paul evaluates the situation. There are two key elements in this process. The first is that he does not focus on the present situation itself but its future implications. If he were to die, he would be with Christ; if he were to live, his imprisonment would be beneficial to the gospel. Paul considers both outcomes to be advantageous. The second element is that Paul always keeps sight of the purpose of his life and ministry. Although he recognizes the benefits of life and death, his focus is not

---

6. Levinsohn, *Discourse Features*, 63; Porter, *Idioms*, 291.

self-centered and he does not disregard the importance of relationships. The benefits that Paul seeks are inherently tied to Christ and his fellow believers. In other words, Paul's greatest joy comes from being with Christ and exalting him. Additionally, Paul finds joy in knowing that his beloved readers will also experience joy because of him. Therefore, while he evaluates his situation from the perspective of "benefit," it is not merely a selfish pursuit for his own sake. The essence of his pursuit is rooted in his love for Christ (a vertical love) and fellow believers (a horizontal love). This love motivates Paul's life and ministry and serves as the criterion for evaluating every situation.

The third observation is why Paul mentions his choice between two alternatives. His primary goal is to comfort the readers by sharing his current circumstances and expressing hope for his release from prison. However, he also aims to provide an example of the criteria for evaluating situations and to demonstrate how to think and discern various circumstances using such standards. In this sense, as in 1:12–18a, Paul's statement can also be seen as an indirect instruction on discerning and maintaining a fruitful life until the end.

PHILIPPIANS 1:27—2:18

OUTLINE:

III. The Body of the Letter (1:12—4:20)
    A. About the situations caused by Paul's imprisonment (1:12–26)
    B. About the real problems of the church (1:27—2:18)
    C. Paul's plan to send Timothy and Epaphroditus (2:19–30)

III. THE BODY OF THE LETTER (1:12—4:20)

B. About the real problems of the church (1:27–2:18)

THIS IS THE SECOND SECTION of the body of the letter and shows both continuity and discontinuity with 1:12–26. In terms of discontinuity, this section begins with an imperative (πολιτεύεσθε [live as a citizen] [1:27]), which is the first command in the letter. This marks a shift from the previous section, which focused on Paul's imprisonment, to a focus on the readers' situation. Another discontinuity aspect is the introduction of those who react negatively to the gospel in 1:28, marking the first time Paul mentions them in the letter.

Despite the discontinuity, however, there are two aspects of continuity. The first aspect is the use of second-person pronouns. Although the topic differs from 1:12–26, this section still focuses on the readers, which is Paul's primary concern. The second aspect is the expression "the gospel of Christ." Just as 1:12–26 begins with the gospel, this section starts Paul's exhortation with the gospel and links it to Christ. This demonstrates that both sections share the overarching theme of Christ and the gospel. According to the observed discontinuity, the progression of the letter so far can be summarized as follows: Introduction of the sender and recipient (1:1-2)—Paul's thanksgiving and prayer for the readers (1:3-11)—Paul's introduction of his situation (1:12-26)—Paul's exhortation on the readers' situation (1:27). Throughout this process, the gospel and Christ serves as unifying elements that provide continuity and permeate all of Paul's explanations.

The endpoint of this section is 2:18 because new characters, Timothy and Epaphroditus, are introduced in 2:19. Since this mark is the first instance where the focus shifts to people other than the readers, it is clearly distinguished from the exhortation about the readers' situation by the use of second-person pronouns.

This section can be divided into four parts based on the two factors: 1:27-30; 2:1-4; 2:5-11; 2:12-18. The first factor is the characters. While 1:27-30 mentions an external group that persecutes the readers, 2:1-4 deals only with the internal group and their relationship with Paul. In 2:5-11, the focus shifts to Jesus Christ and God's work without mentioning Paul or the readers. In 2:12, however, the focus returns to Paul and the readers through the nominative of address "my beloved." In this way, the transition of the characters serves as a crucial indicator of thematic development. The second factor is the use of imperatives. This section contains a total of eight imperatives. Notably, each paragraph begins with an imperative: 1:27 (πολιτεύεσθε [live as a citizen]); 2:2 (πληρώσατέ [make complete]); 2:5 (φρονεῖτε [think]); 2:12 (κατεργάζεσθε [work out]). The remaining four imperatives are all grouped in 2:12-18, where Paul uses the inferential conjunction ὥστε (therefore) to signal a transition to a part that summarizes and applies the previous explanation through a series of commands. In summary, this section follows a thematic flow consisting of (1) a problematic situation caused by an external group(s) (1:27-30), (2) a problematic situation caused by an internal group(s) (2:1-4), (3) an example of Christ Jesus (2:5-11), and (4) summary and conclusion (2:12-18).

1. About the external problem of the church (1:27-30)

According to the Greek text, 1:27-30 consists of two parts: a main clause with an imperative verb, "live as a citizen" (1:27a), and a ἵνα purpose/result clause (1:27b-30), which further clarifies the main clause. The ἵνα clause (1:27b-28a) also contains three types of elaboration (1:28b-30): (1) Paul's evaluation of the readers' situation introduced by the relative pronoun ἥτις (1:28b); (2) a ὅτι reason clause explaining the importance of believing in

Christ (1:29); and (3) an elaboration of Paul's situation through a participial phrase and a relative clause (1:30).

In this structure, the main characters are Paul, the readers, and the readers' opponents. Paul, represented by first-person pronouns, instructs the readers with this letter. The primary interaction takes place between the readers and their opponents. The opponents exert pressure on the readers who are responsible for maintaining their faith by confronting the challenges posed by the opponent according to Paul's instructions. Besides these characters, Christ and the Holy Spirit are also mentioned in the passage, but they are not portrayed as agents of action through verbs. The content and structure of this passage can be summarized as follows.

1. Main clause	Live only as a citizen (1:27a)	The readers
2. ἵνα subordinate clause	So that (ἵνα) whether (εἴτε) I come and (εἴτε) see you or remain absent, I may hear of the things about you (1:27b) That (ὅτι) you stand in one spirit (1:27c) (1) with one mind striving together for the faith of the gospel and (2) in no way alarmed by opponents (1:27d–28a)	Paul, the readers, and the opponents
3. Addition 1 (ἥτις relative clause)	Which (ἥτις) is (1) a sign of destruction for them, but (2) of salvation for you, this from God (1:28b)	The readers and the opponents
4. Addition 2 (ὅτι reason subordinate clause)	For (ὅτι) to you, it has been granted for Christ's sake (1) not only to believe in him (2) but also to suffer for his sake (1:29)	The readers
5. Addition 3 (participial and relative clauses)	experiencing the same conflict which you saw in me, and now hear [to be] in me (1:30)	Paul and the readers

A) 1:27A

Paul begins to address the problematic situations of the readers. The first issue is the hostile external environment that oppresses the church. Philippi was a Roman colony where retired veterans were granted Roman citizenship to reside (Acts 16:12), so the people in that city were naturally loyal to Rome. In such an environment, believers who lived for Jesus rather than Rome faced significant pressure. The pressure was considerable, although it may not have led to deadly persecution. In fact, when Paul first preached the gospel in Philippi, he was flogged and thrown into prison due to the same kind of hostility (Acts 16:19–23). Knowing the situation in Philippi, Paul commands the readers who are experiencing similar hardships with the imperative πολιτεύεσθε, which means to live as a citizen.[1] Although Paul does not explicitly mention the city he is referring to, the use of the cognate noun πολίτευμα (citizenship) (3:20) implies that he is speaking of life as a citizen of heaven rather than of Philippi. Therefore, Paul's command can be seen as an encouragement to live as citizens of heaven.

Paul's command has several implications. First, the readers must recognize their dual identity as citizens of the kingdom of God and residents of the region of Philippi, as mentioned in 1:1. Although believers have been transferred from the realm of darkness to the realm of light through faith in Jesus (John 5:24; Col 1:13), their physical bodies still dwell on this earth. They exist in the world but are not of the world, and they are citizens of heaven but still live on earth. As a result, believers are bound to experience the conflict between light and darkness while living on this earth. Understanding this is key to comprehending believers' present lives and struggles.

Second, the readers should remember to remain loyal to their identity. The true citizenship of believers is in heaven, so their allegiance should be to Jesus Christ and the Father rather than to worldly authorities, such as the Roman emperor. Therefore, Paul's command can be understood as a call to clarify one's identity and life orientation.

Third, the readers should discern the values and cultures of the world. Since they live under the pervasive atmosphere and pressure to be loyal to Rome, it is vital for those who hold heavenly citizenship to discern between the truth and the voice of the world. In this regard, the spiritual warfare of the believers involves deciding which values and voices to hear and follow rather than focusing on a physical aspect.

Fourth, the gospel of Christ is the standard for discernment in the believers' lives, distinguishing them from the world. This is implied in

---

1. "Πολιτεύω," LSJ 1434.

Paul's expression of "in a manner worthy of the gospel of Christ" in 1:27. Therefore, Paul's command can be viewed as a practical application of his intercessory prayer in 1:10, which addresses living a discerning life based on the truth rooted in Christ and the gospel, to the actual lives of the readers.

Fifth, experiencing suffering is inevitable when seeking to live a life that discerns the world through the truth. Paul does not command his readers to avoid suffering. Instead, he focuses on how to live an everyday Christian life based on loyalty to another king, God and Jesus, rather than the Roman emperor.

Finally, there is something more important than any other situation or difficulty. Paul implies this idea by adding "only" before the command. It means that as citizens of heaven, the readers must live a life of discernment and loyalty to Christ and the gospel, which takes precedence over everything else in this world that rebels against God.

B) 1:27B–28A

Paul explains the purpose of his command to the readers using a somewhat complicated structure. The main point is expressed through the ἵνα subordinate clause with the verb and object: "so that I may hear of the things about you." This indicates that Paul's reason for giving this command is to receive updates on the details of the readers' lives because his joy comes from seeing their progress in faith within the gospel. As another expression of Paul's love for the readers, it is consistent with the content of 1:25–26, where he anticipates his release from imprisonment for the benefit of their faith. He expands on this concept by adding a concessional clause with the double conditional conjunction εἴτε (whether): "whether I come and see you or remain absent." It implies that Paul is eager to hear from the readers about the positive results of his command, regardless of his circumstances.

Paul then uses a ὅτι clause and two subsequent participial clauses to describe the specific state of the readers from whom he wants to hear. He expresses that he wants the readers to stand firm (στήκετε) in the one Spirit through the ὅτι clause, which is the object clause of the verb "hear" above. The word στήκετε conjures up the image of a soldier standing his ground amid battle. Furthermore, the use of the present tense implies that Paul expects the readers to maintain this condition continuously rather than as a one-time event. The phrase "one spirit" likely refers to the Holy Spirit rather than the human spirit. Paul then elaborates on how the readers should stand firm using two participial clauses: striving together (συναθλοῦντες) with one mind (μιᾷ ψυχῇ) and not being intimidated by opponents. This additional information also evokes the image of a soldier who is willing to fight with his comrade and face opposition to protect what is valuable.[2]

The state of the readers that Paul expects contains several aspects related to their life as Christians. The first is an understanding of the nature of the Christian life. To be a Christian is to belong to the kingdom of God and live with a dual identity of heavenly and earthly citizenship. As a result, the life of a believer entails spiritual warfare against the powers of darkness and perseverance in undertaking such a battle. Consequently, the readers in Philippi must recognize the dual nature of the Christian life and engage in spiritual warfare against the world.

The second aspect is the purpose of this spiritual warfare. Spiritual warfare involves not only discerning between worldly messages and principles and the truth of the gospel but also persevering through hardship in the grace of salvation that comes from accepting God's truth by faith. Thus, the aim of the readers' warfare is to remain steadfast in their faith in Jesus as Lord and Savior, rather than in earthly powers such as the Roman emperor, and to live according to that faith.

The third aspect is the severity of the spiritual warfare. Battles come with hardships, and not being afraid of opponents implies facing actual fears, which may include physical and economic pressures. Paul acknowledges the readers' situation but encourages them to continue fighting and enduring without being overwhelmed.

The fourth one is that spiritual warfare is a corporate affair. By the expression of "striving together" and the repetition of the concept of unity (ἑνὶ and μιᾷ), Paul emphasizes that this battle should be fought not only by individuals alone but also by the church as a whole. Therefore, the division in the church, as mentioned in 4:2–3, is unacceptable, and efforts should be made to maintain unity, as illustrated in 2:1–4.

The fifth aspect is the necessity of divine assistance. Paul urges the readers to stand firm in one Spirit, recognizing the limitations of relying on human strength alone. As the readers fight against the darkness of the world, seeking divine help is crucial.

In summary, through these five elements, Paul encourages his readers to continue living faithfully in the truth of the gospel, against the pressures caused by the citizens of Philippi, and to live as faithful citizens of heaven.

---

2. "Συναθλέω," *EDNT* 3:296.

C) 1:28B–30

Paul provides three additional explanations regarding his command and expectations for his readers, encouraging them to persevere and obey his instructions. The first explanation emphasizes the importance of standing firm for the sake of the gospel, even in the face of suffering (1:28b). Using the relative pronoun ἥτις (which), Paul asserts that the steadfastness of the readers is a sign of their salvation, but for the opponents, it is a sign of destruction. He does not imply that the actions of the persecutors, or even the act of persecution itself, are the cause of salvation or destruction. Instead, he suggests that an individual's actions reveal their affiliation and identity. In other words, those who oppose the readers prove by their actions that they belong to the kingdom of darkness that rejects God. When God judges the darkness, they will also perish. However, the readers' perseverance indicates that they belong to the kingdom of light and are in the salvation process. Consequently, when the Lord perfects the world, they will share in the future fruits of salvation, which God will grant. Therefore, the readers should not be discouraged by present hardships but should stand firm in anticipating future wholeness.

The second explanation is the meaning of receiving grace for Christ's sake (1:29). Paul outlines this in two ways: believing in his name and suffering for his sake. There are two notable points to consider in his explanation. One is the phrase "for Christ" (ὑπὲρ Χριστοῦ), which Paul deliberately includes to affirm the ultimate direction of the readers' lives. It confirms that the only object of loyalty and service for the citizens of heaven is Christ. The other point is that Paul presents believing and suffering as equal components of grace. This expression portrays the readers' present situation, in which they suffer because of their faith in Jesus, but Paul characterizes it as grace. Therefore, their suffering is not merely an unusual and miserable occurrence but a gift of grace bestowed upon them by God, proving their belonging to the realm of salvation through their faith in Christ.

The third additional explanation is about Paul's situation as an example (1:30). Using a participial clause, Paul asserts that the readers' struggles are similar to what they have seen in his past experiences and what they are currently hearing about his present situation. There are three commonalities between him and the readers. First, both are undergoing hardship, with Paul currently in prison and the readers experiencing fear due to their opponents. Second, both have opponents related to Rome. Paul is imprisoned in Rome, and the Philippians, who are loyal to Rome, put pressure on the readers. Third, the hardships Paul and the readers face are due to their faith in Jesus. Paul associates his readers' circumstances with his own to reassure them that the challenges they face in their spiritual battles as citizens of heaven are not unique to them. This reflects his thoughtful concern for his readers.

In conclusion, in 1:27–30, Paul commands his readers to live a life worthy of the gospel of Christ in the face of external problems, particularly the pressure and opposition from Philippian citizens loyal to Rome. He wants the readers to live a life that is not intimidated by the clamor and persecution of the world but instead stands firm in the truth of the gospel. Even amid difficulties, they should remain faithful as citizens of heaven, loyal to Christ. To maintain such a lifestyle, Paul urges the readers to have a clear understanding of the past, present, and future aspects of salvation, with Christ at the center. He reminds them that they have received the grace of Christ in the past, which includes participation in the salvation process through faith and suffering for his sake. Paul emphasizes the coming judgment of Christ in the future, when those opposing his readers will be destroyed, and those who endure suffering will experience complete salvation. In the present, they should continue to stand firm in the truth, relying on past grace and hoping for the future. Paul also helps the readers by connecting his current imprisonment by Rome for the gospel to the suffering of his readers. In doing so, he gives them an example of living by the gospel and encourages them to remain steadfast in the truth. Overall, 1:27–30 presents a clear picture of how believers should live in this world of darkness, despite its short and somewhat complicated structure.

2. About the internal problems of the church (2:1–4)

Paul moves on to the second problem of the church. The nature of the problem can be deduced from two clues. First, 2:1–4 contains only first- and second-person references, indicating that Paul's exhortation is related solely to the situation within the readers themselves. It differs from 1:27–30, which deals with external adversaries through third-person references. Second, Paul's choice of words has two distinct characteristics. One of these is the frequent use of expressions about oneness, such as in 2:2, where the main clause of the conditional sentence is supported by four terms grouped in the conditional sentence (αὐτό, αὐτὴν [same], σύμψυχοι [being of one mind], and ἕν [one]). The other characteristic is the use of words related to pride through competition and comparison, such as ἐριθείαν (rivalry) and κενοδοξίαν (empty conceit) (2:3). Based on these observations, it is evident that, unlike 1:27–30, 2:1–4 addresses the unity of the church in response to the division caused by competition and comparison within the church.

This paragraph can be divided into two parts based on sentence form: 2:1–2 and 3–4. In 2:1–2, Paul uses a conditional sentence to command the readers to maintain unity in the face of their internal conflicts. In 2:3–4, which consists of two participial clauses, Paul provides a specific example of what he commands in 2:2, mainly in the cognitive area. The structure of this paragraph can be summarized as follows.

1. Paul's command on the internal problem of the church (2:1–2)		
1) Protasis	Therefore, if there is any encouragement in Christ, if any consolation of love, if any fellowship of the Spirit, if any affection and compassion (2:1)	Conditional sentence
2) Apodosis	then make my joy complete by having the same mindset, having the same love, [being] of the same mind, thinking the one thing (2:2)	
2. Additional commands (2:3–4)		
1) Cognitive thinking	Do nothing from selfishness or empty conceit, but think of one another with humility of mind as more important than yourselves (2:3)	
2) Cognitive consideration	Do not only look out for your own personal interests but also for the interests of others (2:4)	

A) 2:1–2

Paul introduces a new topic using the inferential conjunction οὖν (therefore) and a conditional sentence in 2:1. Although the conjunction οὖν implies a result, it does not conclude the previous paragraph (1:27–30) because there is no reference to the opponents in this paragraph. It is more appropriate to consider 2:1–2 as the beginning of a new topic. Nevertheless, the use of οὖν indicates that 2:1–4 is not entirely disconnected from 1:27–30. Instead, it reflects Paul's intention to connect the external pressures discussed in 1:27–30 with the internal divisions within the church. In other words, when Paul urges the readers to stand firm together amid external pressures (1:27), he also believes it is necessary to resolve the internal conflicts within the church to deal with the external problem effectively. That is why Paul begins to address the internal problem of the church using οὖν in 2:1.

The conditional statement consists of four conditional clauses (protases) and a main clause (apodosis) containing a command. Additionally, there is a subordinate clause introduced by the conjunction ἵνα to illustrate the means and participial clauses to explain it. The conditional clauses have only four grammatical subjects, beginning with τις and τι (any), without a verb: (1) any encouragement in Christ, (2) any consolation of love, (3) any fellowship of the Spirit, and (4) any affection and compassion. This expression has three characteristics.

First, everything comes from the relationship between the Triune God and the readers. Although none of the lists explicitly mention God, and the second and fourth lists do not express any divine connection, it is evident that God is the ultimate source of these lists. For instance, the term corresponding to affection (σπλάγχνα) in the fourth list is the same word that Paul used to express his love for the readers in 1:8, where he declares that he loves them with the σπλάγχνα of Jesus. Therefore, while it may be debatable whether the fourth list, affection and compassion, is God's attitude toward the believers or the believer's attitude toward another believer, the Triune God is the ultimate source of this attitude.

Second, these lists describe the experiences of readers in the salvation process. It is unclear which specific verb Paul intended to add for clarification, but based on the expression in the conditional clause, it is unlikely that he intends to urge the pursuit of these things. Instead, it is better to understand that Paul assumes the readers have already encountered these experiences.

Third, all the elements in the list pertain to developing inner stability to foster positive relationships with others. Maintaining healthy relationships can be challenging due to the potential for conflict and emotional hurt. Therefore, believers must be equipped with inner comfort, encouragement, and love to sustain positive relationships. This is particularly important in conflict situations, such as the rivalry and competition in the Philippian church (4:2–3). The lists Paul mentioned as conditional clauses are necessary for internal stability. In this sense, his use of conditional clauses is a deliberate way of addressing the internal issues of the church and emphasizing the importance of inner stability for maintaining positive relationships within the church. In other words, Paul urges his readers to utilize their experience of cultivating inner stability through their vertical relationship with the Triune God as a foundation for establishing and sustaining positive horizontal relationships with fellow believers.

In the main clause of the conditional sentence, Paul instructs the readers to complete his joy (2:2a). The content may seem somewhat strange because, although Paul is addressing the church's internal conflict, specifically the discord between Euodia and Syntyche in 4:2–3, the focus is directed at Paul himself, not the readers. Furthermore, he deviates from the standard word order of "noun (χαρὰν [joy]) plus genitive (μου [my])" and emphasizes his joy through placing the genitive first (μου τὴν χαρὰν). While this may appear self-centered, it can be interpreted as a powerful command to the readers, given Paul's relationship with them.

Paul's readers have been his fellow workers in the gospel for the past decade since the church was founded. They have supported his ministry through material contributions and prayer (1:5–7; 4:15–16). Even now, they are providing for his needs through Epaphroditus while he is in prison (4:18). They love and respect Paul for his work in the gospel, and Paul cherishes them in the heart of Jesus as well (1:8). Given this intimate relationship, Paul's command in 2:2a has two implications. First, Paul does not address their problem solely based on his status as an apostle. Instead, he wants to approach it as a partner, working with them and sharing a mutual love for advancing the gospel. This is consistent with the beginning of the letter in 1:1, where Paul intentionally omits mention of his apostleship. Second, the readers' conflict is not only their concern but also a matter of importance to Paul. Therefore, his command suggests that if they love him, they should be more obedient to his admonitions regarding their problem, which is also his problem. Thus, Paul's command embodies his love for the readers and his sincere hope that their problem will be resolved.

In 2:2b, Paul suggests specific ways for the readers to carry out his command to complete his joy through a subordinate clause with the ἵνα conjunction ("by having the same mindset") and subsequent participial clauses that expand on it ("[being] of the same mind and thinking the one thing"). There are three features in his explanation: (1) All the instructions relate to interpersonal relationships. (2) There is an emphasis on cognitive thinking. Paul advises that the process of resolving conflict should begin in the realm of thought by repeating the verb φρονέω (to think). It can be seen as an example of applying the "inside-out" principle mentioned in Paul's intercessory prayer (1:9–11) to the actual situation of the readers. In other words, for a fruitful life, believers should begin with discernment in the inner realm of thought and then manifest it in the outward expression of life. (3) There is an emphasis on unity. Paul emphasizes the concept of oneness using four words: αὐτὸ, αὐτὴν (same), σύμψυχοι (being of the same mind), and ἓν (one). Since these expressions occur frequently throughout the letter, they suggest that the readers are facing conflict and division, and that Paul proposes unity as the solution. In summary, Paul's command to the readers concerning the internal problem of the church is to maintain healthy relationships with one another, beginning with unity in their thinking.

B) 2:3-4

Using hortatory participles with comparison and contrast, Paul asks his readers to adopt certain attitudes to resolve their internal conflicts. The first attitude pertains to the cognitive aspect of comparing and competing with others (2:3). English Bibles use the verb "do" to describe the issue in terms of action. However, the Greek text just states "nothing from selfishness or empty conceit" and contrasts it with a participle form of ἡγέομαι (to consider), which belongs to the same semantic domain as φρονέω (to think).[3] It indicates that Paul's main objective is to change his readers' thinking. In other words, Paul urges that instead of approaching their relationships with others from a comparative and competitive perspective, they should think (ἡγούμενοι) of others as better than themselves with humble thinking (ταπεινοφροσύνῃ). This is a specific way to achieve unity in the area of thinking mentioned in 2:2b.

The second attitude pertains to unity. Paul instructs each reader to look out (σκοποῦντες) not only for their own interests but also for the interests of others (2:4). Since the word σκοποῦντες pertains to cognitive learning ("being concerned about"),[4] it can be said that Paul emphasizes a change of mindset over mere action. He urges his readers to pay attention to other members of the church, cultivating a sense of togetherness and being of the same mind (σύμψυχοι), as seen in 2:2b. To achieve a change of mindset, the readers must first be equipped with the elements mentioned in the conditional clauses in 2:1. That is, through divine help obtained from their relationship with the Triune God, they can overcome their obsession with seeking comfort, recognition, and love for themselves. As a result, their eyes will be opened to the needs of others, and true unity can begin to take shape. In this sense, Paul's method is both appropriate and practical: he first uses conditional statements to remind the readers of divine help, and then teaches practical steps for solving their problems by changing their way of thinking and perspective.

---

3. "Φρονέω, ἡγέομαι," L&N 364.
4. "Σκοπέω," L&N 351.

3. Jesus Christ, the supreme model for the church (2:5–11)

Paul's exhortation regarding the church's problem continues. This paragraph has long been the subject of significant scholarly debate because it portrays Jesus's ministry. Is 2:6–11 prose or poetry? What is the theological background for understanding Jesus's ministry? Is it derived from the Old Testament, Second Temple Judaism's theology, or the influence of Hellenistic myth? Was this part written by Paul or quoted from the early church creed?[5] Despite the extensive scholarly debate, the more important question is why Paul includes this content here. To answer this question, we must consider the role of 2:5–11 in its context.

The position and role of this paragraph can be identified by its continuity and discontinuity with 2:1–4. One indication of continuity is the imperative φρονεῖτε (think/have [this] mind) (2:5). The second-person imperative indicates that Paul continues to address the situation of his readers. The verb φρονέω is the same one he used in 2:2 to urge the readers to change in the area of cognitive thinking. Thus, the use of φρονεῖτε indicates a close link between 2:5–11 and 2:1–4 in terms of cognitive thinking. In addition, the description of Jesus at the beginning of the paragraph reinforces this connection, as it highlights what he thought (ἡγήσατο). However, there is a discontinuity concerning the characters involved. Jesus Christ appears as the subject of the sentence and takes on the role of the agent of a series of actions, unlike in 2:1–4. Moreover, Paul's words describing Jesus's actions exhibit both continuity and discontinuity. In describing Jesus's incarnation and humiliation in 2:5, Paul uses the verbs ἐκένωσεν (emptied) and ἐταπείνωσεν (lowered), which show continuity with the call to humble thinking (ταπεινοφροσύνη) and the avoidance of vainglory (κενοδοξίαν) (2:3). However, the use of these verbs in 2:5 also signifies discontinuity because they refer to actions rather than thinking. Based on these observations, we conclude that Paul mentions Jesus in 2:5–11 not to explain a theological doctrine unrelated to the context but to provide a comprehensive example of thinking and behavior by linking the case of Jesus to his command on the cognitive thinking given in 2:1–4.

The paragraph of 2:5–11 is divided into two parts: an introduction in 2:5 and the description of Jesus in 2:6–11. The latter can be further divided into three segments based on time, space, and characters. The first segment (2:6) describes a heavenly event in the distant past before Jesus's incarnation. The second segment (2:7–8) deals with Jesus's recent incarnation and death on the cross. Last, 2:9–11 delineates the events following Jesus's death. While Jesus is the main character in the first two segments (2:6–8), God

---

5. For the explanation of the different views on these questions, see Keown, *Philippians 1:1—2:18*, 351–72.

appears in the third segment as the subject of the process that exalts Jesus. It is a heavenly event that includes the ultimate consummation point at the end of history.

This structure presents an interesting observation that the explanation of Jesus's journey proceeds as an inside-out approach. The verbs in which Jesus is the subject progress from his existence (ὑπάρχων [being]) to his thought (ἡγήσατο in 2:6) and to his actions (ἐκένωσεν, λαβών [taking], γενόμενος [being born], ἐταπείνωσεν). This pattern is also related to the position and function of this paragraph. After mentioning cognitive thinking in 2:1–4, Paul presents Jesus's thoughts, actions, and results in 2:5–11 as the basis for his command regarding the readers' behavior and attitude in 2:12–18. Therefore, 2:5–11 serves as an example of Paul's exhortation to his readers and as a bridge linking his teaching on their inward cognitive thinking with their outward behavior. The content of 2:5–11 can be outlined as follows.

1. Introductory command (2:5): Think this in yourself, which was also in Christ Jesus	
2. The example of Jesus (2:6–11)	
1) Preexistence of Jesus (2:6)	* Jesus's thinking * Past in heaven
a. Jesus's existence: He existed in the form of God	
b. Jesus's way of thinking: He did not regard equality with God as a thing to be grasped	
2) Incarnation and cross of Jesus (2:7–8)	* Jesus's action * Relatively recent past on earth
a. Incarnation: He emptied himself to be a human (2:7)	
b Jesus's ministry: He lowered himself even to the death on the cross (2:8)	
3) After Jesus's death (2:9–11)	* God's action * Relatively past in heaven with the future consummation
a. God's action: God highly exalted Jesus and gave the name that is above every name (2:9)	
b. Its result: All who are in heaven and on earth will bow in the name of Jesus, and every tongue will confess the lordship of Jesus for the glory of God the Father (2:10–11)	

A) 2:5

Paul continues his exhortation regarding the internal conflicts in the church by using another imperative. He commands the readers to have the same mindset as Christ. There are several points to notice in his expression. The first one is the use of the imperative φρονεῖτε (think/have [this] mind), which is the same verb Paul used in 2:1–4 when he urged the readers to solve the internal problem of the church. This verb links back to 2:1–4 and serves as a reminder of what needs to be done to overcome the problem.

The second point is Paul's use of Jesus as an example. He intends to present Jesus as the focus of faith and loyalty in the salvation process and as a paradigm for living in a relationship with God. It is noteworthy that Paul does not simply encourage the readers to think about Jesus himself but rather to concentrate on what it means to be in Christ, how Jesus thinks, and how he demonstrates this in his life.

The third point is the use of cataphoric reference for emphasis. A pronoun typically refers to a preceding noun or clause as an anaphoric reference. However, when a pronoun is placed before the corresponding noun or clause, it creates emphasis and is known as a cataphoric reference. In this passage, Paul uses the pronoun τοῦτο (this) first and then provides the corresponding relative clause later, drawing the readers' attention to Paul's message.

From these points, it can be deduced that Paul's purpose in using the example of Jesus is twofold: (1) to emphasize the importance of resolving internal conflicts within the church and (2) to affirm his command that, just as in the case of Jesus, restoring their relationships should begin with a change in mindset and be demonstrated by action. Therefore, the readers should follow Paul's instructions and the example of Jesus to resolve the internal problems of the church.

B) 2:6

Paul begins to explain Jesus's example by presenting two elements of his preincarnate state in heaven. The first element pertains to Jesus's existence: "being [ὑπάρχων] in the form [μορφή] of God." The second element relates to Jesus's way of thinking: "he did not regard equality with God as something to be grasped [ἁρπαγμόν]." These two elements are connected through a participial clause (the first element) and a main clause (the second element). The participial clause functions as a concessive clause, providing background information for the main clause. Paul's primary focus is on the content of the main clause, which concerns the way Jesus thought, rather than the participial clause, which offers the theological or doctrinal explanation for his existence. Therefore, it is not appropriate to approach this part solely as a theological teaching. Instead, it should be viewed as an illustration that provides a specific example of Jesus for the readers' problem, as mentioned in 2:1–4. In particular, Jesus's way of thinking is connected to the change in the readers' mindset that Paul commanded in 2:1–4.

What, then, is the mindset of Jesus that Paul wants to communicate to his readers? Although this passage is not intended to provide theological doctrine itself, it raises several questions about the meaning of certain expressions. Does ὑπάρχων refer to the pre-incarnation of Jesus? What does μορφή imply? Does it refer to his physical body or not? What does ἁρπαγμὸν mean? What does it mean to be "equal with God"? Although there is a complex and lengthy debate, let us simplify it. It would be better to start with the word μορφή, which generally focuses on external form rather than internal essence. The key to understanding its meaning is "the form of a servant" in 2:7. This phrase does not refer to the outward appearance of a particular being, such as a servant. Instead, in the following description, it refers to a created person with a lower status as a servant in comparison to God, the Lord and Creator. Therefore, the phrase "form of God" in 2:6 can also be interpreted as a symbol of God's status and identity as a being adorned with glory and dignity that sets Jesus apart from the rest of creation rather than as a physical or material form of God.

This understanding provides insight into the question of ὑπάρχων. The statement that Jesus became a created man in 2:7 implies that he was not human before. If we think of ὑπάρχων as a post-incarnate form of Jesus, then it would be odd to say that Jesus, who had already become a creature (2:6), became again like a man (2:7). Furthermore, since the use of the adversative conjunction ἀλλὰ in 2:7 distinguishes the situations in 2:6 and 2:7, it is awkward to interpret these verses as happening simultaneously. Therefore, it logically makes sense to view ὑπάρχων in 2:6 as referring to the preincarnate state, which is contrasted with Jesus's incarnation as a human being.

The noun ἁρπαγμὸν appears only in this passage of the Bible and is derived from the verb ἁρπάζω (to grab or seize by force [Matt 11:12; John 6:15; Acts 8:39; etc.]). This word can be interpreted in an active sense, focusing on the process of taking, or in a passive sense, focusing on the result. Of the two, it seems better to understand ἁρπαγμὸν as referring to the result of forcibly taking something, especially something that has been selfishly exploited. The context supports this interpretation. Paul is addressing the internal problems within the church and using Jesus as an example to reinforce his exhortation. What he points out in 2:1–4 is not the outward actions of how the readers are fighting, but their motivation, which is driven by vain desires to elevate themselves through comparison and competition (2:2). In this context, when Paul presents Jesus as a model for the readers, the primary point of contrast is likely to be the motivation to exalt themselves through competition rather than their actions. Therefore, it is more appropriate to understand ἁρπαγμὸν as focusing on the result of the process of taking something by force with the motivation of selfish competition or desire for personal gain.

This understanding can also shed light on the meaning of the phrase τὸ εἶναι ἴσα θεῷ (to be equal with God). Although this phrase is connected to ἁρπαγμὸν, there is no explicit explanation of its meaning. Since Paul has already portrayed Jesus as a being in the form of God, this phrase cannot imply that the relatively inferior Jesus becomes like the superior God the Father. Instead, it indicates an attempt to assert dominance or superiority over the Father God, reflecting a self-centered attitude that prioritizes oneself over the relationship with God. It resembles Adam and Eve's attempt to become like God by disobeying his command in Gen 3, which the Bible identifies as sin. The essence of their sin is not the action of eating the fruit of the knowledge of good and evil but the motivation to exclude God from the realm of thought and set oneself up as the standard of good and evil. Romans 1:28 describes this process as excluding God from one's knowledge and making oneself the center of thought and judgment. In this regard, the concept of sin in the Bible is intrinsically linked to one's relationship with God the Creator, consisting of two phases. The initial state is characterized by a person's exclusive focus on themselves within their cognitive thought world, ignoring the relationship with God. It can be called "the sin" or the fundamental sin. The subsequent phase is the manifestation of "the sin" in various aspects of life, which is called "sins." This twofold process of sin also shows an inside-out pattern.

In summary, Jesus held the status and position of God and was adorned with glory and honor. However, he had no thoughts of selfish and vain ambition that would disrupt his relationship with God or take the initiative. If this was the mindset of Jesus as the Son of God, how should the readers, who have entered into the salvation process through him and are now in a relationship with God/Jesus, respond? Paul delivers his message as an indirect instruction to the readers.

C) 2:7-8

Using an adversative conjunction ἀλλά (but), Paul shifts the focus from Jesus's preincarnate state in 2:6 to what happened afterward. He introduces two processes concerning Jesus with two main verbs: Jesus emptied himself (2:7) and humbled himself (2:8). Paul also elaborates on each process by adding two participial clauses to each.

Concerning the first process, Paul adds the expressions "taking the form of a servant" and "being made in the likeness of men" (2:7a). These two expressions form a hendiadys, indicating that Jesus became human. However, Paul does not solely focus on Jesus's humanity itself, because he first mentions that Jesus took on "the form of a servant." This expression contrasts with "the form of God" in 2:6 and emphasizes two distinctions. First, there is the difference between God as the Creator and a human as a creature. Second, there is the contrast between the Lord, who is the highest above all, and the servant, who is the lowest among humans. After all, Paul highlights the contrast between the highest and the lowest to convey that Jesus, who held the status and position of Lord and Creator before the incarnation, humbled himself and took on the lowest state of a creature, a human being.

Regarding the second process, Paul adds two participial clauses before and after the main verb (ἐταπείνωσεν [humbled]) to describe Jesus humbling himself (2:7b-8). The first is "being found in appearance as a man" before the main verb (2:7b). As another expression of the result of the first process above, it is a premise for Jesus's humble action. The second participial clause, "becoming obedient to the point of death, even death on the cross," refers to Jesus's subsequent action after the main verb (2:8). Jesus's death is a striking expression in several ways because (1) it represents that the Lord of life, who had the status and honor of God before the incarnation, lost his life as a man, a creature; (2) his crucifixion was an execution of a criminal by Roman authority; and (3) his death was considered by the Jews, as a death on a wooden cross, as under the curse of God (Deut 21:22-23). In other words, God the Son was considered the most heinous criminal in the world and died under God's curse. It is unbelievable nonsense! Paul emphasizes this aspect of Jesus's death by adding the phrase "death on a cross." However, he also points out that Jesus's death had another aspect, obedience. Although his death was a humanly and socially humiliating outcome, it was not only an act of defiance against the self-centered desire to take control but also a humble obedience that willingly participated in God the Father's plan of salvation.

Overall, there are two aspects to consider in Paul's description of Jesus's life after the incarnation in 2:7-8. The first aspect is the use of action-oriented verbs, which is distinct from 2:6, which focuses on cognitive thinking with ἡγήσατο ([he] thought). Furthermore, except for the participle εὑρεθεὶς (being found) (2:7b), Jesus is the subject of all the verbs. The progression through these verbs illustrates a series of logical sequences: Jesus emptied himself → became human → humbled himself → obeyed to the point of death on the cross. The post-incarnate process is the pivotal phase in fulfilling God's plan of salvation. Paul describes the entire process as Jesus's proactive and voluntary action, encapsulating it as obedience.

The second aspect is its relationship to 2:1-4. Two indicators in 2:7-8 demonstrate a connection with 2:1-4. One is the use of the verbs ἐκένωσεν (emptied) and ἐταπείνωσεν (made low). These verbs differ from those in 2:1-4, which deal solely with cognitive thinking, in that they refer to behavior. However, there is also a connection with the language Paul uses to exhort his readers in 2:2-3 (κενοδοξίαν [empty conceit] and ταπεινοφροσύνῃ [humility of mind]). Based on this connection, it can be inferred that Paul presents Jesus as the model for the behavioral dimension in 2:7-8 while encouraging his readers to prioritize humility over competition in cognitive thinking in 2:1-4. Another indicator is the expression of servant and servitude. The term "servant," which implies low status, is related to Paul's exhortation to regard other believers as better than oneself in 2:3. Additionally, the presentation of Jesus as a servant in 2:7-8 is intended to introduce him as the best model for the readers to follow in terms of humility. This intention is already reflected in Paul's self-introduction in 1:1, where he refers to himself as a servant of Jesus rather than an apostle. If Paul, whom the readers love and respect, is a servant of the humble Jesus, then the readers should imitate Jesus as Paul does. Their relationship can be summarized as Jesus, the supreme model—Paul, the follower of Jesus—the readers, the followers of Jesus and Paul.

However, the humility that Paul advocates is not an end in itself. Jesus's act of emptying himself to become incarnate and dying on the cross was ultimately an act of obedience to fulfill God's plan of salvation. Similarly, the readers' learning of Jesus's humility is necessary for the unity of the church and for living a life worthy of the gospel on earth as citizens of heaven. Therefore, the readers should strive to embody Jesus's thoughts and behaviors related to humility, so they abandon conflict driven by competition and keep in mind the big picture of the salvation process.

D) 2:9–11

The explanation of Jesus moves on to its third stage through the double conjunction διὸ καὶ (for this reason also). The inferential conjunction διὸ (for this reason) indicates that 2:9-11 is the result of the preceding process mentioned in 2:8 that covers Jesus's preincarnate state and his life on earth until his crucifixion. 2:9-11 deals with the subsequent events and results, namely Jesus's resurrection and ascension to heaven. This passage consists of the main clauses that mention God's actions (2:9) and a ἵνα subordinate clause that explains their consequences (2:10-11).

In the main clauses, Paul mentions two actions of God: highly exalting Jesus and granting him the name above all names. There are several observations to make here. The first is that God appears as the subject and actor in these processes. While the process in 2:6-8 centers on Jesus, this part introduces God's response to Jesus's thoughts and actions. The second is the meaning of what God has done. Paul uses the preposition ὑπερ to describe God's action in a superlative sense: God exalted Jesus to the highest position (ὑπερύψωσεν) and gave him the most excellent name, which is above (ὑπὲρ) every name. Although these two processes can be understood as a hendiadys that God gave Jesus the highest status and position, it does not mean that God gave Jesus something higher than his preincarnate status. Rather, it refers to the restoration process. Jesus initially possessed the glory of God (2:6) but chose to empty himself of that glory to live a life of obedience and die on earth. Then, God restored Jesus to his original state of glory (John 17:5). It is also unnecessary to interpret this process as a reward for Jesus's obedience. It would be awkward to assume that Jesus humbly came to earth to regain his original status or that God restored Jesus's original status as a reward for his obedience. Instead, it is more appropriate to understand this as God's vindication of Jesus's obedience. In other words, God restored Jesus's original status and glory because he recognized that Jesus voluntarily became a creature for the sake of God's plan of salvation for the world and humankind and completed his ministry with obedience.

The subordinate clauses mention the twofold results of God's actions (2:10-11). The first is that every knee, of those who are in heaven, on earth, and under the earth, will bow to the name of Jesus (2:10). The second is that every tongue will confess that Jesus Christ is Lord, to the glory of God the Father (2:11). While the subject of 2:9 is God, the subject in this passage is every knee and tongue. This indicates that the focus is on the response of all creation to the restored status and authority of Jesus, and their response is characterized by submissive kneeling and a confession of recognition. What is noteworthy here is the implication of obedience and confession, and several things must be considered to understand it.

The first thing to consider is the existence of a realm of rebellion. If we reverse the statement that all creation will recognize and submit to the lordship of Jesus, it implies that this has not always been the case. Jesus was originally Lord and Creator alongside God the Father, but a rebellion arose around Satan at some point. Perhaps this rebellion took place before God created the world. This rebellion later extended to humanity through the seduction of the woman by the serpent in Gen 3. As a result, the world that God created became a field of rebellion against him. In this situation, God is not recognized as God in the realm of rebellion, even though he still rules the world as its Lord and Creator. The case of Jesus was even more severe. Although he was the Lord before his incarnation, he did not receive the worship he deserved after the rebellion. The world failed to recognize Jesus's status, despised his humble incarnation, and eventually led him to a humiliating death on the cross. However, the situation changed after the crucifixion and resurrection. Jesus's ministry was to break the rebellious reign and restore the kingdom of God (Mark 1:15; 3:27), and his crucifixion and resurrection marked the culmination of that ministry, signifying victory over darkness (Col 2:15). Jesus's earthly ministry was recognized by God, and his original status and glory were reinstated through his resurrection and ascension. As a result, Jesus will receive full worship in the restored kingdom of God. In this sense, the processes of both the restoration of Jesus's original position and authority and the response of all creation to him are set against the backdrop of the conflict between the kingdom of God and the realm of darkness, along with the beings within it.

The second thing to consider is that the complete worship of Jesus is directed toward a future consummation. Although Jesus ascended and God restored his original status and position, not all creation currently worships him. This complete worship will be fully realized in the future consummation of the salvation process through Jesus's second coming and the final judgment. Therefore, 2:10–11 reflects a coexistence of present restoration and future consummation concerning the authority of Jesus and the kingdom of God.

The third point is that those who will genuinely kneel and confess to Jesus include all beings in heaven, on earth, and under the earth. Although it is unclear who this group encompasses, it can be interpreted as all creation, including spiritual beings. Notably, it even includes the Roman emperor, to whom the citizens of Philippi, who are currently oppressing the church, are loyal. Paul's use of the active (κάμψῃ [bow]) and middle voice form (ἐξομολογήσηται [confess]) implies that the creatures' submission and confession will be voluntary. It will indeed happen someday!

The fourth point is the phrase "to the glory of God the Father." The ultimate goal of the entire process is the glory of God, who initiates, fulfills, and completes the entire plan of salvation.

Based on these observations about the content of the subordinate clauses, it is evident that the restoration of Jesus to his original position and authority was more than a return to his former status. Although the status and authority remain the same, the creatures' responses to him will differ. This is because, through Jesus's obedience to God's will for the kingdom of God and salvation, the realm of rebellion began to be subdued. The kingdom of God will eventually be fully restored, and the worship of Jesus will also be completely restored. Therefore, 2:9–11 can be understood as an explanation of the completion of God's plan, which began before creation and centered on Jesus (Eph 1:4–6).

In conclusion, Paul's description of Jesus in 2:5–11 contains two significant aspects centered on Jesus. The first aspect is a sequence in God's plan of salvation. The story of Jesus is told in chronological order, beginning with his preincarnate state, followed by his incarnation and earthly ministry leading to the cross, his resurrection and ascension, and the ultimate completion of the plan of salvation. Spatially, the process begins in heaven, moves to the earth, and ends with Jesus's return to heaven. Although Paul does not explicitly mention elements such as human sin and the rebellious world against God, the description of Jesus's incarnation and the subsequent process presupposes these elements and their resolution. Overall, this process fulfills the overarching goal of restoring the kingdom of God and bringing salvation to humanity in the context of a world that has rejected God's authority. The second aspect is the inside-out pattern. According to Paul, Jesus's participation in God's redemptive process began in the cognitive realm of thought and progressed into action. Jesus's way of thinking involves abandoning the motive of competition and preemption, while his action demonstrates humble obedience to God's will by lowering himself.

However, it is important to note that Paul's primary focus is not merely to convey theological doctrine but to provide a foundation for practical guidance to his readers facing both internal and external challenges. Concerning the internal conflict within the church, Paul seeks to inspire them to adopt Jesus's inside-out approach and to transform their mindset toward other believers, demonstrating this transformation through tangible actions that promote unity and togetherness. Regarding external issues, Paul shows that since Jesus is the true Lord to whom all creation must submit and recognize, there is no reason to fear or retreat from living a life for Jesus and the gospel, even in the face of suffering and pressure. In light of this, how should the church respond to both internal and external situations? Paul deals with and summarizes this question in the following 2:12–18.

4. Concluding exhortations on the problems of the church (2:12–18)

The place and role of 2:12–18 can be identified by its continuity and discontinuity with the preceding paragraph. Several pieces of evidence indicate the discontinuity. First, there is a shift in the focus of the characters. While 2:6–11 focuses on Jesus, 2:12–18 transitions to second-person references, directing attention to the readers. Second, the series of imperatives in 2:12–18 contrasts with 2:6–11, which contains no imperatives. Third, the nominative of address ἀγαπητοί μου (my beloved) serves to redirect the readers' attention to themselves.

However, these signs of discontinuity also function as indicators of continuity. For example, the use of the second-person imperative indicates that 2:12–18 is consistent with previous passages that addressed the readers' problems through imperative, such as 1:27 (concerning the external problem), 2:1–4 (concerning the internal problem), and 2:5 (concerning the example of Jesus). Moreover, the use of ὥστε (therefore) indicates that 2:12–18 serves not only as a concluding application based on Jesus's example but also as a summary of Paul's exhortations thus far, starting from 1:27. The nominative of address, while signaling discontinuity, also emphasizes to the readers that this is a concluding part, thus serving as a marker of continuity with the previous paragraphs. Therefore, 2:12–18 can be understood as a summary of Paul's solution to the internal and external problems of the church, following the example of Jesus.

This paragraph features four participants: Paul, the readers, God, and the world. Throughout 2:12–18, Paul and the readers are depicted in a relationship of command and obedience. Within this relationship, God appears as a helper in the lives of the readers (2:12). At the same time, the world is portrayed as both an object and environment that the readers must deal with appropriately according to Paul's commands (2:14–16). These participant elements are crucial for understanding the structure of the passage, which can be divided into three parts.

The first part (2:12–13) includes Paul, the readers, and God. The readers are the recipients of both Paul's exhortation through the second-person imperative and God's work (each [2:11] and in you [2:12]). This suggests that this part relates to Paul's exhortation regarding internal problems within the church.

The second part is 2:14–16. Although Paul addresses the readers using the second-person imperative, unlike 2:12–13, he does not use second-person pronouns. Instead, he uses expressions such as "generation" (γενεᾶς) and "in the world" (ἐν κόσμῳ), which pertain to matters outside the church. This indicates that Paul focuses on the readers' behavior concerning their external problems.

The third part (2:17–18) shifts the focus to Paul, employing a conditional sentence with first-person verbs (σπένδομαι [I am being poured out] and χαίρω [I rejoice]). Although a second-person imperative appears in 2:18, its content differs from the previous ones because it pertains to Paul's relationship with the readers. Overall, 2:12–18 summarizes the solution to the readers' internal and external problems. This passage also encourages obedience to Paul's commands, which will bring him joy.

1. Command 1: On the internal problem (2:12–13) 　1) Call the readers: My beloved 　2) Command: Just as you have always obeyed, work out your salvation with fear and trembling (2:12) 　3) Reason: It is God who is at work in you, both to will and to work for good pleasure (2:13)	* Paul, the readers, and God * Direction of command: To the church members (Each and "in you")
2. Command 2: On the external problem (2:14–16) 　1) Command: Do all things without grumbling or disputing (2:14) 　2) Purpose: You will prove yourselves to be blameless and innocent, children of God above reproach in the midst of a crooked and perverse generation (2:15a) 　3) Addition: Among whom you appear as lights in the world, holding fast the word of life for the boast of me in the day of Christ (2:15b–16)	* Paul, the readers, and the world * Direction of command: To the outer world (generation and "in the world")

3. The rejoicings of Paul and the readers (2:17–18) 1) Paul's joy: Even if I am being poured out as a drink offering upon the sacrifice and service of your faith, I rejoice and share my joy with you all (2:17) 2) Command: You, too, rejoice in the same way and share your joy with me (2:18)	* Paul and the readers * Direction of Command: Paul * Conditional structure

A) 2:12–13

Paul uses the nominative of address ἀγαπητοί μου (my beloved) to capture the readers' attention and concludes his exhortations concerning their internal problems with the inferential conjunction ὥστε (therefore). He commands the readers to work out (κατεργάζεσθε) their own (ἑαυτῶν) salvation with fear and trembling (2:12). Although this may seem like an unexpected command, there are two things to consider.

First, the imperative κατεργάζεσθε pertains to the dimension of action. Up to this point, Paul's exhortations regarding the readers' internal problems have included commands about their thinking (2:1–4), a command to adopt the same mindset as Jesus (2:5), Jesus's example of thinking (2:6), and Jesus's example of action (2:7–8). Therefore, it is appropriate that Paul's conclusion consists of commandments concerning the dimension of action.

Second, the meaning of salvation in this context can be understood in two ways: as the personal salvation of the readers[6] or as the wholeness of the church that has resolved its conflicts.[7] The precise interpretation of this term is challenging due to its broad range of meanings. However, it is questionable whether these two views should be considered mutually exclusive for three reasons.[8] (1) The reflexive pronoun ἑαυτῶν is used. The same expression appears in 2:3–4, where Paul addresses individual readers, not the church as a whole, asking them to change their way of thinking. Thus, the use of ἑαυτῶν in the context of commanding the readers to act can also be interpreted as having individual responses in mind. (2) There is a connection with 2:1–4. Since this passage serves as a summary of Paul's exhortations to the church's internal problems, his command can also be viewed as a solution to the divisions within the community. (3) Paul views the church as

---

6. O'Brien, *Philippians*, 277–80; Fee, *Philippians*, 235; etc.
7. Hawthorne and Martin, *Philippians*, 99; Bruce, *Philippians*, 81, 83; etc.
8. Bockmuehl, *Philippians*, 151; Cohick, *Philippians*, 134–35.

the gathering of God's people, as he presents in his other letters (1 Cor 1:2). This perspective suggests that the church community and the individual members are inseparable. For Paul, the wholeness of the church community inherently includes maintaining the integrity of relationships among its members. Therefore, it is appropriate to interpret Paul's command in 2:12 as encompassing both the communal and individual aspects of the readers.

If Paul's command encompasses both communal and individual aspects of the readers, what does Paul mean by salvation? In order to answer this question, two additional elements need to be examined. The first element is the description of Jesus in 2:6–11, presupposing God's grand plan of salvation. In particular, 2:9–11 is set against the backdrop of the future consummation of salvation and the glorification of Jesus in the complete restoration of the kingdom of God. According to Paul, salvation is not merely a static concept, such as the forgiveness of sins and acceptance into the kingdom as one of his children. Instead, it is a progressive concept that involves the fulfillment of God's pre-creation plan. It includes the complete restoration of the kingdom of God over the realm of darkness that rebelled against him and the eternal enjoyment of a new covenant relationship with God. Therefore, Paul's command in 2:12 can be understood as a call to remain faithful in the salvation process, anticipating the future consummation described in 2:9–11.

The second element is Paul's reason for calling for the unity of the church. His approach to the internal problem of the church is not solely to maintain the church's well-being or structure. Earlier in the letter, Paul expresses his concern that the church, as citizens of God, should remain steadfast in serving Jesus as Lord and that their lives should reflect the gospel of Jesus. Therefore, resolving conflicts within the church is essential for each member to live faithfully in anticipation of the future consummation of salvation as God's people.

In summary, the command in 2:12 urges the readers, who have participated in the salvation process through faith in Jesus, to continue living a life worthy of the gospel. It involves shaping the life of the church on earth as God's people in accordance with his will.

To effectively communicate his command, Paul adds two elements before and after the main clause. The first is a comparative clause using καθὼς (just as) before the main clause: "just as you have always obeyed [ὑπηκούσατε], not as in my presence only, but now much more in my absence" (2:12). This clause refers to the readers' attitude toward Paul, which is essentially a human factor. Paul intends to urge them to obey his command now, just as they have obeyed him. There are two noteworthy points in this expression. One is the verb ὑπηκούσατε, which relates to behavior and is linked to Jesus's obedience in 2:8. Although it is not a direct command, Paul encourages his readers to act obediently, just as Jesus expressed his humble mindset through obedience. The other point is the emphasis on time. By using "always" and the expression "not only in my presence but much more in my absence," Paul emphasizes that the readers' obedience should persist regardless of time or circumstance.

The second thing that Paul adds to the main clause is a reason clause introduced by γάρ (because) that follows the main clause: "for it is God who is at work in you, both to will and to work for his good pleasure" (2:13). Unlike the previous case, this addition is about the divine factor and carries two implications. One is that living faithfully toward the completion of the salvation process involves obeying Paul's instructions and ultimately fulfilling God's will and delight. Therefore, the readers who love God must obey his will and live a life worthy of the gospel in unity, beyond internal conflict. The other implication is that there is divine help for those who obey this command. God is the one who not only brought the readers into the salvation process through Jesus but also provides them both the desire to live faithfully within it and the power to do so. Therefore, they should not lose heart or give up but follow Paul's command and God's will and live faithfully in their relationship with God.

In conclusion, Paul's exhortation regarding the internal problems within the church in 2:12–13, which is related to 2:1–4, can be summarized as follows: (1) The readers should renounce competitive and comparative mindsets and follow the example of Jesus, who fulfilled God's plan of salvation through humble obedience. (2) They should also change their perspective on fellow church members and demonstrate this change through acts of humble obedience. (3) Communally, they should build and maintain the church's unity. (4) Individually, they should strive to live faithfully as members of God's people toward the end of the salvation process.

B) 2:14–16

This is the second part of the summary of Paul's commands regarding the problems within the church. Here, he addresses the unbelieving world outside the church. Using a verb with an action component (ποιεῖτε [do]) as in 2:12–13, Paul commands the readers to do all things without grumbling or disputing (2:14). This does not mean that the readers should be passive and not respond to those in their city who hate and oppress the church. Instead, the readers must actively respond by living a different way of life in the gospel.

Paul's intention is evident in the following ἵνα purpose clause (2:15a). He states that the purpose of the command in the main clause is for his readers to be blameless, innocent, and above reproach as God's children amid a crooked and perverse generation. To fully understand this statement, several elements must be considered. The first element is the dual identity of the believers. Paul characterizes the readers as God's children living in an evil generation that rebels against God. This is similar to his description of the readers in 1:1 as those who are in Jesus but living in Philippi. It means that while they are involved in the salvation process because of Jesus, they are still in an "already and not yet" situation. Due to this dual identity, they face external pressure and suffering. The second element is Paul's focus. In the subordinate clause, he uses the verb of being (γένησθε) instead of an action verb. This indicates that his interest lies in the existence of the readers, including their realms of thought and action. The third element is holiness. The three adjectives with the negative prefix α- (ἄμεμπτοι [blameless], ἀκέραιοι [innocent], and ἄμωμα [above reproach]) relate to the holiness that God's children should possess, which contrasts with the characteristics of the world. Based on these elements, Paul's expectation of his readers regarding their external problems is that they become holy beings who are distinct from the world as the children of God.

Continuing on, Paul uses a relative clause (ἐν οἷς [among whom]), which is linked to "the children of God" mentioned in 2:15a and further elaborates on the purpose of his command and specific ways to live according to it (2:15b–16). Regarding the purpose of the command, he states that it is for the reader to shine like lights in the world (2:15b). Here, "light" and "the world" symbolize the conflict between the kingdom of God and the rebellious realm of darkness. Thus, Paul's statement urges the readers to manifest the reign of God in the dark world through their very existence, including their thoughts, words, and actions. Such life is not only an extension of the ministry of Jesus, who revealed God's reign and salvation in the rebellious world, but also the priestly role of the covenant people, bridging the gap between the world and God (Exod 19:6; 1 Pet 2:9–10).

Paul then provides the readers with two more ways to live as lights in a dark world (2:16). The first way has to do with the truth. He encourages them to hold fast to the truth, using the participle ἐπέχοντες (to hold fast). This indicates that since the truth is the standard by which believers discern the voices of the dark world, holding fast to the truth is a crucial way to live as lights in a dark world. The second way relates to their relationship with Paul. He states that the readers should hold fast to the truth for his boasting on the day of Christ, which refers to the day of judgment. In other words, Paul desires to demonstrate that all his labor for the gospel, both past and present, has not been in vain. Although this may not seem directly related to Paul's command to the readers, emphasizing the close and intimate relationship between Paul and the readers can strengthen the legitimacy of his command. This is because the readers received the word of life, the gospel, through Paul's preaching and have been working together with him until now. Thus, if they stand firm in the word of Christ (1:6) and live a life distinct from the world, they will receive commendation and bring joy and pride to Paul. Since the readers hold Paul in high regard, they have no reason to ignore his expectations.

In summary, Paul's exhortation in 2:14–16 regarding the external issues of the church, which relates to 1:27–30, can be distilled into several key points. The readers should (1) recognize their dual identity as partakers in the salvation process and as inhabitants of this world, (2) hold fast to the truth of the gospel despite persecution and hardship in the city of Philippi, (3) follow Paul's example and honor their relationship with him (1:30), (4) live holy lives consistent with their identity as citizens of heaven and God's people, and (5) ultimately become a presence in the world that reveals God's reign.

C) 2:17–18

This is the final part of Paul's exhortations to the church regarding internal and external matters. Here, he shifts the focus to himself, using first-person verbs. His intention is to connect his previous message in 2:16 and emphasize what is important to him, thereby motivating the readers to obey. He communicates this intent in several ways.

The first way is the use of a conditional sentence and sacrificial language about Paul's impending death (2:17). In the conditional clause, he depicts the readers' lives as an offering and service to God in faith, while his own death is described with the term σπένδομαι (to pour out). The word σπένδομαι refers to the act of pouring wine or other liquid on an already offered sacrifice to make it even more valuable to God (e.g., Hos 9:4; Lev 23:18), symbolizing Paul's death (e.g., 2 Tim 4:6). Thus, the conditional sentence means that even though Paul's present situation ends in his death, he rejoices in that death because it makes the readers' lives of faith more precious. Although Paul does not explain why his death will positively affect the lives of his readers, he seems to present his life as another example for those who follow Jesus (3:17). In other words, Paul is willing to embrace his death because he believes that his faithful life and death for the gospel will inspire his readers to live their faith with greater courage (1:12–14). Thus, this conditional statement conveys two things to the readers. First, it reveals Paul's concern and affection for his readers. He is more concerned about their situation than his own death. Second, it highlights Paul's expectation and joy. His joy is that his readers will live faithfully in the salvation process, living in unity with one another and standing firm as God's people in the world in obedience to his commands. This is what the readers who love Paul should keep an eye on.

The second way is the use of imperatives. Paul commands his readers to share his joy in 2:18. While the conditional statement in 2:17 introduces Paul's expectation and joy, these imperatives urge the readers to respond. This is a practical request for them to make their lives of faith in the salvation process their joy. Accordingly, Paul's use of "joy" can be seen as a way to convey his expectation and hope for his readers, encouraging them to embrace his hope as a source of joy in their lives.

The third way is the use of emphasis. Paul effectively communicates his intentions to the readers by employing several emphatic expressions. One of these is repetition. In the main clause of the conditional sentence (2:17), he expresses his joy by rejoicing in himself (χαίρω) and with the readers (συγχαίρω). He also commands the readers to rejoice (χαίρετε) and to rejoice with him (συγχαίρετέ), using imperatives. This repetition underscores the joy deeply rooted in the relationship between Paul and the readers. Another form of emphasis is the use of the second-person pronoun (ὑμεῖς). In general, the nominative pronoun is not necessary for the imperative mood. However, when it appears, it serves as a device for emphasis, intensifying the command. Through these emphases, Paul conveys his hope that the readers will continue to live a life of faith grounded in the truth and remain steadfast in the salvation process.

In conclusion, in 2:17-18, Paul wraps up his earlier exhortations regarding the internal and external challenges faced by the church, which begin in 1:27. Regarding internal issues, he encourages his readers to remain faithful until the end of the salvation process, including maintaining the unity of the church. Regarding their external problems, he instructs them to live as lights, holy and distinct as children of God, setting themselves apart from the darkness of the world. Finally, Paul emphasizes that his joy lies in the faithful lives of his readers and urges them to live with the same expectations and interests.

Overall, Paul's instructions on the problems of the church follow a clear structure: (A) external problems (1:27-30)—(B) internal problems (2:1-4)—(C) the example of Jesus (2:5-11)—(B′) internal problems (2:12-13)—(A′) external problems (2:14-16)—(D) the joy of Paul and the readers (2:17-18). The content of his instructions has several distinctive features.

1. Paul focuses primarily on the practical aspects of his readers' lives rather than doctrinal matters.
2. The exhortations are presented in the context of salvation, which involves the conflict between the kingdom of God and the rebellious world, the dual identity of the believers, and the "already and not yet" nature of the salvation process.
3. Paul urges his readers first to transform their cognitive thinking and then to express this transformation outwardly in their lives.
4. Jesus is both the object of the readers' faith and service and the role model for their daily lives.
5. Paul's exhortations are rooted in a close relationship with the readers.

All of these elements can be summarized as a call to the readers to live faithfully to the end as God's people and children, following the example of Jesus. They are to uphold the truth of the gospel and practice humble love for one another, despite the external and internal challenges they face in the world.

PHILIPPIANS 2:19–30

OUTLINE:

III. The Body of the Letter (1:12—4:20)

    A. About the situations caused by Paul's imprisonment (1:12-26)

    B. About the real problems of the church (1:27—2:18)

    C. Paul's plan to send Timothy and Epaphroditus (2:19-30)

    D. About the potential problems of the church (3:1—4:1)

III. THE BODY OF THE LETTER (1:12—4:20)

C. Paul's plan to send Timothy and Epaphroditus (2:19–30)

THIS IS THE THIRD SECTION of the letter's body. The appearance of Timothy and Epaphroditus marks a discontinuity from the previous sections. The content can be divided into two paragraphs, each focusing on a different character. The first paragraph (2:19-24) deals with Timothy, while the second (2:25-30) focuses on Epaphroditus. Both Timothy and Epaphroditus are individuals whom Paul intends to send to the Philippian church.

1. Paul's plan to send Timothy (2:19–24)

Paul recommends Timothy to the Philippian church. The content can be divided into three parts based on the logical progression indicated by conjunctions. The first part is 2:19, where Paul signals a shift from 2:18 through the use of the adversative conjunction δέ (but) and introduces Timothy as a new character. He expresses his desire to send Timothy to the church to learn about their situation. The second part is 2:20-22, where Paul uses the causal conjunction γάρ (because) to explain his choice of Timothy. He contrasts the plural "they" and the singular Timothy, highlighting Timothy's unique qualities. The last part is 2:23-24. Paul concludes his discussion of Timothy with the inferential conjunction οὖν (therefore). As a whole, this paragraph demonstrates an *inclusio*, marked by the use of the expression ἐλπίζω πέμψαι (I hope to send) at both the beginning (2:19) and the end (2:23-24). It indicates the internal cohesion of the paragraph, which is distinct from the surrounding contexts.

This paragraph has four groups of characters: Paul, the readers, Timothy, and an unidentified group referred to as "they." Paul is the one sending Timothy, while the readers are those expected to receive him. The group referred to as "they" is described as unfaithful to the Lord, contrasting with Timothy. The structure of 2:19-24 is as follows.

1. Paul's plan to send Timothy (2:19) 1) Paul's plan: He hopes to send Timothy quickly to the readers 2) Purpose: For Paul to be encouraged by knowing things about the readers	Paul, the readers, and Timothy

2. A reason to choose Timothy (2:20-22)
 	
1) There is none like Timothy, who shows genuine concern for the readers (2:20)
 	
2) A contrast between Timothy and others
 	
   a. They all seek their own things, not those of Jesus (2:21)
 	
   b. But Timothy has served with Paul for the gospel (2:22)
	Paul, the readers, Timothy, and other people

3. Reiteration of Paul's plans (2:23-24) 1) Plan 1: Paul hopes to send Timothy immediately (2:23) 2) Plan 2: Paul will visit the readers soon (2:24)	Paul, the readers, and Timothy

A) 2:19

After addressing his imprisonment situation (1:12–26) and the internal and external problems of the church (1:27—2:18), Paul shifts his focus to introduce and recommend two individuals whom he plans to send. The first person is Timothy. Paul uses the verb ἐλπίζω (I hope) to express his intention to send Timothy quickly and adds the ἵνα purpose clause to indicate that he hopes to be comforted by learning about the readers' circumstances through Timothy. Several points are noteworthy in his statement.

The first point is that Paul has yet to determine a timetable for sending Timothy. This can be inferred from two expressions in this text. First, the use of the verb ἐλπίζω suggests that Paul's plan remains in the realm of hope despite the inclusion of the term ταχέως (quickly). Second, the phrase "in the Lord Jesus" indicates that Paul desires his hope to be guided by the grace of Jesus, implying that the plan to send Timothy is not yet finalized. Perhaps Paul intends to send Timothy to Philippi depending on the outcome of his trial (2:23).

The second point concerns the role of Timothy. Although Paul does not explicitly mention what Timothy is supposed to do in Philippi, his role is likely to take news about Paul to the readers to comfort them and then to return to Paul with updated news about the church to comfort him. In this sense, Timothy acts as a link between Paul and the readers, encouraging them all.

The third point to note is Paul's intention in sending Timothy. He expresses his desire to receive comfort from the news about the church that Timothy will report to him. He emphasizes this expectation with the emphatic expression κἀγώ (I also), implying that Paul, who is currently in prison, is deeply concerned about the church and longs to be comforted by the news that his readers are doing well. Probably, the news he desires to hear pertains to how the readers are living faithfully as God's people in the gospel of Christ, as instructed in 1:27—2:18, regarding the internal and external challenges of the church. In this sense, Paul's decision to send Timothy can be seen as an expression of his concern and affection for the integrity of his readers in the salvation process.

B) 2:20–22

Paul explains his choice of Timothy using the causal conjunction γάρ (because). The primary reason is that Paul has no one else who cares and loves the church as sincerely as Timothy does (2:20). Immediately after this,

Paul contrasts Timothy with others to highlight his qualifications. In Paul's estimation, all people (πάντες) pursue their own interests and works, not those of Christ Jesus. However, Timothy is different (2:21). Paul reinforces Timothy's trustworthiness by pointing out that the readers already know his reliability and integrity, making a detailed description unnecessary (2:22). Overall, this part primarily focuses on reaffirming Timothy's positive reputation and character.

This passage is about Paul's recommendation of Timothy to the Philippian church. However, certain aspects might confuse someone unfamiliar with the relationships among Paul, Timothy, and the readers. For instance, does 2:20 suggest that only Timothy loves the Philippian church? Does Paul's use of "all" in 2:21 imply that every believer except Timothy disregards the work of Christ? Two factors need to be considered in order to understand Paul's language. The first factor is Paul's current situation. As he is in prison, he may not have many coworkers nearby on whom he can rely. The exact number of individuals present with him is unknown, but Timothy is both available and capable of carrying out tasks on Paul's behalf. The second factor is the history of the ministry relationship between Timothy and the Philippian church. Timothy was part of Paul's team, along with Silas and Luke, that established the church in Philippi during Paul's second missionary journey in the early AD 50s (Acts 16:11–40). Subsequently, Timothy visited the Philippian church several times as Paul's representative (Acts 18:5 [see also 2 Cor 11:9], early AD 50s; 19:22, mid–AD 50s). Thus, it is not surprising that Paul refers to the church's familiarity with Timothy's character, since the Philippian church had known both Paul and Timothy for about a decade by the time of this letter (early AD 60s).

Why, then, does Paul write about recommending Timothy when the church already knows him and such a recommendation seems unnecessary? This recommendation may reflect Paul's hidden intentions. Several clues can be inferred from the text to discern his intentions.

The first clue is the portrayal of two characteristics of Timothy. One is his genuine concern (μεριμνήσει) for the church (2:20). This Greek term signifies a state of mind that is divided and unable to concentrate on one thing, indicating that Timothy was deeply concerned about the condition of the readers. In connection with this, the word ἰσόψυχον (like-minded) also demonstrates that Timothy shares Paul's love for the readers. Another characteristic is Timothy's faithful service to the gospel (2:22). This service is what Paul does, and he states that Timothy serves him as a son serves his father. Notably, the verb ἐδούλευσεν (he [Timothy] served) is a cognate of δοῦλος (servant), which is used to describe both Paul and Timothy in 1:1, as well as the humble service of Jesus in 2:7. It implies that Timothy, like Paul, serves for the sake of the gospel and ultimately follows the example of Jesus. These expressions primarily concern Timothy, but they also reflect Paul's love for his readers and his desire for them to live faithfully for the gospel.

The second clue is Paul's comparison of Timothy with others (2:21). Paul is not suggesting that only Timothy is a faithful minister; rather, he seeks to commend Timothy while warning against those who are not true ministers, employing a bit of rhetorical hyperbole. Although it is unclear whom Paul means by "them," he likely knows of such people from his extensive experience in ministry (e.g., 3:1–4, 18). He wants to convey that, unlike these individuals, the readers should live according to the gospel, following the example of Timothy. In this sense, Timothy can be viewed as another model for the life of the readers (3:17).

Based on these factors, Paul's additional description of Timothy here serves to (1) express his and Timothy's love for the readers, (2) introduce Timothy as another example for the readers to follow in the gospel, and (3) encourage the readers to be faithful to the gospel in the salvation process, as Paul commands.

C) 2:23–24

Paul concludes his recommendation of Timothy with the inferential conjunction οὖν (therefore) and provides two pieces of information. The first is his plan to send Timothy. Although Paul had already stated in 2:19 that he intended to send Timothy, using the phrase ἐλπίζω πέμψαι (I hope to send), he now adds the expression "as soon as I see how things go with me," to make it clear that the exact timing has not yet been determined. It indicates that he will send Timothy as soon as his circumstances permit. The second piece of information is Paul's tentative plan regarding his own visit. While he remains uncertain about the outcome of his trial, his use of πέποιθα (I am convinced) conveys confidence in his release (1:25). If God grants him this favor, Paul plans to visit the church quickly (ταχέως).

2. Paul's plan to send Epaphroditus (2:25–30)

Paul introduces Epaphroditus as the second person he plans to send to the Philippian church. This passage can largely be divided into two parts based on personal pronouns and verb forms. The first part is 2:25–28, where Paul states his intention to send Epaphroditus using the first-person indicative verbs ἡγησάμην (I considered) (2:25) and ἔπεμψα (I sent) (2:28). This part (2:25–28) can be further divided into three smaller units based on the conjunctions. In 2:25, Paul mentions his plan to send Epaphroditus. He then uses the causal conjunction ἐπειδὴ (because) (2:26–27) to explain why he wants to send Epaphroditus. In 2:28, he summarizes his reasoning with the inferential conjunction οὖν (therefore). The logical structure of 2:25–28 is similar to that of 2:19–24, where Paul recommends Timothy. The second part is 2:29–30, where Paul urges the readers to welcome Epaphroditus, using imperatives. This part includes the main clauses with the imperatives (2:29) and a subordinate clause of reasons introduced by the conjunction ὅτι (2:30). This paragraph involves three participants: Paul, the readers, and Epaphroditus, with the primary focus on Paul and the readers.

1. Paul's plan to send Epaphroditus (2:25–28)	
1) Paul's thought to send Epaphroditus (2:25)	* The first-person indicative verbs
2) The reasons for sending Epaphroditus (2:26–27)	
3) Conclusion: Paul sent Epaphroditus to the readers (2:28)	
2. Paul's command regarding Epaphroditus (2:29–30)	
1) Command: Receive Epaphroditus in the Lord with all joy (2:29)	* The second-person imperatives
2) The reason for the readers to receive Epaphroditus well (2:30)	

A) 2:25

Paul speaks of his plan to send Epaphroditus to his readers, and his intention can be identified by two key differences from the case of Timothy. The first difference is the language used. Paul states that he thought it necessary to send Epaphroditus, whereas, in the case of Timothy, he uses the phrase "I hope" to indicate his intention to send him, with the timing still undetermined. Additionally, Paul's use of ἀναγκαῖον (necessary) to describe sending Epaphroditus suggests that he intends to send him immediately due to both his own situation and that of the readers. This is confirmed in 2:28, where Paul explicitly states that he sent Epaphroditus immediately. It is likely that Epaphroditus will deliver this letter to the readers.

The second difference is the length of the description. While Paul offers only a brief recommendation for Timothy, he provides a more detailed introduction to Epaphroditus. Although Epaphroditus was sent by the church and does not require a formal introduction, Paul intentionally provides a lengthy description of him. Paul's intention is revealed through two aspects of how he introduces Epaphroditus. One aspect is Epaphroditus's relationship with Paul. By referring to Epaphroditus as "my" brother, coworker, and fellow soldier, Paul identifies him as a fellow believer who accepted Jesus through Paul's gospel and diligently works for the same gospel. This depiction also signifies that Epaphroditus is steadfast like a soldier, reflecting the qualities Paul urges his readers to embody in 1:27–30. The other aspect is Epaphroditus's relationship with the readers, as Paul refers to him as "your" messenger and minister to Paul's needs. Unlike the typical Greek word order of noun(s) plus genitive, Paul places the genitive pronoun ὑμῶν (your) before the nouns, emphasizing the readers' relationship with Epaphroditus. The church had sent Epaphroditus to deliver the necessary provisions to Paul in prison. Epaphroditus's delivery of money from Philippi in Macedonia to Rome for Paul's benefit demonstrates both his sacrificial dedication to the gospel and his unwavering integrity when handling money. This act also highlights the church's trust in Epaphroditus to fulfill this crucial responsibility. Thus, Paul's lengthy description aims to convince the readers that Epaphroditus is indispensable to both Paul and the church in their work for the gospel and to encourage them to warmly welcome Epaphroditus upon his return (2:29–30).

B) 2:26–27

Paul explains his decision to send Epaphroditus back by using the causal conjunction ἐπειδὴ (because), which elaborates on ἀναγκαῖον (necessary) mentioned in 2:25. He provides two reasons for his decision. First, Epaphroditus ardently longs (ἐπιποθῶν) to see the readers. The term ἐπιποθῶν is the same one Paul used in 1:8 to describe his affection for the readers. This indicates that Epaphroditus has a strong desire to see the readers, just as Paul does. Second, Epaphroditus is distressed because he knows that the readers have learned about his illness (2:26). Paul briefly explains in 2:27 that Epaphroditus was seriously ill and almost died, but he has now recovered by God's grace, which has also brought comfort to Paul.

Although the information provided by Paul is limited, it is possible to reconstruct the situation regarding Epaphroditus as follows.

1. The church sent Epaphroditus to deliver provisions Paul's needs, likely accompanied by a few other church members since he was carrying money.

2. Epaphroditus became severely ill, and some members of the group returned to the church to report the news. It is unclear when Epaphroditus fell ill. He might have become ill either after arriving in Rome, prompting him to send someone back to the church with the news, or on the way to Rome, causing part of the group to return and inform the church.
3. Epaphroditus was distressed by the church's concern for his illness and suffered both physical and emotional pain.
4. God had mercy on Epaphroditus, and he recovered from his illness.
5. This event also alleviated two of Paul's concerns: Epaphroditus's illness and the church's worry for him.
6. Epaphroditus wanted to return to ease the readers' hearts, so Paul decided to send him back.

Overall, three interrelated aspects are evidence in this process: Epaphroditus's commitment to the gospel and affection for the church, Paul's love for Epaphroditus and the church, and God's grace for his people.

C) 2:28

Paul concludes his intention regarding Epaphroditus with the inferential conjunction οὖν and states that he has sent him to the readers with even greater eagerness. Two points are worth noting. The first is the difference in wording from 2:25. In 2:25, Paul uses ἡγησάμην (I thought) to describe his decision to send Epaphroditus in his mind. Here, however, he uses the action verb ἔπεμψα (I sent) to indicate that he actually sent him. This exemplifies Paul practicing the way of life he prayed for his readers in 1:9–11: right discernment and judgment in the inner realm of thought is well expressed in the outer life. The second point is the difference between the cases of Epaphroditus and Timothy. While Paul uses the phrase "I hope" for Timothy (2:19, 23), implying an intention yet to be realized, he opts for an actual verb to depict the sending of Epaphroditus (2:28). This distinction also suggests that Epaphroditus is likely the one delivering the letter to the readers.

Paul then uses the ἵνα subordinate clause to restate the reason for sending Epaphroditus, which is twofold: (1) to please the readers by allowing them to see healthy Epaphroditus again and (2) to relieve Paul's anxieties through their reunion. These reasons also demonstrate Paul's love for his readers.

D) 2:29–30

Using second-person imperatives, Paul shifts the focus to the readers who will receive Epaphroditus. He makes two requests: (1) to receive him in the Lord with all joy, and (2) to hold such people in high esteem (2:29). While the first command is understandable, the second command might have come as a surprise to both Epaphroditus and the readers. However, it reflects Paul's other intention in sending Epaphroditus, possibly to present him as an example for the readers. This intention can also be inferred from 2:30, where Paul uses the causal conjunction ὅτι (because) to explain why the readers should hold Epaphroditus in high esteem: because Epaphroditus had devoted himself to the work of Christ by serving Paul, even to the point of losing his own life, which the readers had not done.

However, it is important to note that Paul's words should not be misconstrued as mere praise for Epaphroditus's service. His statement is based on several assumptions. First, Paul's ministry and imprisonment are solely for the work of Christ, that is, a process of service for the sake of the gospel (1:16). Second, the church's act of sending Epaphroditus to support Paul represents their participation in the work of the gospel (1:7). Third, Epaphroditus came to Paul, who was in prison for the sake of the gospel, despite being seriously ill. This act demonstrates both his participation in the work of the gospel and his faithfulness in fulfilling the task entrusted to him by the church. In particular, the phrase μέχρι θανάτου (to the point of death) in 2:30 is the same expression used to describe Jesus's death on the cross in 2:8. It implies that Epaphroditus obeyed the gospel of Christ to the point of death, following Jesus, who obediently died according to the will of God. This portrayal of Epaphroditus provides a valuable model for carrying out Paul's command regarding the gospel in 1:27–30 and for obeying Paul's admonition in 2:1–4 to prioritize the unity of the church over individual preferences. He also serves as an example of making every effort for the salvation process, as Paul commands in 2:12. Epaphroditus fully deserves the church's respect. Thus, when Paul commands the readers to respect Epaphroditus, he also wants to encourage them to follow the example of Epaphroditus by abandoning self-centered living and continuing to live for the gospel with the church. Here, Paul's use of the plural reference (τοὺς τοιούτους [such people]) implies that there are others who deserve respect, with Timothy likely being one of them. It indicates that although Paul addresses the issues of Timothy and Epaphroditus in 2:19–30, his focus remains on the readers' lives and their faithful commitment to the gospel of Christ in the salvation process.

PHILIPPIANS 3:1—4:1

OUTLINE:

III. The Body of the Letter (1:12—4:20)

    A. About the situations caused by Paul's imprisonment (1:12-26)

    B. About the real problems of the church (1:27—2:18)

    C. Paul's plan to send Timothy and Epaphroditus (2:19-30)

    D. About the potential problems of the church (3:1—4:1)

    E. Final exhortations to the church (4:2-9)

III. THE BODY OF THE LETTER (1:12—4:20)

D. About the potential problems of the church (3:1—4:1)

THIS IS THE FOURTH SECTION of the letter's body, following the discussion of Paul's situation in 1:12-26, the internal and external problems of the church in 1:27—2:18, and Paul's plans to send Timothy and Epaphroditus in 2:19-30. This section exhibits both continuity and discontinuity with the previous one.

The first indication of discontinuity is the absence of references to Timothy and Epaphroditus. Instead, using plural references, 3:2-3 contrasts "they" and "we." The use of first-person plural references appears here for the first time since 1:2 and continues in 3:15-21 through verbs (φρονῶμεν [let us think] [3:15], ἐφθάσαμεν [we attained] [3:16], and ἀπεκδεχόμεθα [we eagerly awaited] [3:20]) and pronouns (3:17, 20, 21). This feature is unique compared to the rest of the letter because, except for this section, the only other occurrence of the first-person plural pronoun is in 4:20, near the end of the letter.

The second indication of discontinuity is the use of terms related to Jewish identity, such as "circumcision" (3:3, 5) and "the law" (3:5-6, 9). These are also the first instances in the letter addressing these topics, further illustrating the discontinuity of this section.

The third indication is the use of the term λοιπόν in 3:1. This term sometimes appears in Paul's other letters as a marker to draw the readers' attention to a topic, signaling a transition to a new topic (1 Thess 4:1; 2 Thess 3:1) or the conclusion of the entire letter (2 Cor 13:11). In Philippians, λοιπόν is also used to conclude a previous command and as a transition marker (4:8). In 3:1, while it does not indicate the end of the letter, this term can be seen as a sign of discontinuity from the previous section.

Despite the discontinuity, there are also signs of continuity with the previous section. The first is the imperative verb in 3:1, 2 (x3), 17 (x2). This verb form has been used since 1:27, when Paul began to deal with the external problem of the church, indicating that his interlocutors in this section are still his readers.

The second evidence is the word χαίρετε (rejoice) (3:1). The verb (συγ)χαίρω has already appeared ten times in the letter, excluding this section (1:18 [x2]; 2:17 [x2], 18 [x2], 28; 4:4 [x2], 10), with four instances in the imperative form (2:18 [x2]; 4:4 [x2]). Consequently, the use of χαίρω with the imperative form in this section demonstrates continuity with the overall progression of the letter.

The third evidence is the noun πολίτευμα (citizenship) (3:20). While this noun appears only here in the Bible, Paul had already expressed his thought with its cognate verb (πολιτεύεσθε [live as a citizen] [1:27]). The use of πολίτευμα shows the connection of this section with the previous parts of the letter.

The fourth evidence is the pattern of Paul's exhortation to the reader, particularly the combination of cognitive thought and outward behavioral expression, as well as the use of exemplary role models. Regarding the combination of cognitive thought and outward behavior, in describing his own case, Paul presents a value comparison of what is more important in the realm of thought (3:7-8) and then describes his act of pursuing the Lord (3:12). Furthermore, he exhorts the reader to think as he does (3:15) and to act accordingly (3:16). This combination was first presented in his intercessory prayer for the reader (1:9-11) and then used as a framework for his subsequent exhortations, such as in the introduction of his own situation (1:12-26) and his exhortations about the reader's external and internal problems (1:27—2:18). In 3:1—4:1, Paul also presents himself and others who follow his example as role models for the reader's life (e.g., 3:15–17). This is consistent with his earlier use of Jesus (2:6-11), Paul himself (1:12-26, 30), and Timothy or Epaphroditus (2:29) as exemplary models.

In conclusion, based on these observations of continuity and discontinuity, 3:1—4:1 can be understood as Paul's ongoing exhortation to his readers, addressing a new issue related to the Judaizers, referred to as "they," who place value the outward markers of Jewish identity.

The evidence for continuity provides insights into how to respond to various perspectives on the position and nature of this section, which has been influenced by discontinuity. For example, one extreme view emphasizing the discontinuity of this section considers it an interpolation from another letter of Paul. This perspective is primarily based on the abrupt shift to the topic of Judaism, marked by the term λοιπόν and the somewhat strong expressions and tone in 3:2, which seems to be incongruous in the context of Philippians. However, as noted above, interpreting this section in such a way because of λοιπόν is an overreach. Furthermore, the strong language and change in tone in 3:2 do not necessarily indicate that it originates from a different letter. Instead, they could reflect Paul's intent to warn the readers about individuals who might cause problems from outside the church. In fact, although Paul uses strong expressions in 3:2, his tone becomes gentler when he exhorts the readers in connection with his own situation. Thus, the case of 3:2 can be understood as a rhetorical strategy to introduce the topic forcefully, aiming to capture the readers' attention and prepare them for the subsequent exhortation. Above all, the elements of continuity mentioned above cast doubt on the notion that this section should be considered content from a completely separate letter.

A more moderate view considers this section as a digression from Paul's continued logic.[1] However, there is no evidence to suggest that the shift in subject matter to the Judaizers represents a departure from Paul's intended purpose in this letter. It is important to acknowledge that, since we cannot fully grasp Paul's underlying rationale, it would be unwise to assume that our interpretation of the logical progression is more accurate than the way Paul has presented the topics in the text.

Another perspective is to understand this section as a cluster of Paul's ethical exhortations, known as paraenesis.[2] This view differs from the previous ones in that it sees Philippians as a single letter and this section as part of Paul's ongoing message development. Moreover, it considers this

---

1. Hawthorne and Martin, *Philippians*, lix. They consider 3:1–21 to be one section.
2. Porter, *Apostle Paul*, 348–49.

section as part of the epistolary form found in Paul's other letters. While this interpretation seems quite plausible, there is some hesitation about fully adopting this view for several reasons.

The first reason is that there is little evidence to justify distinguishing this section separately as paraenesis. Paraenesis generally refers to a section that focuses primarily on exhortation for the believer's life based on doctrinal teaching.[3] In Philippians, however, Paul does not clearly differentiate between doctrine and exhortation for the believer's life. Strictly speaking, no section of Philippians deals with doctrine per se. Even the account of Jesus in 2:6–11 is not intended to expound doctrine itself. Instead, it is presented as an example to encourage internal unity of the church, with a focus on the believer's life. Furthermore, given the elements of continuity mentioned earlier, it is difficult to define this section as an isolated ethical exhortation because Paul continues using the imperative verb and hortatory subjunctive to exhort the readers before this section.

The second reason is the nature of 4:2–9. According to this view, the paraenesis extends through 4:19 or 20.[4] However, 4:2–3 is connected to 2:1–4 and 12–13 in that it deals with internal divisions within the church, and 4:4–5 corresponds with 1:27–30 and 2:14–16 in that it offers exhortations to those outside the church. Additionally, 4:8–9 illustrates a pattern that combines exhortations in the realms of cognitive thought and outward behavior, which has served as an overarching paradigm for admonishing the readers since its introduction in 1:9–11. Moreover, 4:8–9 demonstrates its function as a conclusion to the previous teachings through the use of λοιπόν (finally). Based on these interconnections, it is more appropriate to view 4:2–9 as a summary and conclusion of the exhortations previously presented to the church. Consequently, rather than regarding 3:1—4:19 as a distinct epistolary form separate from the preceding material, it is preferable to understand 3:1—4:1 as another teaching directed to the church, with 4:2–9 serving as the conclusion to the exhortations that began in 1:27.

In order to understand the structure of this section, it is necessary to consider where its endpoint lies. Scholars have suggested various possibilities, such as 3:21; 4:1, 3, 9.[5] The key lies in understanding 4:1. The inferential conjunction ὥστε (therefore) (4:1) itself provides little help in identifying the endpoint, as it can signify either the conclusion of the previous paragraph (3:17–21 or 3:1–21) or the beginning of a new paragraph separate from the

3. Hwang, "Paul's Letter Paraenesis."

4. Porter regards 3:1—4:19 as the paraenesis, whereas Andrew Pitts concedes that paraenesis commences at 3:1 but understands 4:20 as its endpoint (Pitts, "Philosophical and Epistolary Contexts," 301).

5. Greenlee, *Exegetical Summary of Philippians*, 150.

previous one. However, the relationship between 4:1 and 2–3 is noteworthy. The use of proper names in 4:2 to refer to Euodia and Syntyche suggests a clear discontinuity with the content that began in 3:1. Furthermore, what Paul said in chapter 3 has little to do with the internal divisions within the church stemming from Euodia and Syntyche. Additionally, the nominatives of address in 4:1 (ἀδελφοί μου ἀγαπητοὶ καὶ ἐπιπόθητοι [my brothers whom I love and long for]) are masculine, whereas Paul's interlocutors in 4:2 are female. Thus, the adverb οὕτως (in this way) used by Paul in 4:1, when addressing the second person, cannot be linked to the situation in 4:2. Based on these observations, there is a relatively significant discontinuity between 4:1 and 2–3. Consequently, it is preferable to understand the inferential conjunction ὥστε in 4:1 as serving the conclusion of the content introduced in 3:1 rather than as leading to the beginning of 4:2. Therefore, it is advisable to consider 3:1—4:1 as one section.

This section can be divided into four parts based on logical development through participants and conjunctions. The first part (3:1–3) contains Paul's command directed to his second-person plural readers. However, it also includes a contrast between the third-person plural (they) and the first-person plural references (we).

The second part (3:4–14) contrasts the first-person singular (Paul) with the third-person singular (anyone else), without any first-person or third-person plural references. The only second-person reference is the call to the readers in the nominative of address (ἀδελφοί [brothers and sisters] [3:13]) to shift the tone. Notably, although Jesus is not the subject of the verb, he appears as Paul's primary interactive counterpart throughout the passage, e.g., Jesus (3:8, 12, 14) and Christ (3:7, 8 [x2], 9, 12, 14). These observations suggest that, in this part, Paul presents his own case as an example, focusing on his relationship with Jesus, in contrast to the Judaizers. 3:4-14 can be further subdivided into pre-conversion (3:4–6) and post-conversion situations (3:7–14).

The third part is 3:15—4:1. Paul applies his situation from 3:4–14 to his readers using the inferential conjunction οὖν (therefore), the hortatory subjunctive, the infinitive with an imperative connotation, and the first-person plural references in 3:15–16. He then continues his exhortation with the second-person plural imperative in 3:17. The endpoint of this paragraph is unclear, as it could be 3:21; 4:1; or 4:3. The least likely endpoint is 4:3 because 4:2–3 introduces brand-new participants, Euodia and Syntyche, whose issues are less relevant to the preceding passage. A more probable endpoint is 4:1, as it contains the inferential conjunction ὥστε (therefore), which connects it to the previous part. In addition, 4:2 creates a thematic discontinuity by introducing Euodia and Syntyche. Furthermore, παρακαλῶ

(I urge) (4:2) is a common epistolary language used to introduce a new topic in several Pauline letters (Rom 12:1; 1 Cor 1:10; 2 Cor 10:1; Eph 4:1; 1 Tim 2:1, etc.). Therefore, it is appropriate to conclude that the second application of Paul's situation, which began in 3:17, ends with another imperative in 4:1.

1. A warning against the Judaizers (3:1–3)

This paragraph introduces the fourth major theme in the body of the letter, which deals with the issues related to the Judaizers. The structure can be divided into two parts. The first part is 3:1, where Paul addresses the readers as "my brothers and sisters" and commands them to rejoice. The second part is 3:2–3, where Paul issues a series of commands to be cautious of "them" (3:2). He then uses the causal conjunction γάρ (because) to explain the reason for the commands by contrasting the situation of "them" with that of "us" (3:3).

1. Introduction: Rejoice in the Lord (3:1) 1) Command: Rejoice, my brothers and sisters, in the Lord 2) Addition: To write the same things to you is not a hesitation for me and a safeguard for you	* Paul and the readers
2. A warning against the Judaizers (3:2–3) 1) Three commands: Beware of dogs, beware of evil workers, and beware of the mutilation (3:2) 2) Reason: Because we are the circumcision, worshipping in the Spirit of God, boasting in Christ Jesus, and putting no confidence in the flesh (3:3)	* The readers * A contrast between "they" and "we"

A) 3:1

Using the phrase τὸ λοιπόν (further or finally) and the nominative of address ἀδελφοί μου (my brothers and sisters), Paul draws the attention of the readers and transitions from his plan to send Timothy and Epaphroditus (2:19–30) to the issue of the Judaizers. He instructs the readers to rejoice in the Lord (3:1a) and adds that writing the same thing is not burdensome (ὀκνηρόν) for himself and is safe for his readers (3:1b). Despite its brevity, several observations are necessary to understand this expression.

At the outset, there are two things to consider regarding 3:1a. One of these is the use of the expression τὸ λοιπόν, which Paul uses as a connector for larger units. Some point to its use in 2 Cor 13:11, where it indicates the beginning of the conclusion of the entire letter, and argue that this passage is a fragment of Paul's other letter.[6] However, this phrase often serves as a topic introducer to shift the focus of discussion in other letters (e.g., 1 Thess 4:1; 2 Thess 3:1). Therefore, it is better to interpret it here as a transition marker introducing a new topic for the Philippian readers, rather than as the opening phrase of a hypothetical fragment of another letter. In this regard, translations such as "further"[7] or "as for the other matters"[8] are more appropriate in this context than "finally."

Another thing to consider in 3:1a is the imperative χαίρετε (rejoice). The verb χαίρω has been used five times so far (1:18 [x2]; 2:17, 18, 28; see also συγχαίρω [2:17, 18]), and this is the second instance where it appears in the imperative form, following 2:18. In light of its previous usage, what matters to Paul is "what to rejoice in." Thus, this verb carries both emotional and functional dimensions, conveying to the readers what Paul values as a Christian and an apostle (see also χαρά [joy] [2:2]). In particular, the imperative χαίρετε is an invitation to the readers to share his concern. Here, Paul adds the expression "in the Lord," which appears for the first time in the letter. If this addition is intentional, it implies that the joy Paul speaks of is not simply the easy life or happiness of the readers but a call to consider with equal importance what Paul values in the salvation process in Christ.

On the other hand, there are also a few things to consider regarding 3:1b. The first is the relationship between 3:1a and 3:1b. Paul links them with asyndeton, which implies a close relationship.

The second thing to consider is the structure of 3:1b. "To write the same things to you" serves as the subject, and two clauses are connected by the correlative conjunction μέν . . . δέ. This expression typically conveys a sense of contrast (not A but B), but it is used differently here. This is because both cases have a positive process and outcome, although ἐμοὶ (to me) and ὑμῖν (to you) are being compared. In this case, Paul uses the phrase οὐκ ὀκνηρόν (no trouble), a typical hesitation formula in letters of the day,[9]

---

6. E.g., Reumann, *Philippians*, 452.
7. Keown, *Philippians 2:19—4:23*, 89; Hansen, *Philippians*, 212.
8. Banker, *Semantic and Structural Analysis*, 114.
9. Reed, *Discourse Analysis of Philippians*, 229–38.

which indicates his willingness to write something because of his intimacy with his readers. In the case of the readers, he says that his writing will make them safe. Therefore, Paul's message conveys his willingness to write the same things because it benefits his readers.

The third thing to consider is τὰ αὐτὰ (the same things). There are two possible interpretations of this pronoun. One interpretation is to see it as a cataphoric reference to Paul's warning against the Judaizers, which will be addressed later.[10] The difficulty with this view is what "the same things" refers to in this context. Is it a warning against the Judaizers themselves, or is it Paul's example and exhortation regarding them? In addition, the reason Paul mentions "the same" is also problematic. Since the topic of the Judaizers appears for the first time in this letter, Paul's use of "the same" implies that he had already discussed similar content with his readers in an earlier letter. This creates another issue, as it requires speculation about a situation not verified by the letter itself.

Another interpretation of τὰ αὐτὰ is to see it as an anaphoric reference that refers back to previous content.[11] In this case, possible candidates for the antecedent of this phrase include the command to rejoice (3:1a), the content following the command to rejoice (2:18), or Paul's instruction to the readers (1:27—2:17). However, due to the discontinuity with the previous part, as signaled by τὸ λοιπόν, and the close connection between 3:1a and 3:1b, it appears more appropriate to interpret τὰ αὐτὰ as referring to the χαίρετε (rejoice) in 3:1a. This means that the instruction to "rejoice in the Lord" in 3:1a is a repetition of the same command given earlier in the letter. Some may question why Paul adds the content of 3:1b when he is repeating the command to rejoice. However, considering the context and the implications of the command to rejoice, the addition of this content is reasonable. As noted earlier, the command to rejoice in the Lord is not solely about the emotional state of the readers but rather about what Paul considers essential to the Christian life and asks the readers to share with him. Therefore, it can be inferred that Paul emphasizes the importance of rejoicing in the Lord by adding 3:1b. This emphasis on the command to share his genuine concern may make sense, especially since the issue that Paul will deal with is the Judaizers who have plagued the churches throughout his ministry.

In summary, through both command and comments, 3:1 conveys to the readers that the subject of the Judaizers, which Paul will address, is quite important and serious. The command to rejoice in the Lord in 3:1a is an exhortation to his readers to consider what Paul values for their progress

---

10. E.g., Fee, *Philippians*, 292–93.
11. Hawthorne and Martin, *Philippians*, 173; Bockmuehl, *Philippians*, 180.

in the faith (2:18) and for their lives in the salvation process (2:12). Furthermore, the comments in 3:1b serve not only as a demonstration of Paul's love for his readers but also as a means of helping them in standing firm in the truth. Overall, 3:1 functions as an introduction that directs the readers' attention to the topic presented from 3:2 and emphasizes the significance of Paul's exhortation.

B) 3:2–3

Using imperatives, Paul warns his readers about the Judaizers who spread false teachings (3:2). His language is quite forceful and harsh in several ways. First, he repeats the command "beware of" three times using the imperative verb βλέπετε. While a single command would have sufficed to refer to the same group, Paul repeats it three times to emphasize his command. Second, he refers to the Judaizers as "dogs." This term was highly offensive to both Jews and non-Jews, making Paul's expression derogatory toward the Judaizers. Although the Judaizers might have considered non-Jewish readers to be "dogs," Paul insists that they are the ones who truly deserve the label. The use of such harsh language and its position as the first warning against the Judaizers may startle the readers, but it can be seen as a shock tactic to create a strong impact. Third, he uses the term κατατομήν (mutilation). Paul calls them mutilators in reference to their insistence on circumcision, which is the ritual cutting off of part of a man's foreskin. Such language would also have been considered a significant insult to the Judaizers and a provocative choice of vocabulary for Paul's readers. In addition, Paul describes the Judaizers as evildoers. Although that may be relatively mild compared to the other two expressions, it conveys the same negative evaluation of them. These distinctive expressions leave a strong impression on Paul's readers, forcefully urging them to be cautious of the Judaizers.

There are a few more observations to be made regarding Paul's command. First, Paul does not engage with the Judaizers as interlocutors nor directly criticize them. He does not provide specific information about the Judaizers. Despite his negative portrayal of them, he does not further explain their identity or claims. There may be two reasons for this. One reason is that his readers already possess some knowledge of the Judaizers. The book of Acts reports the heated debate with the Judaizers (around AD 48–49) after Paul's first missionary journey. If Philippians was written in the early AD 60s, Paul's disputes with the Judaizers had already been ongoing for twelve to thirteen years. It is possible that the Philippian church, which had maintained close contact with Paul during that time, was aware of the

Judaizers' existence and ongoing debates with Paul. Therefore, Paul might have believed that a simple warning would suffice to convey his intentions to the readers without needing detailed explanations about the Judaizers. Another reason may pertain to Paul's intention in mentioning the issue of the Judaizers here. It is relevant to the second additional observation that Paul does not address the Judaizers directly. Throughout chapter 3, Paul's interlocutors are the readers. Although he provides commands and reasons with the Judaizers in mind, his primary focus is on the response of the readers. Paul does not aim to argue with the Judaizers directly; therefore, he does not give a detailed explanation of them to the readers.

These two observations lead to a third one. Paul's language suggests that the Judaizers were not present in the Philippian church when the letter was written. If they had been among the readers at the time of writing, Paul would have addressed them more extensively as a more serious problem. This is because, as in Galatians, their presence would have threatened the stability of the church. However, Paul only warns the readers about the Judaizers in strong terms, without the urgency of Galatians or the lengthy and direct argument found in 2 Cor 10-13. It appears that the situation in which the Judaizers directly influenced the readers' church had not yet occurred. Nevertheless, Paul recognizes the potential danger of the Judaizers' teachings and believes that warning his readers is necessary. Therefore, he encourages an appropriate response from the readers in this passage.

In 3:3, Paul employs the causal conjunction γάρ to present the reason for the commands and contrasts the state of "they" with that of "we" (Paul and the readers). The main point of contrast is identity, which is expressed by the verb ἐσμεν (we are). Paul then uses participles to add three privileges derived from identity: worship, boasting, and confidence. Although the content of 3:3 is about "we," Paul's statement implies, in reverse, that the Judaizers emphasize circumcision, the outward symbol of one's relationship with God in the old covenant, even while believing in Jesus. They probably argue that circumcision remains necessary even in the new covenant fulfilled through Jesus, citing Gen 17:13-14, which describes circumcision as evidence of the everlasting covenant and warns that those who are not circumcised will be cut off from God's people. Furthermore, the Judaizers seem to claim that circumcision is essential for the covenant people to truly worship God and maintain their relationship with him. They view circumcision as a mark of pride, a definitive sign of salvation, and seem to insist that even non-Jewish Christians must become "Judaized" to be genuine members of the covenant people.

Paul presents a counterargument to the Judaizers and provides a correct perspective for himself and his readers (we) based on the premise of the salvation process that includes the fulfillment of the new covenant through Jesus the Messiah. His reasoning is as follows:

1. The Old Testament promised the Jews the new covenant, which includes the forgiveness of sins (Jer 31:31–34). Therefore, both non-Jews and circumcised Jews must enter into the new covenant.

2. The Old Testament promised that the new covenant would be fulfilled through the Messiah, a descendant of David (Ezek 37:24–26), and that the Holy Spirit would dwell with the new covenant people (Ezek 36:27).

3. Jesus, the promised descendant of David and the Messiah, came to earth to fulfill these prophecies (2:7; Rom 1:3).

4. Through his work on the cross, Jesus fulfilled the promised new covenant (2:8; 1 Cor 11:25).

5. Those who believe in Jesus have their sins forgiven, enter into the new covenant (Rom 3:24), receive the seal of the Holy Spirit (Rom 8:15–16), and become God's covenant people, the children of God and his Israel (Gal 6:16).

6. Therefore, the readers who believe in Jesus are God's new covenant people, who are spiritually circumcised, even though they are not physically circumcised.

7. The readers can worship God through the Holy Spirit and boast in Jesus alone for making such salvation possible, and do not need to depend on physical circumcision as proof of salvation.

In short, Paul argues that the false teachings of the Judaizers, who focus on circumcision, should not be followed since the new covenant people have a new identity and true privileges through Jesus. It is as if he is condensing the long argument of Galatians into a single sentence. Paul's explanation does not end there. In the following explanation from 3:4, he provides practical examples and exhortations based on his personal experience to elicit positive responses from his readers.

2. The example of Paul's past and present (3:4–14)

The issue of the Judaizers continues. The function of this part can be inferred by examining its discontinuity and continuity with 3:1–3. The most notable evidence of discontinuity is the use of singular rather than plural references. While 3:1–3 refers to the readers (plural "you") or the Judaizers in the plural, 3:4–14 shifts to the first-person singular, focusing on Paul's situation. Even the hypothetical person contrasted with Paul is presented in the singular (τις ἄλλος [someone else]). However, there are also elements of continuity here. Three pieces of evidence are noteworthy. First, the concessive conjunction καίπερ (although) links the content of 3:3 to Paul's situation. Second, Paul contrasts the hypothetical person with himself to strengthen his argument. Last, Paul addresses the issue of relying on the flesh. These three elements demonstrate a connection to the content of 3:3, highlighting the contrast between the situation of the Judaizers and "we" (Paul and the readers). Therefore, 3:4–14 can be understood as introducing another reason for the command to the readers regarding the Judaizers, especially by using Paul's own situation as an example.

The structure of 3:4–14 can be divided into three parts based on temporal elements. The first part (3:4–6) introduces Paul's pre-conversion state as the starting point of his response to the arguments of the Judaizers. The second part (3:7–11) deals with Paul's transformation after participating in the salvation process through Jesus. This part focuses primarily on his past transformation and present situation, particularly in relation to his cognitive thinking. The third part (3:12–14) describes Paul's present situation, emphasizing his pursuit of a future reward and presenting his cognitive thinking and its outward expression in attitudes and behaviors. The structure involves three participants: (1) Paul, the protagonist of the story; (2) Jesus, the central object of Paul's life and pursuits; and (3) God, who is a relatively hidden participant because he does not appear as the subject of a sentence. However, God is the one who grants Paul salvation (3:9) and a calling (3:14).

1. Paul's situation before being saved (3:4–6)

    1) Introduction: Paul had more reasons for confidence in the flesh (3:4)

    2) The list of Paul's boastful seven things:

        a. Being circumcised on the eighth day

        b. A member of the people of Israel

        c. Of the tribe of Benjamin

        d. A Hebrew of Hebrews

        e. A Pharisee as to the law

        f. A persecutor of the church as to the zeal

        g. Being faultless as to righteousness in the law (3:5–6)

2. Paul's situation after being saved 1 (3:7–11)

    1) Paul's situation (new way of thinking): Paul considered whatever he gains as a loss (3:7)

    2) Explanation 1: Rationale (3:8a–b)

        a. New way of thinking: Paul considered everything a loss (3:8a)

        b. Rationale: Because the knowledge of Christ is far superior to other things (3:8b)

    3) Explanation 2: Purpose (3:8c–11)

        a. New way of thinking: Paul considered whatever he gains as rubbish (3:8c)

        b. Purpose 1: To gain Christ (3:8d)

        c. Purpose 2: To be found in him (3:9a)

        d. Addition 1 to purpose 2: Concerning righteousness, Paul has righteousness not from the law but from God through faith in Christ (3:9b)

        e. Addition 2 to purpose 2: Concerning the Christian life, Paul wants to know Jesus, the power of his resurrection, and the sharing in his sufferings, becoming like him in his death, so that he may attain the resurrection from the dead (3:10–11)

* Cognitive thinking
* Focus on the past and present situation

3. Paul's situation after being saved 2 (3:12–14)
 	
  1) Paul's situation (3:12)
 	
    a. Recognition: Paul does not consider that he has already obtained or become perfect
 	
    b. Pursuit: Paul presses on to make it his own because Christ Jesus has made him his own
 	
  2) Explanation (3:13–14)
 	
    a. Recognition: Paul does not consider that he has made it his own (3:13a)
 	
    b. Pursuit: Forgetting what lies behind and straining toward what lies ahead, Paul presses on toward the goal for the prize of the upward call of God in Christ Jesus (3:13b–14)
	* Cognitive thinking and attitudinal behavior
	* Focus on the present and future situation

A) 3:4–6

This is the beginning of the second reason for the command to beware of Judaizers, given in 3:2. Unlike 3:3, which provides the first reason, Paul uses his personal story as an example and contrasts his life before and after his conversion. He begins his explanation with his past as a Jew in the old covenant. Paul employs the concessive conjunction καίπερ (although) to link the phrase ἐν σαρκὶ πεποιθότες (putting confidence in the flesh) mentioned in 3:3. He explains that, although he no longer trusts in the flesh as he did before, there were things he trusted in the flesh in the past (3:4a). In this context, the term "flesh" symbolizes Jewish identity and privilege centered on circumcision, indicating that Paul possessed the qualities that the Judaizers valued. Furthermore, Paul highlights the superiority of his former status by comparing himself to a hypothetical interlocutor who trusts in the flesh. He argues that if someone, such as a Judaizer, has reason to trust in the flesh, then he has even more reason to do so (3:4b). Paul's aim is to emphasize the contrast between his current state as a member of the new covenant person and the fleeting nature of the Judaizers' assertions. He employs two methods to convey this intent. First, he repeatedly uses the first-person pronoun ἐγώ (I myself) in 3:4a and 3:4b, drawing the readers' attention to his own condition. Second, he elaborates on his boasting in 3:5–6, explaining why he is superior to the Judaizers, thus culminating the portrayal of Paul before his conversion.

Paul lists seven elements of pride that he possessed as a member of the old covenant people and as a Jew before his conversion, which surpassed the boasts of the Judaizers. These elements consist of four inherited privileges and three acquired qualifications. The first inherited privilege was circumcision, which Paul received on the eighth day after his birth, marking him as a member of the old covenant people like the Judaizers. The second privilege is that he is a genealogical descendant of Abraham, as he belongs to the people of Israel. The third privilege is that Paul is from the tribe of Benjamin, identifying him as an orthodox Jew. This means that he is not a descendant of northern Israel or the Samaritans, whom the Jews regarded as half-breeds or non-Jews. In particular, his Jewish name, Saul, is identical to that of the first king of Israel and a prominent figure in his tribe, which seems connected to this privilege. The fourth privilege is that he is a Hebrew of the Hebrews. It likely indicates that he is a Jew who can speak Hebrew or Aramaic. Despite being from Tarsus, Paul maintained ties to Palestine, unlike other diaspora Jews, who spoke only Greek. These four elements demonstrate Paul's Jewishness, but he may not have been dissimilar to the Judaizers in certain respects.

However, the qualifications that Paul had acquired were distinctive. He differentiates these elements from the previous ones using the term κατὰ (in regards to), which signifies that they were unique to Paul and set him apart from the Judaizers. The first qualification was that he was a Pharisee in regard to law (κατὰ νόμον). According to Acts 22:3, Paul was a Pharisee who had moved from Tarsus to Jerusalem and studied under Gamaliel, a grandson of the great Jewish scholar Rabbi Hillel. What Paul is saying is that he was superior to the Judaizers, who emphasized circumcision according to the law (κατὰ νόμον), because he was a scholar who had studied the law orthodoxically.

The second acquired qualification was that he was a persecutor of the church in terms of zeal (Acts 8:1–3; 9:1–2). Paul's primary reason for such actions was that he could not accept the early church's proclamation of Jesus as Lord. He seemed to have had several reasons for rejecting Jesus as the Messiah promised in the Old Testament. One reason was that Jesus was not from Bethlehem. Since the Messiah, who was to come from the line of David, had to be born in Bethlehem (Mic 5:2), Jesus of Nazareth could not be the Messiah. This argument appears in the Gospels as a reason for the people's skepticism about Jesus's messiahship (John 7:41–42), and Paul, a Pharisee, would have been familiar with this reasoning. Another reason was that Jesus was crucified on a tree, which was considered cursed by God (Deut 21:22–23). From the Pharisees' perspective, it was inconceivable that God's chosen one could die under God's condemnation. However, the most crucial reason for Paul's rejection of Jesus was that Paul did not believe in Jesus's resurrection. Considering these reasons together, for Paul before his conversion, (1) Jesus was not the Messiah promised in the Old Testament, (2) his resurrection was a fabrication created by the church, and (3) the church's teachings about Jesus were heretical and a threat to God's truth. Therefore, as a zealous Pharisee committed to God and the law, Paul believed it was his duty to eradicate the church to prevent God's wrath from falling on his fellow Jews. Consequently, based on his convictions, he persecuted the church with great zeal. In this sense, Paul was far more faithful to the old covenant in the past than any of the Judaizers plaguing the church.

The third qualification Paul acquired was that he was faultless regarding the righteousness of the law. This statement pertains to the context of the old covenant relationship with God. In this relationship, the law serves as a means through which God reveals his will to the covenant people, enabling them to maintain their relationship with him. By observing the law, the covenant people maintain their relationship with God and receive life before him (Ezek 20:11). The Scripture calls this state righteousness (Deut 6:25), which is the state of righteousness by law that Paul is referring to in this passage. Since this is a state attained through the meticulous observance of the law, Paul's claim to be blameless means that he faithfully kept the law as a Pharisaic scholar. Although this state cannot lead to salvation in the new covenant through the Messiah, it also underscores Paul's faithfulness to the old covenant, surpassing even the Judaizers, who boasted the signs and privileges of the old covenant.

All three acquired qualities are relevant to the old covenant centered on the law. These qualities represent the very state of being that the Judaizers seek and the very example they hope to persuade the church to follow. Therefore, it is understandable why Paul insists he had more things to trust in the flesh than the Judaizers. He shares their Jewish identity, belonging to the old covenant, and embodies the best of what they aspire to achieve.

B) 3:7

Paul reassesses his past, a condition superior to what the Judaizers boasted of in the old covenant. He states that everything that was once a benefit to him now counts as a loss because of Christ. His statement contains three noteworthy expressions.

The first point to note is the use of the verb ἥγημαι (I thought), which refers to cognitive thinking. It indicates that the fundamental contrast between Paul's past in the old covenant and his present in the new covenant lies in a shift in his thinking. Moreover, it illustrates where repentance should begin in the salvation process. In Rom 1:28, Paul attributes the root cause of God's wrath to the rejection of God in one's knowledge. According to this teaching, the fundamental nature of sin relates to internal cognition, where one places oneself at the center instead of God, before manifesting outward actions or attitudes. Therefore, human repentance, which is one of the ways to turn God's wrath into salvation, must begin with a change in the thought process that focuses on God instead of oneself. In this light, Paul's transformation can be viewed as a significant reconfiguration of his cognitive structure or worldview regarding his relationship with God rather than merely a religious transition from Judaism to Christianity.

The second point is the term "Christ," the Messiah, which refers to the one who will fulfill the new covenant as promised in the Old Testament (cf. Ezek 37:24–28). Therefore, all Jews, including Paul, who belonged to the old covenant, must believe in Christ to participate in the new covenant of salvation. While the early church proclaimed Jesus as the promised Messiah, Paul did not accept the message because he did not believe in Jesus's resurrection. Instead, he actively persecuted those who followed Jesus. However, everything changed when Paul encountered the risen Jesus on his way to Damascus (Acts 9:1–9). He recognized Jesus as God's promised Messiah and fully embraced the early church's proclamations about Jesus. As a result, Paul transitioned from the old covenant to the new covenant of salvation through Jesus, the Messiah. For Paul, therefore, Jesus became the central reason for the change of worldview and the starting point, foundation, and driving force of his subsequent life in the new covenant.

The third point is the economic terms, specifically "profit" (κέρδη) and "loss" (ζημίαν). In this context, the language indicates that Paul's change in thinking was not the result of uncritical acceptance, such as brainwashing, but rather the consequence of evaluating what was truly important by comparing values. It involved a judgment about whether to prioritize his inherited privileges and acquired qualifications in the old covenant or the new life gained in Christ Jesus. In this process, Paul chose the latter. This cognitive discernment process was already introduced in his intercessory prayer for the readers in 1:9–11. He also applied this approach in describing his own situation (1:12–26, especially 1:21) and in exhorting the readers regarding their problems (1:27—2:4). Therefore, Paul's mention of this process while recounting his transformation aims to reaffirm the readers that this comparison and choice of values centered on Jesus is crucial not only for believing in Jesus but also for maintaining the lives of believers thereafter.

C) 3:8–11

Starting with the phrase ἀλλὰ μενοῦνγε (what is more), Paul provides a detailed explanation of how his mindset changed because of Jesus. The content can be divided into two parts based on the double use of ἥγημαι (I thought), which addresses the reason and the purpose behind his transformation.

First, regarding the reason, Paul states that he considers everything a loss because of the surpassing value of the knowledge of "Christ Jesus my Lord" (3:8a–b). Two aspects are noteworthy here. One is the repetition of the phrase that he counts all things as loss, which emphasizes the clarity of Paul's change in thinking. The other is the use of various expressions about Jesus. In addition to the term "Christ," Paul also uses other expressions to refer to Jesus, such as "Jesus," "my Lord," and a prepositional phrase that explains who caused Paul to count everything else as of no value. This is significant in comparison to 3:7, which mentions only Christ. The reference to "Jesus" indicates that he is the Messiah who fulfills the promised new covenant. "My Lord" implies that Paul's knowledge of Jesus is not simply a matter of objective doctrine but is rooted in a personal relationship of intimate fellowship. Based on these observations, Paul viewed his past boasting in the old covenant as a loss because he regarded the knowledge and fellowship with Jesus in the new covenant as much more valuable. In this sense, Jesus is not only the cause of Paul's change of mindset but also the reason for his new life.

Second, as to the purpose, Paul explains that he regards all his past gains as rubbish to gain something new (3:8c–11). This new thing is to gain Christ and be found in him, which means to exist and live in a relationship with Jesus. Paul then elaborates on two further aspects of this state.

One aspect is the fundamental state he has attained in the new covenant (3:9). Using the participle ἔχων (having), Paul contrasts the righteousness he previously had in the old covenant with the righteousness he now possesses in the new covenant. The term "righteousness" refers to an appropriate state of being and living consistent with one's identity. Regarding God, righteousness means his faithfulness as the Creator, including his judgment toward his creatures (Ps 9:8; 50:6; 96:13; etc.) and his love and faithfulness to those in the covenant relationship with him (Ps 25:10; 110:19; etc.). Regarding humans, on the other hand, righteousness is the state of responding appropriately to God, their Creator, and remaining faithful to their covenant relationship by fully keeping the law that reveals God's will (Deut 6:25). In this passage, Paul contrasts his faithfulness to God in the old covenant with that in the new covenant. As stated in 3:6, when he was in the old covenant, he believed he had kept the law blamelessly and, therefore, had the righteousness that comes from being faithful in his relationship with God. However, attaining a state of righteousness in the new covenant through the Messiah is entirely different. Contrary to Paul's earlier boast and belief, no one can attain righteousness by keeping the law because the law is not a solution to the problem of sin but merely a means of revealing God's will (Rom 3:20; 7:7). Moreover, even Paul, who believed himself to be faultless in keeping the law, could not escape the curse of the law unless he always fulfilled everything written in it (Gal 3:10–11). The solution lies in the grace of the forgiveness of sins promised in the new covenant (Jer 31:34). As the promised Messiah, Jesus fulfilled this promise through his crucifixion. He opened the way for those who believe in him to be counted righteous through the forgiveness of sins. This means that they are recognized as faithful in their covenant relationship with God. Paul also believed in Jesus and received the grace of forgiveness of sin and righteousness before God through his faith. This brought him into the new covenant relationship. In the new covenant, he received a new relationship and identity that far surpassed his previous boasting in the old covenant.

Another aspect that Paul adds to his new state is the purpose of life in the new covenant (3:10–11). Using the infinitive (γνῶναι [to know]), Paul articulates this purpose as knowing three things: Jesus, the power of his resurrection, and participation in his suffering. While the knowledge of Jesus mentioned in 3:8 refers to a broad knowledge gained through a relationship with him, the knowledge here is more specific to the life and work of Jesus, particularly his sacrificial death on the cross. Paul likely includes this because he has in mind his imprisonment for the gospel. In other words, just as Jesus obeyed God's will to the point of death and experienced the glory of the resurrection as a result (2:8–11), Paul desires to persistently live a life faithful to the gospel by imitating (συμμορφιζόμενος [conforming to]) Jesus's death now, in order to obtain the resurrection of the dead in the future.

In summary, according to Paul's confession, Jesus is the promised Messiah (Christ), who fulfilled the promise of the new covenant through his crucifixion and resurrection. He also became the gateway to the forgiveness of sins, which could not be obtained by following the law in the old covenant. Furthermore, Jesus called Paul to give salvation, a new life, and a mission as an apostle in the new covenant. In this sense, Jesus is both the reason for and purpose of Paul's ministry and life. This is why Paul considers his past boasting in the old covenant as worthless, recognizing the value of his new identity and privileges in Jesus in the new covenant. Moreover, even as he is facing death, Paul understands that it is more valuable to continue to live according to God's call and will in the gospel, following the example of Jesus.

D) 3:12–14

In this passage, Paul elaborates on his ongoing experience in the new covenant salvation process. While 3:7–11 addresses Paul's assessment of his past boasting in the old covenant, he shifts his focus here to the attitudinal and behavioral aspects toward the future state in the new covenant through διώκω (I pursue [3:12, 13]). Acknowledging that he has neither obtained it yet nor achieved perfection, he confesses that he strives to make it his own because Christ Jesus has made Paul his own (3:12). To understand Paul's statement fully, it is essential to consider several elements.

The first element to consider is the transition from the realm of thought to that of action in his expression. Although there is no explicit mention of the realm of thought in 3:12, the use of the verb λογίζομαι (I consider) in 3:13, where Paul elaborates on the same content, indicates that his statement about not yet achieving or being perfected pertains to his self-assessment within the realm of thought. In this sense, 3:12 has a progression from the cognitive evaluation to the outward action of pursuit.

The second element is the content of what Paul desires to attain and complete. It relates to 3:10–11, where Paul expresses his desire to be conformed to the death of Christ in his ministry and life, to participate in Jesus's sufferings and the power of his resurrection, and ultimately to gain a more profound knowledge of Christ through this process. Paul acknowledges that he has not yet fully attained this state and is still striving toward it. This implies that, while the relationship with Jesus has no end, Paul's earthly ministry does, and he seeks to fulfill his calling by imitating Christ until that time. In this sense, 3:12–14 is more future oriented than 3:7–11.

The third element to consider is the motivation behind Paul's pursuit. Using the phrase ἐφ' ᾧ (because) (see also Rom 5:12) and the emphatic καὶ (indeed), he explains that his pursuit is motivated by the fact that he was seized (κατελήμφθην) by Christ Jesus. The verb κατελήμφθην is the passive voice of the same word (καταλαμβάνω) that Paul uses to introduce the content of his pursuit ("to make [καταλάβω] it my own"). This indicates that the initial stage of the salvation process experienced through Jesus, such as entering into the new covenant, beginning a new life, and being called to ministry, is closely linked to Paul's subsequent pursuit.

Combining these elements, Paul's statement in 3:12 reveals that he does not stop at the transition from the old to the new covenant and at the change in the realm of thought. Instead, by taking Jesus, who saved him and gave him a mission (Acts 9:15-17; 26:16-18), as both the starting point and the model for his new life and ministry, Paul desires constantly to strive to live a life that fulfills the gospel witness to Christ until the end of his life.

In 3:13-14, Paul elaborates the content of 3:12 by addressing the readers with the nominative of address ἀδελφοί (brothers and sisters) and emphasizing his own situation with the first-person pronoun ἐγώ (I). He provides two explanations: one regarding his perception of the current situation, using the verb λογίζομαι (I consider) (3:13a), and the other regarding the behavioral aspect of his life, using the verb διώκω (I pursue) (3:13b-14). Overall, this passage describes Paul's situation in the form of "not A but B," employing the negative adverb οὐ (not) and the adversative conjunction δέ (but).

In the "not A" part (3:13a), Paul expresses that he has not attained (κατειληφέναι) what he expected. The use of the same verb καταλαμβάνω that is mentioned in 3:12 indicates that he has his ministerial calling in mind. In other words, although Paul is in prison for the sake of the gospel, he does not consider that he has failed to fulfill his calling, because his life is not yet over. Instead, he remains focused on one thing, which will be mentioned in the "but B" part.

The "but B" part (3:13b-14) consists of three components. The first component introduces the pursuit process in the realm of action through the main verb διώκω. It is the same word used in 3:12, but Paul adds the phrase κατὰ σκοπόν (toward the goal) to describe his pursuit of ministry in the new covenant as a race toward the finish line. This is consistent with 2:16, where he describes his ministry as a race to preach the word of life (1 Cor 9:24).

The second component is the premise situation for Paul's pursuit (3:13b): forgetting what lies behind and straining toward what lies ahead. He addresses it by linking two participles with the correlative conjunction μὲν .. δέ (on the one hand ... on the other hand) and placing them before the main verb, which creates a contrast in both the position and direction centered on time. The phrase "what lies behind" refers to his past ministry, which was quite successful, according to Paul's confession in other letters. He preached the gospel from Jerusalem through Asia, Macedonia, and Achaia, reaching as far as Illyricum (Rom 15:17-19). Even his current imprisonment in Rome can be seen as evidence of the success of his work since it resulted from the Jews' anger over his successful ministry and the persecution he faced in Jerusalem (Acts 21:28). However, Paul says that he does not consider all of this a complete accomplishment. Instead, he continues his life of pursuit with the attitude of fulfilling ministry set before him until the end.

The third component in the "but B" part is the goal of Paul's pursuit (3:14). Using a prepositional phrase with εἰς (for), he describes this goal as the prize of the upward call of God in Christ Jesus. To better understand this expression, a few things need to be considered. One is the meaning of "in Christ Jesus." The preposition ἐν (in) can have various interpretations, such as indicating means or place. However, in this context, it refers to a place that signifies one's relationship with Jesus. The other thing is the use of the adverb ἄνω (upward). Together with the subjective genitive τοῦ θεοῦ (of God), this word indicates that Paul's calling came from God, the author of the new covenant salvation, rather than from a human decision.

The more difficult thing in Paul's expression of the goal is the term "prize" (βραβεῖον). It is the same word used in 1 Cor 9:24 to describe the reward given to the winner in the race of the Christian life. It is also combined with σκοπὸν (goal), just mentioned to describe his ministry as a race (3:14). The difficulty lies in the specific meaning of the word. Its meaning is symbolic and can only be inferred from the current and previous contexts in the letter. Four clues are worth examining.

The first clue is Paul's intercessory prayer for the readers in 1:9–11. He expresses his hope that their lives of discernment through knowledge and wisdom will continue until the end of history, when Jesus returns, and that their lives will bring glory and praise to God. Although believers may receive praise and recognition from God (Matt 25:14–30), Paul's ultimate focus is that the name of God, who brings salvation and new life, will be glorified through their lives. Therefore, Paul would have the same perspective on his life and ministry.

The second clue is the verb καταλαμβάνω (take hold of). In introducing and describing his pursuit of ministry, Paul uses this verb to express that the goal of this process is to know Christ. Therefore, the prize he speaks of also seems to relate to this goal, i.e., complete fellowship with Christ.

The third clue is that the prize in the present context is related to a state after death. In 3:10–11, Paul expresses his desire to know Christ through his participation in Christ's death and resurrection. This indicates that his goal in life and ministry is future oriented.

The final clue is Paul's reason for hoping for the resurrection. In 3:20–21, Paul expresses his eagerness for the return of Jesus Christ, who will transform Paul's lowly body into a glorious one, like that of Jesus. Here, Paul's main expectation is not just a transformation of the body but, through the resurrection, a complete and face-to-face fellowship with the Triune God, which is impossible in the fleshly body (1 Cor 13:12). With these clues in mind, it can be understood that Paul's expected reward here is (1) to praise and glorify God by living faithfully until the end, in response to the expectations of the God/Jesus who saved and called him, (2) to experience the resurrection from the dead after the end of his life and ministry, and (3) to gain a deeper relationship with Christ by knowing him and enjoying full fellowship with him.

In summary, Paul explains his case in chronological order. He first presents his past situation in old-covenant Judaism before being saved, then describes his situation in the new covenant attained through Jesus (3:4–6). He goes on to evaluate his past change and describes his present pursuit of Christ (3:7-9), and finally points to the future complete salvation, which includes the resurrection (3:10–11). Within this framework of salvation, he does not consider his life and ministry a complete success after being saved from the old covenant to the new covenant through Jesus. Instead, he strives to live faithfully to his calling, with the ultimate goal of enjoying eternal fellowship with Christ in the resurrection after fulfilling his calling (3:12–14). To achieve this goal, he employs two methods. The first is to use value comparison to discern what is more important in the realm of thought and then to live out the outcome in daily life. This inside-out progression has been consistently applied to various issues since its initial introduction in the intercessory prayer of 1:9–11. Thus, it can be inferred that Paul presents this pattern as a key principle for the lives of the readers. The other method is to evaluate the past and present in light of the overarching salvation process and to live faithfully in the present with the future consummation in mind. Paul's presentation of his life and ministry is not intended for self-promotion but to encourage the readers, who, like Paul, had experienced the transition from the outside to inside the new covenant relationship, to approach the issues of the Judaizers from the same perspective. This intention is further developed in the following paragraph (3:15—4:1)

3. APPLICATION TO THE READERS AND PAUL'S COMMAND (3:15—4:1)

This paragraph shows both discontinuity and continuity with the previous one. Three elements contribute to the discontinuity. The first is the shift in the participants. Unlike 3:4–14, which focuses on Paul's personal situation through first-person singular references (I), 3:15—4:1 primarily uses second-person plural references (we) with third-person plural (they) after 3:17 referring to people other than the readers. The second element is the change in mood. In 3:4–14, Paul uses only indicative verbs to describe his situation, but 3:15—4:1 contains exhortations to the readers with a hortative subjunctive (3:15), an infinitive with an imperative connotation (3:16), and a series of imperatives (3:17; 4:1). The third element is the inferential conjunction οὖν (therefore) (3:15), which signifies a transition to a conclusive statement based on what Paul has previously explained. This conjunction also provides a thematic link, creating continuity. As a result, 3:15—4:1 serves as the conclusion of the second reason for the warning given in 3:2 about the potential threat of the Judaizers.

This paragraph can be divided into three subunits based on the participants, the mood of the verbs, and the conjunctions. The first part (3:15-16) focuses on the conversation between Paul and the readers, using first-person plural and second-person plural verbs and employing the hortatory subjunctive and the infinitive. The second part (3:17-21) differs from 3:15-16 in that it uses the nominative of address (ἀδελφοί [brothers and sisters]) and the second-person imperatives in 3:17. This passage introduces two other groups besides Paul and the readers: one group is those whom the readers are to imitate (3:17), and the other is those whom the readers are not to follow (3:18-19). The flow of 3:17-21 can be identified by the use of imperatives, participants, and the causal conjunction γὰρ (because): (1) Paul's two commands (3:17); (2) reason 1: Paul, negative examples of people, and the readers (3:18-19); (3) reason 2: Paul, positive examples of people, and the readers (3:20-21). The third part (4:1) is distinct from 3:21 due to the use of the nominative of address (ἀδελφοί), the reappearance of the imperative verb, and inferential conjunction ὥστε (therefore). In this structure, Jesus is presented as the one who initiates salvation through the cross and brings it to its final consummation through the resurrection of believers. God appears as the agent responsible for the process of the believers' resurrection.

1. Concluding Exhortations (3:15-16)	
1) Exhortation 1: Share Paul's way of thinking (3:15a)	
2) Addition: If you, the readers, think differently about anything, God will reveal that also to you (3:15b)	* Paul and the readers
3) Exhortation 2: Live up to the standard that Paul and the readers have attained (3:16)	

2. Concluding commands 1 (3:17–21) 　1) Command 1: Be joint imitators of me 　2) Command 2: Watch carefully those who live according to the pattern you have in us (3:17) 　3) Reason 1 (negative examples): Many live as the enemies of the cross of Christ (3:18–19) 　4) Reason 2 (positive examples): As the heavenly citizens, we live eagerly waiting for a Savior who will transform our lowly body into the body of Jesus's glory (3:20–21)	* Paul and the readers * Two other Christian groups: one is those who live focusing on earthly things, and the other is those who live waiting for the future resurrection
3. Concluding command 2: Stand firm in the Lord (4:1)	

A) 3:15–16

Paul connects his own examples in 3:4–14 to the situation of the readers by using the inferential conjunction οὖν (therefore). In 3:15, he employs the first-person plural subjunctive verb φρονῶμεν (let us think) and exhorts them to have the same way of thinking as he does. Using a conditional sentence, Paul states that if others have a different way of thinking, God will also reveal it to them. Then, in 3:16, he exhorts the readers to live in conformity with whatever state of thinking they have reached, using the infinitive στοιχεῖν (walk or live) with an imperative connotation. In order to understand Paul's statements, a few observations are necessary.

The first point is an inside-out pattern in Paul's admonition. He begins with the hortatory subjunctive form of the verb φρονέω (think), which pertains to the realm of thought (3:15). This is the same verb that Paul used to introduce Jesus's way of thinking (2:5), to present Paul's solutions to the internal problems of the church (2:2), and to introduce his cognitive attitude toward them (1:7). In this context, τοῦτο (this) (3:15a) can be understood as referring to Paul's transformation of values and way of life described in 3:7–11. Paul then uses the infinitive form of the verb στοιχέω (walk or live) (3:16), which carries an imperative connotation and belongs to the semantic domain of behavior. This sequence of "think and do" aligns with the inside-out principle consistently observed throughout the letter. It conveys Paul's intention to encourage his readers (1) to have the same perspective that Paul has and (2) to live in accordance with what God is enlightening them to think, irrespective of their current level of understanding, for example, whether they agree with Paul's perspective or have not yet reached that level.

The second observation is Paul's respectful attitude toward the readers, evident in several expressions. For instance, he describes the readers as mature (τέλειοι), indicating that they have made significant progress in the salvation process. This is not to say that the readers have completed the entire process. Although they still have more to accomplish in their journey of faith, what Paul means is that they (1) have transitioned from the realm of darkness into the kingdom of light through Jesus and have experienced the fulfillment of the promise of the new covenant, (2) currently prioritize Christ as their highest value and work together with Paul for the gospel (1:5), and (3) eagerly anticipate completing their journey of faith. Even though the readers need to hear Paul's exhortation, he acknowledges and respects their current state of faith. Another example of Paul's considerate attitude is his addressing those who disagree with him. Using the second-person plural verb φρονεῖτε (you think) and the pronoun ὑμῖν (to you), Paul continues to include them among the readers he loves, despite their different states of faith. They are likely newer believers rather than opponents of Paul. The reasons for mentioning them seem to reflect his considerate and loving heart rather than an attempt to impose his way of thinking. Paul expresses his expectation of their maturity in faith by acknowledging that God's commands and teachings will continue to shape their lives.

The third observation is the use of the first-person plural verbs. One example is the hortatory subjunctive φρονῶμεν (3:15). It includes Paul in the content of the exhortation, unlike the second-person plural imperative, which is addressed only to the readers. The other is the verb ἐφθάσαμεν (we arrived) (3:16). This verb serves as the basis for the action of στοιχεῖν and signifies reaching a particular state in relation to the realm of thought. Although the infinitive στοιχεῖν does not specify person and number, it can be inferred that ἐφθάσαμεν reflects the necessity for both Paul and the readers to express an inside-out pattern of life. Consequently, the use of first-person plural verbs demonstrates that what he is urging is essential for all who want to live faithfully in the Lord, including Paul himself.

In summary, Paul invites his readers to consider his case as an example of the journey of faith shared by all believers, including themselves. He places discernment in the realm of thought as a starting point. It reflects his expectation that his readers will continue to take steps toward upright living through sound thinking and discernment regarding the claims of the Judaizers. However, Paul does not seek to impose his thoughts on the readers, regardless of their state of faith. He wants the weak in their faith to adopt his perspective but leaves room for divine intervention and waits for their maturity. He then exhorts his readers to live according to the degree of maturity they have attained in their understanding. Overall, Paul's statement reflects his sincere love for the readers (1:7).

B) 3:17

Paul presents a second application based on the description of the readers' situation. He addresses his readers with the nominative of address ἀδελφοί (brothers and sisters) and commands them directly in the second-person imperative. Paul's command is twofold. The first one is to imitate him. His wording is unusual in that he uses the term συμμιμηταί (fellow imitators) instead of μιμηταί (imitators). It implies that there are individuals who already follow Paul's example, and he encourages the readers to join them in imitating himself. Timothy and Epaphroditus may be among those who are already following Paul's example. The second command is to carefully observe those living according to the example that the readers have in "us." The first-person plural reference refers to Paul and his companions, excluding the readers. This command serves as a means of fulfilling the first command, especially about the way of life (περιπατοῦντας) that expresses their transformed thinking outwardly. In other words, to imitate Paul, the readers must closely observe those who live according to the same pattern of life as Paul and his companions and follow their example.

There are several considerations regarding the purpose of these commands. The first is the aspects of his life that Paul expected his readers to imitate. According to Paul's teaching in 3:1–14, the pattern (τύπον) of his life and ministry includes three key aspects: (1) focusing on the new-covenant salvation through Jesus, rather than being influenced by the old-covenant privileges centered on circumcision, as claimed by the Judaizers; (2) pursuing a more profound knowledge of Jesus through the process of value comparison and expressing inner discernment outwardly; and (3) avoiding complacency regarding past and present success and continuing instead to run the race of ministry and life of faith while anticipating the future consummation of the salvation process. If these are the characteristics of Paul's life, Paul likely expected his readers to embrace and live according to these principles as well.

The second thing is the role models for the life of the readers. In 3:17, two groups serve as role models: Paul himself and those who imitate Paul. Furthermore, Jesus the Messiah is the ultimate model whom Paul seeks to emulate (3:10) because Jesus humbly relinquished his glory, took on human form, and obediently fulfilled God's will through self-sacrifice (2:6-8). In this context, Paul describes an interconnected sequence of learning and imitation: The readers are encouraged to imitate those who strive to imitate Paul, who in turn imitates Jesus, the ultimate model. This creates a pattern: Jesus ← Paul ← those who wish to imitate Paul ← the readers.

The third point is the reason for Paul's commands. While he expects his readers to follow the pattern of his life, there seem to be two additional reasons for mentioning those who imitate him. One is to demonstrate that the way of life Paul exemplifies in the following Jesus is already a true pattern adopted by other faithful believers. The other reason is that he hopes the readers will warmly receive Timothy and Epaphroditus, whom he is sending to them, and imitate their faithful lives in the gospel.

C) 3:18–19

Paul provides the first reason for his commands issued in 3:17, using the causal conjunction γὰρ (because), and introduces a new group who walk (περιπατοῦσιν) differently than him and those who follow his example. He states that although he has mentioned this before, he now repeats it with tears (3:18). The purpose of this repetition is twofold: to refresh his readers' memory and to convey his affection while emphasizing the importance of not following negative examples.

Paul refers to the negative examples as enemies of the cross of Christ (3:18). Identifying whom he is explicitly referring to and what he means requires interpretation, as this is a symbolic expression. However, several clues provide guidance.

First, the use of the verb περιπατοῦσιν (they walk) suggests that Paul's focus is on their moral lives rather than refuting their theological claims. Thus, the expression "enemies of the cross" may refer to those who live in opposition to Jesus's life and ministry, which are characterized by humility, obedience, and sacrifice to fulfill God's will (2:6-8).

Second, since there is no indication of those who reject the gospel among the readers of this letter, it is unlikely that these negative examples belong to the members of the Philippian church.

Last, they are likely fellow believers. If the people described in 3:18-19 were unbelievers, it is unclear why Paul would weep while admonishing the church about "their" situation. This is because, in 1:27-30, Paul is resolute about the unbelievers who are pressing on the church, referring to them as those who will perish and stating that he is confronting them through conflict (ἀγῶνα). Therefore, it is more reasonable to conclude that he is grieving over those among the believers who live contrary to the gospel while warning his readers against their influence.

Given these factors and the present context, it is difficult to completely exclude the Judaizers from the πολλοί (many) that Paul mentions. However, it is not necessary to limit this group to the Judaizers alone. Since it represents believers who live differently than Paul, it is better to think of the Judaizers and others outside the Philippian church who profess to be believers but live in opposition to the way of Jesus's life and ministry as represented by the cross.

In 3:19, Paul further explains the situation of those who are enemies of the cross with four descriptions. He first introduces three aspects using the relative pronoun of possession ὧν (whose). The first aspect is their destiny, which Paul describes as destruction. This is the opposite of the final stage of salvation through the resurrection (3:12) and represents a different outcome than what they expect through their faith. The second and third aspects are that their god is their belly, and their glory is their shame. These reveal why their end is destruction. Despite their professed faith, they are, in a sense, idolaters because they prioritize their eating, drinking, and pursuit of gain above all else. As a result, their fate can be only judgment and destruction. Furthermore, since the glory they seek has nothing to do with God, it will bring them only shame before him. Paul sharply contrasts the results of their pursuit of glory with those such as Jesus, himself as a follower of Jesus, and those who follow Paul's example.

The fourth description Paul provides is that, using a participle, he depicts them as those whose minds are set on earthly things. This is the primary reason their lives differ from the example of Jesus. According to Paul's explanation of an inside-out process, their way of thinking (φρονοῦντες) is fixed solely on what the world, which rebels against God, offers in terms of benefits rather than on their relationship with God/Jesus and its outcome. Their situation exemplifies Jesus's teaching that what comes from the heart defiles a person (Mark 7:20–23) and that no one can serve both God and money (Matt 6:24). Their way of thinking is reflected in their way of living (περιπατοῦσιν) as enemies of the cross of Christ, and consequently, their end is destruction.

D) 3:20–21

Paul presents the second reason for his commands issued in 3:17 with the causal conjunction γάρ (because). This time, he refers to those who pursue a lifestyle contrary to that described in 3:18–19, using the first-person reference (we), which includes himself, those who follow his example, and the readers. Unlike the simple descriptions of the negative examples, Paul's explanation of the case of "we" is somewhat complex. In 3:20a, the main verb ὑπάρχει (it exists) introduces the second reason for the command mentioned in 3:17: our citizenship is in heaven. Paul then elaborates on this using two relative pronouns. The first is ἐξ οὗ (from which) (3:20b), which refers to heaven in 3:20a and explains that "we" eagerly await a Savior, the Lord Jesus Christ, who is in heaven. The second is ὅς (who) (3:21), which refers to Jesus in 3:20b. According to the text, Jesus will transform "our" lowly bodies to be like his glorious body by God's power, which enables Jesus to bring everything under his control. The complexity of this structure reflects Paul's intention to provide the readers with a criterion for discernment and conviction by giving more information on important matters.

There are several notable points in Paul's statement. The first is the phrase "citizenship [πολίτευμα] in heaven." The term πολίτευμα is a cognate word of πολιτεύεσθε (live as a citizen), which he used in 1:27 to encourage the readers to stand firm in the gospel despite the hostile environment in Philippi. Here, he intends to clarify the belonging and identity of "we." The key point is that "our" citizenship is in heaven, which is central to the contrast between "we" and "they." According to Paul's evaluation, those described in 3:18 are the people who, despite having entered the kingdom of God by faith and experiencing the salvation of the new covenant, continue to live as if they were citizens of this world. In a sense, they resemble the unbelievers in Philippi, who cling to their earthly citizenship and oppress the church. However, "we" are different in that "we" set "our" minds on heaven and live with an identity as citizens of the kingdom of God. To emphasize this contrast, Paul reverses the normal order of noun plus genitive and places the genitive (ἡμῶν [our]) before the noun (πολίτευμα), thus emphasizing the people who possess such citizenship.

The second point is why "we" focus on heavenly citizenship. In brief, it is because Jesus is there. Paul's explanation relates to Jesus's identity and his future work. Regarding Jesus's identity, Paul refers to Jesus as the Savior (σωτήρ). This term, used for the first time in this letter, signifies the one who restores the kingdom of God and fulfills the promise of the new covenant, specifically referring to the one who will bring the process of salvation to completion in the future. This Savior is the Lord, God the Son, and the promised Messiah. However, for the readers in Philippi, a Roman colonial city, the statement that Jesus is the Savior might have conveyed another meaning. They were under pressure from their fellow citizens loyal to the Roman emperor, who was considered as the savior of the Roman world at that time. However, Paul declares that Jesus, not the Roman emperor, is the true Savior and the ultimate finisher of all historical processes. This statement would have confirmed the readers' faith and hope.

Regarding the future work of Jesus, on the other hand, Jesus will transform "our" lowly bodies, "our" present physical bodies, into bodies like his glorious body. This refers to the final work of Jesus for the believers. Paul's phrasing here is unique. In his other letters, he typically refers to God as the agent of the resurrection of believers (Rom 8:11; 1 Cor 15:38; 2 Cor 3:18) and the Holy Spirit as the channel through which the power of the resurrection is imparted (Rom 1:4; 8:11). However, the idea of Jesus as the subject of the resurrection is not foreign to Paul since Paul introduces Jesus, the last Adam, as the life-giving spirit in 1 Cor 15:45. Furthermore, this concept was already present in the teaching of Jesus that those who see the Son and believe in him will be raised again on the last day (John 6:34).

The third point in Paul's statement is that God's plan and power work together in Jesus's final act. Using the prepositional phrase with κατὰ (according to), Paul explains that Jesus's work of transforming the bodies of believers will be accomplished according to God's power, which brings everything under the authority of Jesus (3:21). This expression is related to 2:9–11, where God restored Jesus to his original position and glory after his resurrection and ascension. It declares that all creatures, including the Roman emperor, will kneel before the name of Jesus and acknowledge him as Lord. Therefore, the resurrection of the individual believers is not only the final stage of God the Father's plan for believers, in which the Triune God participates and fulfills, but also part of the future consummation of the universal salvation process. In this process, all rebellious powers against God will be judged, and God's rule will be fully restored in Christ (Matt 6:9–10; Eph 1:10).

The fourth point is why "we" eagerly await the resurrection of the body through Jesus. Although not explicitly stated in this passage, the reason can be inferred from the third observation above and Eph 1:5. In this context, Jesus's work of transforming the believer's body represents one of the final phases of God's plan of salvation. It can be said that this process fulfills God's grand plan of salvation for humans. According to Eph 1:5, God's plan of salvation dates back to his pre-creation plan, which centers around the adoption (υἱοθεσίαν) of human beings as members of his family. It indicates that God had a plan before creation to create human beings and have them share and enjoy a loving relationship with the Triune God as one family. Creating the first man and woman in Gen 1:28 was the first step in carrying out this plan. Despite human rebellion against God, his plan has continued to progress through the earthly and heavenly ministries of Jesus, culminating in Rev 21:7, where believers will be declared as God's children after completing all stages of salvation. Therefore, "we," who have participated in the salvation process by believing in Jesus, the Messiah, hope for the future resurrection because "we" desire to enjoy full fellowship with the Triune God by passing through the final stage of God's grand plan of salvation.

To summarize these observations, "we," including Paul, are not like the negative examples who prioritize their interests over God's and cling to earthly things that will soon pass away. Although following Christ may involve suffering (1:28–30; 3:10), "we" are on a life journey consistent with our identity as citizens of heaven. "We" think and hope for true glory in the future, which includes being clothed in resurrection bodies through the work of the Triune God and enjoying loving fellowship with God forever. The readers are encouraged to observe positive and negative examples of people and adopt a mindset distinct from worldly thinking, as commanded in 3:1. This way of thinking should be expressed in their lives, following the examples of Paul and his followers.

E) 4:1

Paul concludes his discussion of the potential threat of the Judaizers, which began in 3:1, and his subsequent exhortations with the inferential conjunction ὥστε (therefore). He commands the readers to stand firm (στήκετε) (see also 1:27) in the Lord in this way (οὕτως). The adverb οὕτως can refer either to the preceding or the following content. In this case, however, it is more appropriate to interpret it as referring to the preceding one since 4:1 serves as a conclusion to the issue of the Judaizers. Thus, the meaning of Paul's final command to stand firm in the Lord can be understood in four ways:

1. Do not be misled by the arguments of the Judaizers.

2. Build the readers' Christian lives on their identity and privileges as the people of the new covenant, who have believed in the work of Jesus proclaimed by Paul and have been transferred into the kingdom of God's grace.

3. Anticipate the future stage of the salvation process, in which God will complete the restoration of his kingdom by subjecting all things to Jesus. By God's power, Jesus will transform the lowly bodies of believers into new bodies like his glorious body, and they will enjoy full fellowship with the Triune God.

4. Demonstrate the new mindset centered on Jesus as an ongoing way of life in the present.

To emphasize the significance of this command, Paul uses several distinct expressions to address his readers. In addition to the frequently used term ἀδελφοί (brothers [and sisters]) (x6: 1:12; 3:1, 13, 17; 4:1, 8), he also employs the expressions ἀγαπητοὶ καὶ ἐπιπόθητοι (beloved and longed for) and "my joy and crown." The phrase ἀδελφοί μου (my brothers [and sisters]) implies that they belong to the same family under God as their Father. "Beloved and longed for" communicates Paul's deep love for them, while "my joy and crown" indicates that they are the result of his ministry and the source of his pride. These terms of address differ from those used for Epaphroditus in 2:25. Although Paul refers to both groups as "my brother," he also calls Epaphroditus a fellow worker and soldier, which relates to the ministry of the gospel. In contrast, the titles used here are all relational. This difference is due to Paul's different intentions in each case. In the first case, Paul wants to present Epaphroditus as a model of faithful living in the gospel; however, he intends here to encourage the readers to follow his example by adopting a renewed mindset and lifestyle. Nevertheless, despite this difference in rhetorical purpose, it is evident that each title reflects Paul's heartfelt affection for his readers.

In conclusion, several principles for the Christian life can be drawn from Paul's commands and explanations so far:

1. The Christian life begins with the gospel of Jesus. Through Jesus's ministry on the cross and his resurrection, believers are transferred from the realm of darkness, which rebels against God, to the kingdom of light, where they have a new covenant relationship with God. While certain aspects of the old covenant, such as circumcision, are no longer relevant, fundamental principles of the law, such as love for God and love for people, remain essential for the new covenant people.

2. The core of the Christian life is focusing on one's relationship with God/Jesus and extending that relationship to fellow believers. Paul's life is characterized by his pursuit of Jesus and his longing to be with the readers he loves. Likewise, the readers should strive for a relationship with God/Jesus, as Paul and his followers do. This relationship will continue beyond life on earth into an eternal relationship in heaven, where believers will enjoy communion with the Triune God and other believers through their resurrected bodies.

3. The Christian life should be an inside-out process. To properly sustain the Christian life, it is essential to exercise discernment in the realm of

thought before engaging in behavioral aspects. Specifically, it is crucial to distinguish between God's will and the values and interests of the world. The standard for making such discernment is the will of God as revealed in the gospel and the overall process of salvation, which includes the grace that initiated the process in the past, the experience of God's presence in the present, and the completion of the process in the future. Christians should use this standard to assess their current situation and express their discernment through their way of life.

4. The Christian life is not static but progressive. Salvation is not a one-time event but a process and an ongoing journey with God that continues until the individual's personal end or the cosmic culmination of the universe at Christ's return. Christians must continue to walk with God day by day.

5. It is crucial to recognize that there can be risks in the Christian life, including personal suffering and the influence of worldly factors that can potentially jeopardize one's relationship with God. Therefore, Christians must acknowledge the dual nature of their identity and remain steadfast in their faith journey by following Jesus, the ultimate example, and imitating those who seek to follow Jesus.

PHILIPPIANS 4:2–9

OUTLINE:

III. The Body of the Letter (1:12—4:20)

    A. About the situations caused by Paul's imprisonment (1:12-26)

    B. About the real problems of the church (1:27—2:18)

    C. Paul's plan to send Timothy and Epaphroditus (2:19-30)

    D. About the potential problems of the church (3:1—4:1)

    E. Final exhortations to the church (4:2-9)

    F. A thank-you note for the gift from the church (4:10-20)

III. THE BODY OF THE LETTER (1:12—4:20)

E. Final exhortations to the church (4:2-9)

ELEMENTS OF DISCONTINUITY AND CONTINUITY help to identify the position of 4:2–9. One element of discontinuity is the introduction of certain participants, such as Euodia and Syntyche, for the first time in this letter. Another element is the use of παρακαλῶ (I urge), which signals a shift in topic from the previous section.[1] Nevertheless, there is also continuity with the previous section. A series of appeals (παρακαλῶ [x2 in 4:3]; ἐρωτῶ [I ask] [4:3]) and commands (x8 in 4:3–9) indicate continuity in that Paul continues to exhort his readers. The end of this section is 4:9 because there is an apparent discontinuity beginning with 4:10, marked by the absence of

---

1. Reed, *Discourse Analysis of Philippians*, 265.

commands and the introduction of a new theme, the gift from the readers to Paul.

The section of 4:2–9 can be divided into two parts based on the participants. The first part (4:2–3) mentions Euodia and Syntyche, who are competing for the gospel. Paul exhorts them to be of the same mind in the Lord and appeals to another individual to help them. The second part is 4:4–9, where Paul summarizes and concludes his exhortations to the readers with a series of imperatives.

1. Toward a unity of the church (4:2–3)

Paul introduces new characters, Euodia and Syntyche, and moves on to a different topic. The content can be divided into two: Paul directly urges Euodia and Syntyche (4:2), and he appeals to his faithful companion, addressed in the singular as "you" (4:3).

1. Appeal to Euodia and Syntyche: Have the same mindset (4:2)
2. Appeal to another person (4:3)
    1) Command: Help these women
    2) Addition 1: They have struggled with Paul in the gospel, together with Clement and the rest of Paul's fellow workers
    3) Addition 2: Their names are in the book of life

A) 4:2

Paul switches the subject and urges the two women in the church, Euodia and Syntyche, to have the same mindset. Despite its brevity, several points are noteworthy. The first point is the repetition of the verb παρακαλῶ (I urge). Paul uses this verb for each woman, indicating that he is not taking sides or showing favoritism. It shows his careful consideration to avoid offending either of them unnecessarily. The second point is the phrase τὸ αὐτὸ φρονεῖν (to be of the same mind). It is the same phrase that Paul used in 2:2 when he urged his readers to complete his joy (τὸ αὐτὸ φρονῆτε [2:2]), suggesting that the issue addressed in both passages is the same. The third point is the phrase "in the Lord," which implies that their unity of mind should go beyond mere human harmony and be rooted in their relationship with the Lord Jesus. This is consistent with how Paul illustrated his exhortations to unity of mind (2:1–4), using the example of Jesus (2:5–11). This phrase also indicates that the situation of Euodia and Syntyche is connected to 2:1–4.

Based on the observations mentioned above, the issue with these two women is that they do not share the same mindset. According to what Paul says about them in 4:3, both are working hard for the sake of the gospel, but they are expressing their zeal through rivalry instead of cooperation. In some ways, they are similar to those mentioned in 1:15–17, who preach Christ with a competitive spirit rather than a pure intention to spread the gospel. Unlike the situation in Corinth, their rivalry does not yet appear to threaten the church since Paul does not rebuke them. However, if left unchecked, it could become a serious problem for the church, making it difficult to maintain a unified voice and stance against external pressure from unbelievers in Philippi. Therefore, Paul explicitly names Euodia and Syntyche and appeals to them to resolve their conflict so that the church can effectively proclaim the gospel and stand firm as citizens of heaven. Furthermore, Paul's appeal to these women, in connection to 2:1–4, can be interpreted as a call to practice his series of exhortations: doing nothing out of selfish ambition or vanity, thinking of others as more significant than oneself in humility, and caring for the needs of others as well as one's own.

B) 4:3

Paul continues his exhortation to Euodia and Syntyche. This time, he appeals to another person with the vocative γνήσιε σύζυγε (genuine companion) and the second-person pronoun σέ (you), commanding him to help these women. He then provides more information about Euodia and Syntyche through two relative clauses. There are several things to note in the structure and content of this passage.

The first point is the identity of the person to whom Paul is appealing and commanding. The vocative σύζυγε, which combines συν (with) and ζυγός (yoke), can mean comrade in a military context or companion in a friendship context. The addition of the adjective γνήσιε (genuine) indicates that Paul is addressing a true fellow worker, but the specific identity of this person is not revealed. Several candidates have been suggested, including Epaphroditus, Timothy, the Philippian church, Silas (Acts 16:19), Luke, and Lydia. However, Epaphroditus cannot be the subject of a second-person reference because he will be sent to the church with this letter. Similarly, Timothy is not a viable option because he is to be sent later. It is uncertain whether Silas was with Paul during his imprisonment in Rome. If Luke wrote the "we" passage in Acts, it is possible that he traveled to Rome with Paul

(Acts 28:16), but it remains unclear whether Luke was in Philippi when Paul wrote this letter. While it is possible that Paul's interlocutor is the Philippian church, the difficulty lies in explaining the shift from the second-person plural, which Paul consistently used to address his readers earlier in the letter, to the second-person singular reference here. A more plausible candidate is one of the overseers and deacons mentioned in 1:1. This is because Paul's reference to church leaders as recipients of the letter is relevant to the body of the letter and would be crucial in resolving the rivalry between Euodia and Syntyche. In addition, if these two women are prominent members of the church and are zealous for the gospel, then the leaders would be the most appropriate people to exhort and help them. However, since Paul does not specify the name of his interlocutor, we must acknowledge that the identity of the second-person singular referent remains a matter of speculation.

The second point to note is Paul's elaboration on the women. He uses two relative pronouns to provide additional information about them, one of which pertains to their commitment to the ministry of the gospel. Using the word αἵτινες (whoever), he states that they struggled with him (συνήθλησάν) in the gospel. The term συνήθλησάν is related to fighting together on the battlefield,[2] and in this context, it means that they became Paul's coworkers and labored for the gospel. It is noteworthy that Paul uses the same word in 1:27 when he addresses his readers about the external problems of the church, specifically, the opposition of the unbelieving citizens of Philippi. By using this word to describe Euodia and Syntyche, he implies that despite their competitive attitude toward each other, they are both devoted to the gospel. Moreover, based on Paul's expression of gratitude to his readers for standing with him in the gospel from the beginning and his expectation that their lives of devotion will continue until Christ's return (1:3–7), the dedication of these two women to the gospel can be seen as another example for the readers to imitate. Paul also mentions Clements and "the rest of my fellow workers" to emphasize that Euodia and Syntyche's faithfulness to the gospel is no less than that of his other coworkers. In this sense, Euodia and Syntyche are faithful workers in the ministry of the gospel, and their dedication is so outstanding that it should serve as a model for others to follow.

Paul, then, adds another piece of information about them with the relative pronoun ὧν (whose), and this time, he focuses on their relationship with God. He notes that their names are recorded in the book of life, similar to genealogies and family registers, where a person's name is added at birth and removed at death. When a person joins God's family through

---

2. "Συναθλέω," *EDNT* 3:296.

Jesus, their name is added to the book of life, which serves as evidence that they will not be condemned in God's final judgment (Exod 32:32; Ps 68:29; Dan 12:1; Luke 10:20; Heb 12:23; Rev 3:5; 13:8; 17:8; 20:12, 15; 21:27).[3] The fact that the names of Euodia and Syntyche are written in the book of life indicates that they are new covenant people, recognized by God as his children in the kingdom of God. In other words, they possess heavenly citizenship (3:20). Based on Paul's explanation, it can be inferred that Euodia and Syntyche are faithful and committed to the gospel in their ministry as born-again children of God.

The third thing to note is why Paul asks a third person to help Euodia and Syntyche and adds positive remarks about them. Given Paul's appeal for the unity of these two women in 4:2 and chapter 2, it is likely that the church members are already aware of the competitive relationship between them. In this context, Paul's mention of the content in 4:3 seems to be for at least two reasons. One is his desire to solve their problem. It is unclear how much effort the women have already made to improve their situation. However, Paul seeks to solve the issue by involving a third party because their problem could have negative consequences for both themselves and the church. That is why Paul uses the expression ναί (yes) to draw the readers' attention and issue a command. Another possible reason is that he wishes to prevent church members from treating Euodia and Syntyche negatively. Despite their rivalry, they remain valuable members and coworkers with whom the church should cooperate in advancing the gospel. In this sense, Paul's command in 4:3 can be understood as a call to handle the situation involving Euodia and Syntyche with discernment and love, guided by sound truth.

2. Toward a proper Christian life (4:4–9)

Paul's exhortation to the church comes near the end of the letter. He gives brief commands to all readers, using the second-person plural rather than addressing Euodia and Syntyche. This paragraph can be divided into four parts based on subject matter and target of commands. The first part is 4:4, where Paul instructs his readers to rejoice. This serves as an introduction to the final instructions and encapsulates his intent throughout the entire letter. The second part is 4:5, where Paul addresses the attitude of the readers toward those outside the church, using the phrase πᾶσιν ἀνθρώποις (to all people). The third part is 4:6–7, which deals with prayer. Finally, the fourth part is 4:8–9, where Paul gives final commands regarding areas of thought and action.

---

3. Stuart, *Exodus*, 685–88.

There are several participants in 4:4–9. As human beings, Paul and the readers are presented as individuals who give and receive commands, respectively. The people outside the church are those with whom the readers should live in a relationship. As a divine being, God appears as the one who hears and answers the readers' prayers (4:6–7) and gives them peace (4:9). In addition, Jesus, referred to as the Lord, is the foundation of the readers' current state of happiness (4:4) and will ultimately bring history to its consummation upon his return (4:5).

A) 4:4

Paul begins his final exhortations to the church. His first command is to rejoice always. The term "joy" is used as both a verb and a noun in this letter to express the emotions of Paul and his readers (Paul's joy: 1:4 [noun], 18 [verb]; 2:2 [noun], 17 [verb]; 4:10 [verb]; the readers' joy: 1:25 [noun]; 2:18 [verb], 28 [verb], 29 [noun]; 3:1 [verb]; 4:1 [noun], 4 [verb]; see also συγχαίρω [Paul and the readers] [2:17–18]). However, the language used in this context also serves to communicate what Paul considers essential in his life and that of his readers (1:18; 2:2, 17–18; 3:1). In particular, the imperative form conveys his expectation that the readers will share what he values (2:18; 3:1). Therefore, Paul's command to rejoice here is not simply a request for their emotional happiness. Instead, he is asking the readers to align their minds, emotions, and wills with his explanation and exhortation of various situations in the church that began in 1:27. This understanding is reinforced by the addition of "in the Lord," which implies that Paul expects the readers to live their lives fully in a relationship with Jesus. In addition, Paul emphasizes his call to rejoice by repeating the same expression.

B) 4:5

The second command in the final exhortations is to instruct the readers to show gentleness (ἐπιεικὲς) to all people (πᾶσιν ἀνθρώποι), referring to those outside the church. Although the adjective ἐπιεικὲς implies forbearance and a gentle approach, the command does not suggest that the readers should passively accept the demands of others without question. In the context of the time when the unbelieving citizens in Philippi were pressuring the relatively weak church, those outside the church could see the readers' gentleness as the submission of the powerless, which might lead to further disregard and ridicule. Nevertheless, Paul's command calls for a proactive attitude toward the unbelievers of the world, as he taught in this letter. Based on the previous content of the letter, it can be inferred that this command contains at least three characteristics. The first is to be aware of the dual identity of a believer. The readers have become children of God through faith in Jesus, but they still have to live in this world, which conflicts with the kingdom of God. The second is to live as citizens of heaven. Despite pressure from Philippi's citizens loyal to Rome, believers should remain steadfast in the gospel as citizens of heaven (1:27–30). The third is to hold fast to the word of truth, live a life set apart from the world, avoid complaining or arguing with unbelievers, and maintain a pure and blameless way of life (2:14–15). In short, what Paul commands is an active life of living in love and truth in the midst of a crooked and perverse world.

Paul emphasizes the nearness of the Lord's return to reinforce his command. In this letter, the return of the Lord is addressed in relation to the readers' lives for the gospel (1:6), their lives of love on earth discerned with knowledge and insight (1:9–11), the beginning of eternal fellowship with the Triune God through the resurrection (3:20–21), and the initiation of the consummation of salvation, in which all beings in heaven and on earth will be subject to Jesus (2:10–11; 3:21). Thus, the expression "the Lord is near" in this context signifies that (1) the final judgment of the realm of darkness is imminent, (2) the oppression and suffering caused by the unbelievers of the world is about to come to an end, and (3) the eternal victory enjoyed with the Lord is close. This should be sufficient for the readers to endure external persecution and actively live a life of truth and love toward those outside the church.

c) 4:6–7

This is the third part of Paul's final exhortations. Here, he focuses on the prayer of the readers. At the beginning of the letter, Paul introduced his prayer for the readers (1:4–11), and now he instructs them to maintain their lives well through prayer. By placing the theme of the prayer at the beginning and end of the letter, Paul structures the letter in a way that reminds the readers of the importance of prayer in their lives.

Paul's instructions on prayer consist of two parts: how to pray and its result. To explain how to pray, he introduces a series of steps using the second-person active imperative μεριμνᾶτε (be anxious) and the third-person passive imperative γνωριζέσθω (let something be made known) (4:6). The first step is to let go of distracting and complex thoughts. The verb μεριμνάω means to be divided in thought, indicating a state of anxiety caused by various thoughts and emotions related to potential or actual problems.

Therefore, Paul's use of the imperative form of μεριμνάω with μηδὲν (nothing) can be understood as an admonition not to allow one's mind to be dominated by circumstances. The second-person active imperative is noteworthy, as it tells the readers to use their will. The readers cannot control every situation they encounter, nor do they have all the solutions. However, their mental responses to these situations are entirely up to them. The active imperative suggests that the readers can control their thoughts and should use this power in response to various situations.

The second step is to inform God of the readers' requests. Paul's choice of wording is noteworthy. In contrast to the first step, where he used the second-person active imperative, here he employs the third-person passive imperative γνωριζέσθω (let something be made known). It indicates that the focus is not on the readers' act of praying but on the process by which their requests are communicated to God. Paul's phrasing appears to reinforce the readers' understanding of the nature of prayer. According to him, prayer is not about reporting solutions or plans for a situation to God and ordering him to carry them out. Instead, it is a humble plea for help, entrusting all aspects related to the timing, method, and outcome of the prayer to God's sovereignty and anticipating that God will answer the prayers favorably in his own time and manner. In this sense, prayer can be seen as transferring control over a matter or situation from oneself to God.

Paul adds four elements to support this point. The first element is ἐν παντὶ (in everything), which corresponds to μηδὲν (nothing) in the case of worry. This means that just as there is no limit to the situations and objects for which anxiety must be stopped, there is no limit to the area where help from God is requested. In this sense, prayer means acknowledging that everything is under God's sovereignty.

The second element is τῇ προσευχῇ καὶ τῇ δεήσει (by prayer and supplication), which refers to the actual act of praying. There is no need to distinguish the specific meaning of these words because they are used in several places in the Bible to refer to the act of praying to God (1 Kgs 8:38, 54; Ps 102:1; 143:1; Dan 9:3; 1 Tim 2:1). It is better to think of them as a hendiadys, which means prayer itself.[4]

The third element is μετ' εὐχαριστίας (with thanksgiving). This represents a different attitude toward situations and problems than the anxiety mentioned in the first step. It is noteworthy that Paul mentions this attitude in the process of prayer rather than as a result of prayer, indicating that the attitude of thanksgiving is independent of whether the problem is solved or not. Therefore, to pray is to entrust all processes and outcomes to God's

---

4. O'Brien, *Philippians*, 492–93; contra, Reumann, *Philippians*, 614.

faithful sovereignty and to expect his goodness based on the relationship with God. Regardless of the outcome, God is always good to those who pray.

The fourth element of prayer is πρὸς τὸν θεόν (to God), which indicates the recipient of prayer. This expression shows the essential difference between anxiety and prayer. While anxiety is a complex and uneasy state focused on oneself, prayer focuses on God.

Putting these elements together, the prayer that Paul speaks of is a request to God for help in any situation experienced in this life. It includes several components, such as (1) willful control in the realm of thought so that the situation does not dominate the believer's mind, (2) allowing God's intervention in the situation, and (3) thanksgiving by humbly acknowledging God's good sovereignty over the timing, method, and outcome of the answer to prayer.

On the other hand, regarding the result of prayer, Paul states that the peace of God, which surpasses all understanding, will guard the hearts and minds of the readers in Christ Jesus (4:7). This statement contains several observation points.

The first point is the subject and verb of the process. In discussing how to pray, Paul uses the people's actions as the subject of the process. However, when discussing the result of prayer, something God provides appears as the subject, and the effect it has on people is the verb. This highlights that the outcome of prayer is entirely under God's sovereignty.

The second point is the content of God's response to prayer. Paul does not mention the resolution of the situation or problem. Instead, he connects God's peace with the heart and mind of the praying person as a result of prayer. This expression suggests that the essence of God's answer is to change the inner state of those who pray rather than the outer environment. It is related to the anxiety and gratitude mentioned in the case of how to pray. In other words, when believers rely on the sovereignty of God, suppress their complex thoughts about various situations and problems, and pray with gratitude, God responds to their prayer by protecting and helping them to remain anxiety free and grateful in the realm of their hearts and minds. As a result, this inner state enables the readers to focus more on God, regardless of their circumstances, and better understand and discern external problems, recognizing God's work more effectively.

The third point is the emphasis expressed by addition and repetition. Paul emphasizes the peace of God by adding a participle ("surpassing all understanding") and an article (ἡ) plus noun plus article (ἡ) plus modifier form.[5] He also repeats the second-person genitive about the hearts and

---

5. Levinsohn, *Discourse Features*, 57–60.

minds of the readers ("your hearts and your minds"), emphasizing the beneficiaries of the answer to prayer. These emphases convey that God's peace surpasses the readers' thoughts and can alleviate their anxiety, leading to gratitude.

The last point is the phrase "in Christ Jesus." This indicates that the steadfastness in the readers' hearts and minds resulting from answered prayer should be linked to their relationship with Jesus. Therefore, for believers who have a new covenant relationship in the kingdom of God through Jesus, God's answer to their prayer is primarily for their benefit. However, ultimately, it is a divine help to deepen their relationship with God/Jesus.

D) 4:8–9

Paul concludes his exhortations using the nominative of address ἀδελφοί (brothers and sisters) and the phrase τὸ λοιπόν (finally). He provides two instructions. The first one is to think rightly (4:8). He specifies what they should think about by listing eight virtues, introduced with six relative pronouns ὅσα (whatever) and two conditional clauses: whatever is true, whatever is honorable, whatever is right, whatever is pure, whatever is lovely, and whatever is commendable; if there is any excellence and if there is anything praiseworthy. These virtues relates to one's relationship with God as described in the Bible, such as being true, honorable (Prov 15:26), right, pure, excellent (1 Pet 2:9; 2 Pet 1:3), and praiseworthy (Eph 1:6, 12, 14); or with fellow believers, such as being true, honorable (1 Tim 3:8, 11; Titus 3:2), right, lovely, commendable, excellent (2 Pet 1:5), and praiseworthy. These virtues were also highly valued in the Greco-Roman society of the time, including the city of Philippi. Therefore, what Paul urges his readers is to fill their minds with thoughts that align with their dual identity as citizens of heaven in order to maintain good relationships with God and fellow believers, to live a blameless and pure life as those who are in the world but not of it, and to shine as lights in the darkness. Paul conveys this command in an emphatic structure, in which he first states what the readers should think and then uses the plural pronoun ταῦτα (these things) as the object of an imperative verb λογίζεσθε (think). This structure makes the readers focus on what to think.

The second instruction is to act rightly (4:9). Like the first instruction above, Paul emphasizes this command by stating what they should do in a relative clause. Then, he uses the pronoun ταῦτα (these things) to make it the object of the imperative verb πράσσετε (practice). Paul commands his readers to follow two things: the teachings they have learned and received from him; and his life, which serves as an example of how to live according to his teachings. He does not instruct his readers to live like him because he lived a perfect life like Jesus. Instead, as he has written earlier, he has been striving to discern important aspects in various situations and apply that discernment to his daily life, with Jesus as his foundation and role model. Therefore, Paul's instructions on behavior can be understood as an encouragement for readers to continue their journey of faith by following the examples of Jesus and Paul, just as Paul follows Jesus as his model.

Paul adds that the God of peace is with those who live in this way (4:9). While in the context of prayer, he states that the peace of God calms the internal realm, particularly the complexities and anxieties of the mind and thoughts (4:7); here the God who provides peace is present in the lives of his readers as they express right thinking in their actions. This means that God's help for his people encompasses both the realm of thought and practical support, enabling his people to remain steadfast in their faith and persevere through external hardships and pressure.

In summary, Paul's final command regarding the thoughts and actions of the readers in 4:8–9 consists of three elements. The first component is the inside-out pattern of life, which requires internal discernment to be expressed through external attitudes and actions. This pattern is reflected in the structure of the text, where Paul first instructs the readers on what to think and then on what to do. The second element is the emphasis on what to think about and what to do. Paul seeks to ensure his readers remain attentive to the things that truly matter. The third element is the role models whom the readers should imitate.

Among these three elements, the first and third elements appear as overarching principles in this letter. Regarding the inside-out pattern, Paul first mentions this principle as the content of his intercessory prayer in 1:9–11. He then applies it to his own situation in prison (1:12–26) and the problems of the readers (1:27–4:1) as the basis of his exhortations. Regarding the role model, on the other hand, Paul presents Jesus as the ultimate example for all believers (2:5–11; 3:10–11). He describes himself as a follower of Jesus (2:15–17; 3:17) and encourages his readers to imitate others who follow his example (2:19–24 [Timothy], 25–30 [Epaphroditus]; 3:17 [those who live according to Paul's example]). Therefore, Paul's exhortations to the readers in this letter, which could become his last will if he is not released, can be summarized as: "Think and do according to an inside-out way of life in the gospel, following the role models."

PHILIPPIANS 4:10–20

OUTLINE:

III. The Body of the Letter (1:12—4:20)
    A. About the situations caused by Paul's imprisonment (1:12-26)
    B. About the real problems of the church (1:27—2:18)
    C. Paul's plan to send Timothy and Epaphroditus (2:19-30)
    D. About the potential problems of the church (3:1—4:1)
    E. Final exhortations to the church (4:2-9)
    F. A thank-you note for the gift from the church (4:10-20)
IV. Letter Closing (4:21-23)

III. THE BODY OF THE LETTER (1:12—4:20)

E. A thank-you note for the gift from the church (4:10–20)

THE POSITION AND FUNCTION of 4:10-20 can be inferred from its continuity and discontinuity with the preceding parts. Regarding the discontinuity, the most notable feature is the absence of imperatives. In contrast to the previous sections (1:27—4:9), where Paul used imperatives (eighteen times), a hortatory subjunctive (3:15), and an infinitive with an imperative connotation (3:16) to give instructions about the internal and external situations of the readers, including his request to Timothy and Epaphroditus (2:29), this passage lacks such verbs. This absence suggests that Paul's aim here is to establish a friendly atmosphere by complimenting (4:14) and blessing the readers (4:19) rather than making demands. This shift creates a discontinuity within the larger unit, distinguishing it from 1:27—4:9. Another element of discontinuity is the focus of the conversation. This section moves the focus from Paul's communication to the readers to the gift they sent to him through Epaphroditus.

Despite its discontinuity, 4:10–20 contains elements of continuity relevant to the overall content of the letter. The first element is the verb χαίρω (to rejoice), which Paul has used, along with its noun form, to express his emotions and intentions to the readers (2:17–18; see also 1:3; 4:1 [noun form]) and to change the topics (1:18; 3:1; 4:4). Thus, ἐχάρην (I rejoiced) (4:10), which shifts the topic while expressing Paul's feelings toward the readers, also serves as an indicator of the connection with the earlier part of the letter.

The second element is the association between Paul and the readers centered on the gospel. Throughout the letter, Paul presents the gospel as the binding force between himself and the readers. This is evident from his expression of thanksgiving and intercession (1:3–11), the introduction of his situation (1:12), his first command to the readers (1:27), and up to the case of Euodia and Syntyche (4:2–3). In particular, 4:10–20 shares with 1:7 the theme of fellowship in the gospel (συγκοινωνούς [1:7]; ἐκοινώνησεν [4:15]).

The third element is Epaphroditus. He was sent by the readers to deliver what Paul needed, and Paul already mentioned him in 2:25–30.

Based on these elements of continuity and discontinuity, 4:10–20 is the part where Paul expresses his gratitude for their gift after finishing all his admonitions about their situation (4:4–9) and before closing the letter (4:21–23). Furthermore, 4:10–20 is connected to the earlier part of the letter, particularly to 1:3–11, which deals with thanksgiving and intercession based on his relationship with the readers in the gospel.

This passage can be divided into three parts. The first part (4:10–13) focuses on Paul's joy over the gift from his readers. It consists of two subunits based on the participants. In the first subunit (4:10), Paul is the main subject, expressing his joy that the readers have revived their concern for him and sent him a gift. In the second subunit (4:11–13), Paul remains the main subject, but the readers are not mentioned. Instead, Paul recounts how he has effectively dealt with various situations, explaining that his joy in 4:10 is not due solely to the gift.

The second part (4:14–18) addresses Paul's commendation of the readers' gift and can also be divided into two subunits based on the participants. In the first subunit (4:14–16), the readers are the main subject, with Paul commending them for their support in his ministry. In the second subunit

(4:17–18), the focus shifts back to Paul as the main subject, where he elaborates on his evaluation of the readers from 4:14–16. He clarifies that he is not commending them to solicit another gift but for their benefit.

The third part (4:19–20) includes Paul expressing his hope that God will continue to show grace to the readers and giving glory to God.

Throughout this passage, the human participants are Paul, the readers, and Epaphroditus, who is introduced as the one who brought the gift to Paul. The divine participants are the Lord and God. The Lord refers to God and/or Jesus, emphasizing their relationship with Paul. God is depicted as the one who empowers Paul, receives the devotion of the readers, meets their needs, and ultimately receives all the glory and praise.

1. Paul's joy (4:10–13)

    1) Paul's joy over the gift from the readers (4:10)

    2) Additional comment: Paul's clarification (4:11–13)

        a. Paul's clarification: Paul is not expressing his joy due to need (4:11–12)

        b. Reason: Paul has learned self-sufficiency through his experience (4:13)

2. Paul's commendation (4:14–18)

    1) Paul's commendation of the readers (4:14–16)

    2) Additional comment: Paul's excuse (4:17–18)

        a. Paul's clarification: His commendation is not for requesting another gift but for the benefit of the readers (4:17)

        b. Reason: Paul has received everything, including the recent gift from (4:18)

3. Paul's wish and doxology (4:19–20)

    1) Paul's wish: God will supply all the needs of the readers according to his riches in glory in Christ Jesus (4:19)

    2) Doxology: To our God and Father be glory forever and ever. Amen (4:20)

1. Paul's joy (4:10–13)

A) 4:10

Paul changes the subject with the expression ἐχάρην (I rejoiced), using the same transition technique he used in 1:18; 3:1; 4:4. This time, however, he introduces his joy in the passive aorist form, indicating that something outside of him has brought him joy. The reason for Paul's joy is that the readers' concern for him has been revived (ἀνεθάλετε). The verb ἀνεθάλετε conveys the imagery of a plant growing and blooming again. Although the readers had previously thought about Paul, they had not had the opportunity to express their concern regarding Paul's imprisonment. Now they can articulate their thoughts, which makes Paul happy.

Paul emphasizes the gift from his readers and his response in several ways. First, he adds "in the Lord" and "greatly" when speaking about his joy. He implies that the gift is something to greatly rejoice over, not only for Paul personally but also in the context of his relationship with God. This is the only instance in the letter where Paul mentions his joy in such terms, and it conveys his grateful heart as if this situation brings him unparalleled joy. Second, Paul changes the word order to emphasize the readers' concern for him. He does this by inserting a prepositional phrase (ὑπὲρ ἐμοῦ [for me]) to break the close connection between the article (τὸ) and the infinitive (φρονεῖν [to think]). Third, he highlights the readers' previous situation. By using ἐφ' ᾧ (because) (see also 3:12) and the emphatic καὶ (indeed), he shows that they had previously attempted to express their concern for him but had not been given the opportunity. This statement shows that Paul is already aware of his readers' ongoing concern for him and is grateful for their efforts.

B) 4:11–13

Paul's main intention in mentioning the readers' gift as a source of joy in 4:10 is to convey that their concern for him has finally borne fruit, and he appreciates their continued affection. However, since the expression in 4:10 is the most emphatic form of Paul's joy in the entire letter, he might have been concerned that his readers would think his focus was solely on meeting his needs. To prevent this potential misunderstanding, Paul asserts that he is not driven by his own needs (4:11a). He then presents his lessons from past experience to support his defense (4:11b–13). Several points can be noted in Paul's defense.

The first point to consider is the structure of Paul's statement. He presents his ability to be content in all circumstances as the core of his argument in 4:11b. Then, he elucidates his learning process and its content in 4:12–13, following a logical sequence: (1) Paul encountered various situations related to material possessions, such as wealth and poverty (4:12a–b); (2) he learned the secret of being content in all situations, whether experiencing plenty, hunger, abundance, or need (4:12c); and as a result, (3) he can do all things through God who strengthens him (4:13). This well-structured and logical explanation serves to convince his readers of the credibility of Paul's intentions.

The second thing to note is the unique features in each part of the structure. At the outset, Paul's expression of having learned self-sufficiency in 4:11b has two notable features. One is the use of the first-person nominative pronoun (ἐγώ) for emphasis. Although he has already used a first-person verb in the context, he uses the pronoun to emphasize his state of learning. This emphasis can be translated as "I myself." Another feature is the double use of the verb εἰμι (to be). The first instance occurs as an infinitive (εἶναι), referring to what Paul has learned, while the second is used in a relative clause (ἐν οἷς εἰμι) to describe his situation. These usages indicate that his focus is not on a single action or overcoming a particular situation but on existing and living through every stage of his life. In other words, Paul has learned to exist and live without attachment to possessions in all aspects of his life as a Christian in this world.

In addition, Paul's presentation of his learning process and content in 4:12–13 has distinctive features. The first feature is the use of contrast, where he describes his learning in terms of wealth and poverty (4:12). The second feature is repetition. He restates the contrast between wealth and poverty (4:12a–b) as the contrast between (1) fullness and hunger and (2) abundance and lack (4:12c). The third feature is an escalating progression in his learning. Paul's explanation begins by acknowledging situations of wealth and poverty (οἶδα) (4:12a–b) and then expands to "in any and every" situation of wealth and poverty. These features highlight the practicality of his learning through past experience (2 Cor 11:27) and powerfully convey that Paul has learned not to be obsessed with wealth and poverty through his past experiences. The fourth feature is the divine element (4:13). Although Paul does not mention this element in 4:11–12, it is a significant cause and a result of his self-sufficiency, which he has gained through experience. The term πάντα (all things) in 4:13, like "in any and every" in 4:12c, refers to all situations of wealth and poverty in terms of possessions. Therefore, Paul's statement in 4:13 does not imply that he has become a superhero by the power of God or Jesus. Instead, it means that he has learned to rely on God's assistance in all situations, whether in times of wealth or poverty. As a result, he can now be self-sufficient through God's power.

Paul's explanation can be summarized as follows, based on the observations above: (1) he has experienced both poverty and abundance in his life; (2) along the way, he has experienced the help of God/Jesus; (3) he has learned to focus on his relationship with the Lord and the ministry of the

2. Paul's commendation of the readers (4:14–18)

A) 4:14–16

Paul shifts the focus from himself to his readers and commends them for their actions (ἐποιήσατε) with the adverb καλῶς (well) (4:14). He commends them because their gift is a way of sharing in his suffering, which is expressed by the following participle clause ("sharing in my affliction"). Here, he emphasizes his suffering by altering the normal word order of noun plus genitive to genitive μου (my) plus noun θλίψει (affliction).

There is a twofold implication in his evaluation of the gift from the readers. First, Paul's suffering is an extension of his ministry of the gospel. That is, his trial is part of the vindication process of the gospel (1:16) since he has witnessed to the gospel and is now in prison. This leads to the second implication that the gift from the readers is not simply relief for Paul's needs. Instead, they are a way of participation in the defense and affirmation of the gospel and, by extension, in the grace of God that saves believers for the sake of the gospel and enables them to live as channels of life on this earth (1:7, 29). This is consistent with the earlier part of the letter, which introduced the gospel as the foundation of his relationship with the readers. In this sense, it is not surprising that Paul rejoices "in the Lord" over the gift from the readers.

In 4:15–16, Paul provides examples of the reader's participation in his ministry of the gospel. He notes that only the Philippian church engaged with him in terms of giving and receiving from the beginning of the gospel when he left Macedonia (4:15). Furthermore, even when he was in Thessalonica, the readers sent help to meet his needs more than once (4:16). There are several points to note in Paul's expressions.

First, it seems that Paul does not intend to provide an accurate account of all instances of help from his readers. Two pieces of evidence support this inference, one of which is the inversion of the chronological order of events in 4:15 and 4:16. The case in 4:15 most likely refers to the financial support he received from the Philippian church when he left Macedonia and was in the Corinthian region of Achaia (Acts 18:5; 2 Cor 11:8–9). However, 4:16 is the situation when he was still in Thessalonica in Macedonia. Chronologically, the event in 4:16 precedes that of 4:15. Another piece of evidence is the expression καὶ ἅπαξ καὶ δὶς (once and again) (4:16). It does not indicate an exact count or recurring action but, as an idiom, roughly means "more than once" or "several times."[1] Therefore, it is pointless to count how many times the readers helped Paul based on this expression.

Second, the readers' support of Paul was not merely a response to gratitude for his preaching of the gospel to them. In 4:15, Paul uses the commercial expression ἐκοινώνησεν εἰς λόγον δόσεως καὶ λήμψεως ([no church] shared with me in the matter of giving and receiving) to depict the readers' support as monetary exchange. However, since Paul also depicts the readers' gift as supporting his ministry and suffering for the sake of the gospel in 4:14, it is more appropriate to understand this expression as indicating that the readers had been involved in his ministry of the gospel from the beginning through their financial-support "ministry."

Third, the use of the second-person verb (οἴδατε [you know]) indicates that the readers were already aware of the events to which he is referring. At first glance, Paul's expression may seem somewhat odd. Since he is commending the present behavior of the readers, it might seem more appropriate to make it clear that he knows of their past participation in his ministry. However, Paul appeals to their knowledge, which may be related to the first observation above and the phrase "in the beginning of the gospel" (ἐν ἀρχῇ τοῦ εὐαγγελίου). That is, his intention is not to list every instance of the readers' involvement that he remembers but to remind them, as he mentioned in 1:5, that they had been involved in his ministry of the gospel from the very beginning of his founding of the church through his preaching of the gospel. By doing so, he aims to help the readers recognize that his evaluation and praise of their current behavior are well grounded. This may be more effective in communicating his intention than simply giving an example of his case.

Fourth, there are several distinctive expressions for emphasis. One of them is the use of the nominative of address Φιλιππήσιοι (Philippians), which is mentioned for the first time in the letter, to draw the readers' attention. Another feature is the repeated use of second-person nominative pronouns (ὑμεῖς [you]). Since Paul has already used a second-person verb in 4:14, he does not need to use the nominative pronoun in 4:15. Nevertheless, he uses it along with the nominative of address to emphasize the knowledge of his readers. Paul also highlights the readers' church by using the nominative pronoun when contrasting οὐδεμία ἐκκλησία (no church) with the Philippian church in terms of participating with Paul in giving and receiving. The last feature is the emphatic use of καί. In 4:15, it is used with

---

1. "Ἅπαξ καὶ δίς," L&N 608.

the second-person nominative pronoun to emphasize the readers. In 4:16, following the conjunction ὅτι, it emphasizes that the readers assisted Paul even when he was in Thessalonica.

B) 4:17–18

Unlike in 4:14–16, where Paul used second-person references, he now employs first-person references to explain his intention to commend the readers. This is the second explanation following 4:11. Paul expresses his gratitude to the readers because their gift signifies their love for him and participation in the ministry of the gospel. However, he is concerned that his intentions might be misconstrued as a request for more gift due to his own needs, so he uses a bank account metaphor to clarify his intentions. In 4:17, he uses the phrase οὐχ ... ἀλλὰ (not A but B) and the verb ἐπιζητῶ (to seek) to explain that he is not seeking an additional gift but rather abundant fruit that will benefit the readers (εἰς λόγον ὑμῶν). The phrase εἰς λόγον ὑμῶν can be understood as the readers' bank account.[2] In other words, Paul's raise of their gift is not an indirect request to add more money to his account but rather a desire (ἐπιζητῶ) to see the readers' account filled with abundance.

In 4:18, Paul elaborates on the two elements mentioned above: (1) he does not intend to ask the readers for more gifts, and (2) he commends them for the sake of making their accounts full. Regarding the first element, Paul states that he has received everything he needs and has more than enough. He then adds that he has been filled with the gift from his readers through Epaphroditus. It is as if his bank account was fully credited because his readers sent him financial support. In this sense, his praise of the readers is a pure expression of gratitude for their actions. Regarding the second element, on the other hand, Paul describes their gift as a fragrant offering that pleases God. At first glance, the gifts appeared to be given only to Paul. However, since Paul was carrying out God's work, he viewed their gifts as a participation in his ministry and an expression of their devotion to God, as if they were offering a sacrifice. This shifts the perspective of the gift from one related to Paul to one related to God and suggests that, as a result of their devotion, God will respond with blessings that will fill their accounts with abundance.

---

2. "Λόγος," BDAG 601.

3. Paul's wish and doxology (4:19–20)

Paul shifts the agent of action from himself to God and explains how the readers' account of blessing will be filled in their lives. Since the readers offered their gift to God, God will supply their needs (4:19). Here, the readers' needs encompass the various aspects of their lives in this world and the spiritual elements that deepen their relationship with God. These needs pertain both to individuals and to the church community.

Paul adds a few expressions to enhance the meaning of his message. The first is the phrase ὁ θεός μου (my God), which demonstrates his personal relationship with God. It helps the readers understand why supporting Paul is an offering to God and why God will bless them for their service. Since Paul is doing God's work, helping him is also serving the same God with whom he has a relationship. The second is the three prepositional phrases that describe God's blessing. The first phrase κατὰ τὸ πλοῦτος (according to [God's] riches) indicates that God's blessing will be abundant for the readers. The second phrase ἐν δόξῃ (in glory) suggests that all of these things will bring glory to God and honor his name. The third phrase ἐν Χριστῷ Ἰησοῦ (in Christ Jesus) means that since the readers' gift is for the sake of Jesus's gospel, God's fulfillment will also occur in the context of their relationship with Jesus. In this regard, what God provides for the readers goes beyond mere peace or satisfaction and leads them to a deeper relationship with God and Jesus, ultimately manifesting God's glory.

Paul concludes with a doxology (4:20), praising God, who will bring all these things to pass. Overall, what Paul says in 4:19–20 is similar to his intercessory prayer for his readers in 1:9–11. Both passages contain elements such as love manifested through action, which is an outward demonstration of an inward process of discernment guided by knowledge and wisdom. The passage emphasizes the importance of the readers' lives continuing to bear good fruit for God and leading to his glory and praise. This similarity suggests that Paul views his readers' gift as more than just pleasing to him. He sees it as part of the process by which they discern what is important in the gospel, bear good fruit before God, and ultimately experience a fullness of life that reflects God's glory. In this context, Paul might have viewed their gift as evidence that God hears and responds to his intercessory prayer for the readers. Therefore, it is appropriate for Paul to express his gratitude toward them for their actions and a gift.

In conclusion, Paul's expression of gratitude for the readers' gift in 4:10–20 has four key elements. The first is the relationship of love between Paul and the readers. Regarding Paul's love, he shows his love for the readers at the beginning of the letter by thanking God for them and praying for them whenever he remembers them (1:3–5). He even claims that God can attest to his deep love for them (1:8). As for the readers' love, upon learning of Paul's imprisonment, they displayed their affection by sending Epaphroditus to provide for Paul's needs. The mutual concern and affection between Paul and the readers are truly extraordinary.

The second element is the gospel, which is the vital link between Paul and his readers. Paul regards the readers' gift not only as personal help to him but also as their participation in his suffering for the gospel. This theme runs throughout the letter, beginning in 1:5, where Paul mentions that the readers have shared in his suffering for the gospel from the beginning. As the letter progresses, Paul continues to address both his own situation and that of the readers in relation to the gospel. In this sense, the readers are coworkers with Paul in the ministry of the gospel.

The third element is Paul's caution about material support. Although Paul expresses appreciation and gratitude for their gift, he is careful not to give the impression that he desires more support. This shows that he is a good minister who does not seek personal gain through the work of the gospel.

The fourth element is Paul's learning about possessions. Paul says that he has learned through past experiences not to be attached to wealth or poverty but to be self-sufficient by relying solely on God and expecting his help. While this implies that Paul has experienced considerable financial hardship (2 Cor 11:27), this lesson serves as one of the motivations for his unwavering focus on God throughout his ministry and even during his present imprisonment. It also enables Paul to express genuine gratitude and appreciation for the gift he has received, seeing it as active participation in the ministry of the gospel.

The last element is the ultimate purpose of life, which is to glorify God's name through Jesus in the gospel. Paul describes the readers' gift as an offering committed to the kingdom of God and assures the readers that God will respond with abundant blessings. However, Paul clarifies that this grace not only enriches their lives but also reveals God's glory in their relationship with Jesus Christ. Therefore, Paul's gratitude to his readers in 4:10–20 can be understood as another way of teaching, integrating such elements as his relationship with them, their gift, the Lord's response to their commitment, and their resulting lives into the larger picture of the salvation process in the gospel.

PHILIPPIANS 4:21–23

OUTLINE:

III. The Body of the Letter (1:12—4:20)

    A. About the situations caused by Paul's imprisonment (1:12-26)

    B. About the real problems of the church (1:27—2:18)

    C. Paul's plan to send Timothy and Epaphroditus (2:19-30)

    D. About the potential problems of the church (3:1—4:1)

    E. Final exhortations to the church (4:2-9)

    F. A thank-you note for the gift from the church (4:10-20)

IV. **Letter Closing (4:21-23)**

    A. Greetings (4:21-22)

    B. Benediction (4:23)

IV. LETTER CLOSING (4:21–23)

A. Greeting (4:21–22)

THIS IS THE FINAL PART of the letter. The use of the greeting verb ἀσπάζομαι (I greet) not only indicates the discontinuity with the previous section but also signals the transition to the final part of the letter. The content can be divided into two parts: the greeting (4:21-22), which uses greeting verbs, and the closing (4:23), which does not. Both divine and human participants are present in 4:21-23. The human participants are the believers who exchange greetings with the readers (4:21–22), including the brothers who accompany Paul, the people from Caesar's household, and all the saints. The divine participant is Jesus. He is the central figure connecting the relationship between the readers and the saints (4:21) and the source of blessing for the readers (4:23).

1. Greetings (4:21–22)

   1) Command the readers to greet: Greet every saint in Christ Jesus (4:21a)

   2) Greetings to the readers (4:21b–22)

      a. Greeting of those who are with Paul: The brothers who are with me greet you (4:21b)

      b. Greeting of all the saints: All the saints greet you, especially those of Caesar's household (4:22)

2. Benediction: The grace of the Lord Jesus Christ be with your spirit (4:23)

Paul begins to close the letter with the verb ἀσπάζομαι (to greet) (4:21), which was a typical way to end a letter in his day. While the elements such as the greeting, thanksgiving, and prayer at the beginning of the letter establish a connection with the readers and prepare them to receive the rest of the letter, the final greeting serves to reinforce the relationship with the readers and lend credibility to the entire letter. Paul achieves this in two ways.

The first way is to link the readers with other believers by exchanging greetings between the two groups. Paul first uses the imperative ἀσπάσασθε (greet) to command the readers to greet every saint in Christ Jesus. He then says that many believers greet the readers, using the indicative ἀσπάζονται (they greet). By establishing this connection between the readers and other believers, Paul conveys that the readers' situation is not his sole concern. This illustrates another way in which the two groups practice their oneness in the Lord, putting aside rivalry and greeting each other in pure love.

The second way is to introduce the people who are sending greetings to the readers. Paul mentions that the group with him greets the readers (4:21a). Although it is clear that Timothy (1:1; 2:19–24) and Epaphroditus (2:25–30) are with Paul, it is uncertain who else may be present. Paul's intention in mentioning these individuals is to communicate that both he and those with him encourage and support the readers in their lives of faith. He then passes on the greetings of many believers, especially those from Caesar's household (4:22). The people from Caesar's household were likely former slaves or freedmen who were part of the Roman emperor's household. It is unclear how they came to know the gospel, but Paul's mention of them is deliberate. He aims to convey that there are individuals within the heart of the empire who remain loyal to Jesus as their Lord, not the Roman emperor, and that they stand in solidarity with the readers. This reflects Paul's intention to comfort and encourage the readers who are facing difficulties from the citizens of Philippi loyal to Rome.

In summary, while the closing greetings were a customary component of the letter at that time, Paul uses this convention to strengthen his relationship with the readers and reiterate his love and expectations throughout the letter. In addition, he implicitly delivers the importance of maintaining a loving fellowship among the saints (2:1–4) and encourages the readers to stand firm in the face of external difficulties related to Rome (1:27–30).

B. Benediction (4:23)

This is the final blessing for the readers and the end of the letter. Paul expresses his wish without a verb, that the grace of the Lord Jesus Christ may be with the spirit of the readers. Despite its brevity, it contains several aspects concerning the life of believers. First, their existence is rooted in their relationship with Jesus. Second, as the readers walk in this relationship, they will receive the grace or divine help of Jesus. Third, as a result, they will be better equipped to live their lives in Jesus. This final benediction also reflects Paul's love for his readers.

BIBLIOGRAPHY

Banker, John. *A Semantic and Structural Analysis of Philippians*. Dallas: Summer Institute of Linguistics, 1996.
Baur, F. C. *Paul the Apostle of Jesus Christ: His Life and Works, His Epistles and Teachings*. Peabody, MA: Hendrickson, 2003.
Bockmuehl, Markus N. A. *The Epistle to the Philippians*. BNTC. Peabody, MA: Hendrickson, 1998.
Bruce, F. F. *Philippians*. NIBCNT. Peabody, MA: Hendrickson, 1989.
Carson, D. A., and Douglas J. Moo. *An Introduction to the New Testament*. 2nd ed. Grand Rapids: Zondervan Academic, 2005.
Cohick, Lynn H. *Philippians*. Edited by Tremper Longman III and Scot McKnight. SGBC. Grand Rapids: Zondervan Academic, 2013.
Collange, Jean-Francois. *The Epistle of Saint Paul to the Philippians*. Translated by A. W. Attridge. London: Epworth, 1979.
Fee, Gordon D. *Paul's Letter to the Philippians*. NICNT. Grand Rapids: Eerdmans, 1995.
Fowl, Stephen E. *Philippians*. THNTC. Grand Rapids: Eerdmans, 2005.
Garland, David E. "The Defense and Confirmation of the Gospel." *RevExp* 77 (1980) 327–36.
Gnilka, Joachim. *Der Philipperbrief*. HThKNT 10.3. Freiburg: Herder, 1968.
Greenlee, J. Harold. *An Exegetical Summary of Philippians*. 2nd ed. Dallas: Summer Institute of Linguistics, 2008.
Halliday, M. A. K. *Language as Social Semiotic*. London: Arnold, 1978.
Halliday, M. A. K., and Ruqaiya Hasan. *Language, Context, and Text: Aspects of Language in a Social-Semiotic Perspective*. Language Education. Oxford: Oxford University Press, 1985.
Hansen, G. Walter. *The Letter to the Philippians*. PilNTC. Grand Rapids: Eerdmans, 2009.
Hawthorne, Gerald F., and Ralph P. Martin. *Philippians*. Rev. ed. WBC 43. Nashville: Nelson, 2004.
Hays, Richard B. *Echoes of Scripture in the Letters of Paul*. New Haven, CT: Yale University Press, 1989.
Holloway, Paul A. *Consolation in Philippians*. SNTSMS 112. Cambridge: Cambridge University Press, 2001.
———. *Philippians*. Hermeneia. Minneapolis: Fortress, 2017.
Hwang, Young Chul. "Paul's Letter Paraenesis." In *Paul and the Ancient Letter Form*, edited by Stanley E. Porter and Sean A. Adams, 253–68. PSt 6. Leiden: Brill, 2010.

Jewett, Robert. "The Epistolary Thanksgiving and the Integrity of Philippians." *NovT* 12 (1970) 40–53.
Keener, Craig S. *Acts: An Exegetical Commentary*. 4 vols. Grand Rapids: Eerdmans, 2012–15.
Keown, Mark J. *Philippians 1:1—2:18*. EEC. Bellingham, WA: Lexham, 2017.
———. *Philippians 2:19—4:23*. EEC. Bellingham, WA: Lexham, 2017.
Leckie-Tarry, Helen. *Language and Context: A Functional Linguistic Theory of Register*. Edited by David Birch. London: Pinter, 1992.
Lee, Jae Hyun. *Paul's Gospel in Romans: A Discourse Analysis of Rom 1:16—8:39*. LBS 3. Leiden: Brill, 2010.
———. "'Think' and 'Do' Like the Role Models: Paul's Teaching on the Christian Life in Philippians." In *The Language and Literature of the New Testament: Essays in Honor of Stanley E. Porter's 60's Birthday*, edited by Lois K. Fuller Dow et al., 625–43. BibInt 150. Leiden: Brill, 2016.
Levinsohn, Stephen H. *Discourse Features of New Testament Greek: A Coursebook on the Information Structure of New Testament Greek*. Dallas: Summer Institute of Linguistics, 2000.
Lightfoot, John B. *St. Paul's Epistle to the Philippians*. Peabody, MA: Hendrickson, 1999.
Martin, Ralph P. *Philippians*. TNTC. Grand Rapids: Eerdmans, 1980.
McDonald, Lee Martin, and Stanley E. Porter. *Early Christianity and Its Sacred Literature*. Peabody, MA: Hendrickson, 2000.
Melick, Richard R., Jr. *Philippians, Colossians, Philemon*. NAC 32. Nashville: B&H, 1991.
O'Brien, Peter T. *The Epistle to the Philippians*. NIGTC. Grand Rapids: Eerdmans, 1991.
Peterman, G. W. *Paul's Gift from Philippi: Conventions of Gift Exchange and Christian Giving*. SNTSMS 92. Cambridge: Cambridge University Press, 1997.
Pitts, Andrew W. "Philosophical and Epistolary Contexts for Pauline Paraenesis." In *Paul and the Ancient Letter Form*, edited by Stanley E. Porter and Sean A. Adams, 269–305. PSt 6. Leiden: Brill, 2010.
Porter, Stanley E. *The Apostle Paul: His Life, Thought, and Letters*. Grand Rapids: Eerdmans, 2016.
———. *Idioms of Greek New Testament*. BLG 2. Sheffield: Sheffield Academic, 1992.
———. "Paul of Tarsus and His Letters." In *Handbook of Classical Rhetoric in Hellenistic Period (330 B.C.—A.D. 400)*, edited by Stanley E. Porter, 533–85. Leiden: Brill, 2001.
———. "Prominence: An Overview." In *The Linguist as Pedagogue: Trends in the Teaching and Linguistic Analysis of the Greek New Testament*, edited by Stanley E. Porter and Matthew Brook O'Donnell, 45–74. NTMon 11. Sheffield: Sheffield Phoenix, 2009.
Porter, Stanley E., and Matthew Brook O'Donnell. *Discourse Analysis and the Greek New Testament: Text-Generating Resources*. LNTG 2. London: T&T Clark, 2024.
Reed, Jeffrey T. *A Discourse Analysis of Philippians: Method and Rhetoric in the Debate over Literary Integrity*. JSNTSup 136. Sheffield: Sheffield, 1997.
Reed, Jeffrey T., and Ruth A. Reese. "Verbal Aspect, Discourse Prominence, and the Letter of Jude." *FN* 9 (1996) 181–99.
Reumann, John. *Philippians*. AYB. New Haven, CT: Yale University Press, 2008.

BIBLIOGRAPHY

Riesner, R. "Chronology of Paul." In *Dictionary of Paul and His Letters: A Compendium of Contemporary Biblical Scholarship*, edited by Scot McKnight et al., 109–16. 2nd ed. IVP Bible Dictionary. Downers Grove, IL: IVP Academic, 2023.

Schenk, Wolfgang. *Die Philipperbriefe des Paulus*. Stuttgart: Kohlhammer, 1984.

Schnabel, Eckhard J. *Early Christian Mission*. 2 vols. Downers Grove, IL: InterVarsity, 2004.

Schubert, Paul. *Form and Function of the Pauline Thanksgivings*. BZNW 20. Berlin: Töpelmann, 1939.

Silva, Moisés. *Philippians*. BECNT. Grand Rapids: Baker, 1992.

Stuart, Douglas K. *Exodus*. NAC 2. Nashville: B&H, 2006.

Thielman, Frank. "Ephesus and the Literary Setting of Philippians." In *New Testament Greek and Exegesis: Essays in Honor of Gerald F. Hawthorne*, edited by Amy M. Donaldson and Timothy B. Sailors, 205–23. Grand Rapids: Eerdmans, 2003.

Thurston, Bonnie B., and Judith M. Ryan. *Philippians & Philemon*. Edited by Daniel J. Harrington. SP 10. Collegeville, MN: Liturgical, 2005.

Van Dijk, Teun A. "The Study of Discourse Analysis." In *Discourse as Structure and Process*, edited by Teun A. van Dijk, 1–35. Discourse Studies: A Multidisciplinary Introduction. London: SAGE, 1997.

Wanamaker, Charles A. *The Epistles to the Thessalonians*. NIGTC. Grand Rapids: Eerdmans, 1990.

White, John L. *Light from Ancient Letters*. Foundations and Facets. Philadelphia: Fortress, 1986.

Witherington, Ben, III. *Friendship and Finances in Philippi: The Letter of Paul to the Philippians*. NTC. Valley Forge, PA: Trinity, 1994.

Yoon, David I. "Prominence in NT Discourse: Galatians 1, 11–2:10 as a Test Case." *FN* 46 (2013) 3–26.

AUTHOR INDEX

Banker, John, 102, 155
Baur, F. C., 2, 155
Bockmuehl, Markus N., 4, 33, 34, 51, 80, 103, 155
Bruce, F. F., 80, 155

Carson, D. A., 3, 155
Cohick, Lynn H., 4, 80, 155
Collange, Jean-Francois, 29, 155

Fee, Gordon D., 4, 29, 31, 33, 51, 80, 103, 155
Fowl, Stephen E., 33, 155

Garland, David E., 33, 155
Gnilka, Joachim, 33, 155
Greenlee, J. Harold, 99, 155

Halliday, M. A. K., 7, 8, 155
Hansen, G. Walter, 3, 13, 34, 51, 102, 155
Hasan, Ruqaiya, 7, 155
Hawthorne, Gerald F., 3, 29, 33, 34, 51, 80, 98, 103, 155, 157
Hays, Richard B., 51, 155
Holloway, Paul A., 4, 14, 33, 155
Hwang, Young Chul, 99, 155

Jewett, Robert, 33, 156

Keener, Craig S., 5, 156
Keown, Mark J., 3, 6, 14, 68, 102, 156

Leckie-Tarry, Helen, 7, 156
Lee, Jae Hyun, 11, 12, 14, 35, 41, 156

Levinsohn, Stephen H., 35, 54, 138, 156
Lightfoot, John B., 29, 156

Martin, Ralph P., 3, 29, 33, 34, 51, 80, 98, 104, 155, 156
McDonald, Lee Martin, 12, 156
Melick, Richard R., Jr., 51, 156
Moo, Douglas J., 3, 155

O'Brien, Peter T., 4, 33, 34, 80, 137, 156
O'Donnell, Matthew Brook, 11, 156

Peterman, G. W., 33, 156
Porter, Stanley E., 2, 5, 11, 12, 13, 31, 54, 98, 99, 155, 156

Reed, Jeffrey T., 7, 11, 24, 33, 102, 130, 156
Reese, Ruth A., 11, 156
Reumann, John, 3, 13, 29, 33, 51, 102, 137, 156
Riesner, R., 3, 157
Ryan, Judith M., 51, 157

Schenk, Wolfgang, 28, 157
Schnabel, Eckhard J., 3, 157
Schubert, Paul, 33, 157
Silva, Moisés, 4, 28, 33, 51, 157
Stuart, Douglas K., 134, 157

Thielman, Frank, 3, 157
Thurston, Bonnie B., 51, 157

Van Dijk, Teun A., 7, 157

Wanamaker, Charles A., 24, 157
White, John L., 29, 157

Witherington, Ben, III., 29, 157

Yoon, David I., 11, 157

SUBJECT INDEX

Abraham, 110
already and not yet, 83, 86
anaphoric, 35, 37, 70, 103

behavior, 68, 69, 74, 79, 81, 97, 99,
    109, 120, 140, 147
behavioral aspect (dimension), 74, 97,
    115, 116, 129

Caesar's household (Roman
    emperor's), 4, 152, 153
Caesarea, 2, 3, 4
cataphoric, 35, 37, 48, 54, 70, 103
circumcision, 7, 97, 101, 104, 105,
    106, 109, 110, 122, 128
citizen(s)
    live as a, 8, 56, 57, 59, 97, 125
    loyal to Rome, 6, 17, 36, 63, 125,
        136, 153
    of God, 81
    of heaven, 59, 60, 61, 62, 63, 74, 84,
        120, 127, 132, 136, 139
    of the kingdom of God, 59, 125
    of this world, 125
    Philippian (of Philippi), 5, 6, 26,
        36, 40, 46, 61, 63, 76, 133, 135,
        136, 153
citizenship
    earthly citizenship, 61, 125
    heavenly, 59, 61, 125, 134
    noun, 59, 97, 125
    Roman, 5, 8, 40, 59
clause
    concessional, 60 70
    embedded, 10, 11, 12

participial, 31, 38, 62, 70, 73, 146
primary, 10, 11, 12
purpose, 38, 53, 57, 83, 89
reason, 57, 82
relative, 58, 70, 83, 139, 145
result, 57
secondary, 10
subordinate, 48, 58, 60, 65, 66, 75,
    83, 92, 92, 94
Clement, 6, 131
cognitive discernment (evaluation),
    38, 112, 115
cognitive thinking, 64, 66, 68, 69, 74,
    86, 107, 108, 111
competition, 16, 41, 47, 48, 49, 63, 64,
    65, 72, 74, 77
competitive spirit, 47, 132
contextual information, 1, 2, 7, 8
conjunction
    adversative, 71, 73, 88, 116
    causal, 88, 89, 92, 93, 95, 101, 105,
        119, 123, 124
    concessive, 107, 109
    correlative, 45, 102, 116
    inferential, 57, 64, 75, 80, 88, 91,
        92, 94, 99, 100, 119, 120, 127
covenant
    everlasting, 105
    new, 7, 27, 28, 39, 40, 81, 105, 106,
        109, 111, 112, 113, 114, 115, 116,
        117, 118, 121, 122, 125, 127, 128,
        134, 139
    old, 7, 27, 105, 109, 110, 111, 112,
        113, 114, 115, 118, 122, 128

SUBJECT INDEX

(covenant continued)
   people, 27, 28, 39, 83, 104, 105, 106, 110, 111, 128, 134
   relationship, 27, 38, 39, 40, 81, 111, 113, 114, 118, 139

dative, 27, 28, 32, 33
day of Christ Jesus, 31, 34, 39
discernment, 14, 15, 16, 28, 32, 37, 38, 39, 40, 49, 59, 60, 66, 94, 112, 117, 121, 122, 125, 128, 129, 134, 140, 149
discourse analysis, vii, 7, 11, 13, 24, 33, 102, 130, 156, 157
dual identity, 27, 28, 59, 61, 83, 84, 86, 136, 139

emphatic expression (marker, structure, element), 9, 12, 35, 40, 85, 89, 115, 139, 144, 147
Epaphroditus, vi, 3, 4, 6, 15, 16, 18, 19, 25, 37, 46, 56, 57, 66, 87, 91, 92, 93, 94, 95, 96, 98, 101, 122, 123, 128, 130, 132, 140, 141, 143, 148, 150, 151, 152
Ephesus, 3, 4, 157
epistolary form, 2, 99
Euodia and Syntyche, 6, 19, 40, 41, 66, 100, 130, 131, 132, 133, 134, 142
external pressure, 15, 17, 41, 83, 132

faith, 15, 16, 17, 27, 47, 48, 50, 54, 58, 59, 60, 61, 62, 63, 70, 80, 81, 84, 85, 86, 104, 108, 114, 121, 122, 124, 125, 126, 129, 136, 140, 152
false teachers, 6, 7, 15, 26, 28, 41
false teachings, 104, 106
financial support (aid), 6, 33, 146, 147, 148

genitive, 26, 33, 54, 66, 93, 117, 125, 138, 146
gift(s), vi, 13, 14, 15, 19, 28, 29, 33, 34, 62, 130, 131, 141, 142, 143, 144, 146, 147, 148, 149, 150, 151, 156
gospel
   advancing, 66, 134
   content of, 43, 44
   contrary to, 124
   for the sake of (for), 6, 15, 17, 31, 35, 39, 46, 62, 63, 83, 84, 88, 91, 93, 95, 114, 115, 116, 121, 131, 132, 133, 136, 146, 147, 150
   in, 1, 17, 32, 33, 34, 35, 40, 66, 82, 89, 91, 115, 123, 125, 128, 129, 131, 136, 140, 142, 149, 150
   ministry of, 15, 25, 26, 31, 34, 35, 36, 37, 40, 47, 128, 133, 134, 146, 147, 148, 150
   life worthy of, 36, 38, 63, 74, 81, 82
   of Christ (Jesus), 46, 53, 56, 59, 60, 63, 81, 89, 95, 128
   preach (proclaim, spread, witnessing), 6, 36, 41, 43, 44, 45, 46, 47, 53, 132
   truth of, 61, 63, 84, 86

head-tail relationship, 9, 12
hesitation formula, 102
Holy Spirit, 15, 16, 39, 49, 52, 58, 60, 106, 126
Holy Trinity, 52
humiliation (humility), 27, 64, 68, 74, 123, 132

imitate (imitation), 16, 26, 74, 119, 122, 123, 133, 140
imperative, 10, 37, 41, 43, 56, 57, 59, 68, 70, 78, 79, 80, 85, 97, 99, 100, 101, 102, 104, 119, 120, 121, 122, 135, 136, 137, 139, 141, 152
imprisonment, v, 2, 3, 4, 8, 14, 18, 25, 30, 35, 36, 41, 42, 44, 45, 46, 47, 49, 50, 51, 53, 54, 56, 60, 63, 87, 89, 95, 96, 114, 116, 130, 132, 141, 144, 150, 151
in Christ, 25, 27, 31, 36, 46, 47, 50, 60, 62, 64, 65, 69, 70, 101, 102, 108, 109, 112, 117, 126, 138, 139, 143, 149, 152
indicative, 91, 92, 118, 152
infinitive, 45, 100, 114, 119, 120, 121, 141, 144, 145
inside-out, 14, 16, 38, 39, 40, 41, 66, 69, 72, 77, 118, 120, 121, 124, 128, 140

SUBJECT INDEX

integrity, 14, 38, 81, 89, 90, 93, 156
intercessory prayer, 14, 15, 17, 23, 30, 31, 32, 33, 34, 35, 37, 40, 41, 42, 60, 66, 97, 112, 117, 118, 140, 149
internal conflict (division), 15, 40, 41, 47, 49, 53, 66, 77, 82
interpersonal information, 8
ius Italicum (law of Italy), 5

Jewish identity, 97, 98, 109, 111
joy, 19, 25, 34, 48, 49, 50, 51, 52, 54, 55, 60, 64, 66, 79, 80, 84, 85, 92, 95, 102, 128, 131, 135, 142, 143, 144, 146
Judaizers, 15, 19, 98, 100, 101, 102, 103, 104, 105, 106, 107, 109, 110, 111, 118, 119, 121, 122, 124, 127

kingdom
  acceptance (enter, transfer) into, 27, 81, 120, 125, 127
  belongs to, 27, 61, 62,
  of darkness, 62
  of God, 27, 59, 61, 76, 77, 81, 83, 86, 125, 134, 136, 139, 150
  of light, 62, 121, 128
  restoration of his, 76, 77, 81, 124, 127

law, 27, 39, 97, 108, 110, 111, 113, 114, 128
life of love, 15, 16, 37, 38, 39, 40, 41, 48

Macedonia, 5, 93, 116, 146
Messiah, 6, 106, 110, 111, 112, 113, 114, 122, 125, 127
mindset, 48, 64, 67, 70, 71, 72, 77, 80, 82, 113, 127, 128, 131, 132
ministry
  his (Jesus's), 68, 69, 75, 76, 77, 83, 85, 123, 124, 128
  his (Paul's), 15, 35, 36, 37, 52, 66, 103, 115, 116, 117, 128, 142, 146, 147, 148, 150

of the gospel, 15, 25, 26, 31, 34, 35, 36, 37, 40, 47, 128, 133, 146, 147, 148, 150
their (Euodia and Syntyche's), 134
model, 16, 18, 26, 27, 31, 36, 46, 68, 72, 74, 86, 91, 95, 116, 122, 123, 128, 133, 140

nominative of address, 57, 78, 80, 100, 101, 116, 119, 122, 139, 147
overseers and deacons, 24, 28, 133

participation
  in Christ's death and resurrection, 117
  in his (Christ's) suffering, 114
  in the gospel (ministry), 6, 32, 33, 34, 35, 36, 95, 146, 147, 148, 150
  in the salvation process, 63, 77,
participle, 10, 31, 35, 38, 54, 67, 74, 83, 113, 124, 138, 146
persecution, 27, 36, 59, 62, 63, 84, 116, 136
Pharisee, 108, 110, 111
Philippi, 1, 2, 3, 4, 5, 6, 8, 15, 16, 23, 24, 25, 26, 27, 33, 41, 59, 61, 76, 83, 84, 89, 90, 93, 125, 132, 133, 135, 139, 153, 156, 157
praetorian guard, 4, 44, 45
prayer, *see also* intercessory prayer, v, 6, 12, 14, 25, 17, 19, 23, 30, 31, 32, 33, 34, 35, 36, 37, 39, 40, 41, 42, 57, 66, 97, 112, 127, 118, 134, 136, 137, 138, 139, 140, 152
prominence, 11, 156, 157

realm
  of action, 115, 116
  of darkness, 59, 76, 81, 83, 121, 128, 136
  of hope (anticipation), 50, 89
  of light, 59,
  of rebellion (rebellious), 6, 76, 77, 83
  of salvation, 62
  of their hearts and minds, 138
  of thought, 66, 72, 77, 94, 97, 115, 116, 118, 120, 121, 138, 140

rejoice, 43, 44, 45, 48, 50, 51, 54, 79, 80, 85, 97, 101, 102, 103, 134, 135, 142, 144
relationship
  between Paul and his readers, 1, 23, 29, 31, 32, 36, 48, 79, 83, 84, 85
  between the church and the ministers, 1
  between the readers and the saints, 152
  between the Triune God and the readers, 65
  between Timothy and the Philippian church, 90
  with Christ (Jesus), 46, 49, 100, 113, 115, 117, 118, 135, 139, 149, 150, 153
  with God, 17, 27, 32, 33, 37, 38, 39, 40, 70, 72, 81, 82, 105, 111, 112, 114, 124, 128, 129, 133, 138, 139, 144, 149,
  with Paul, 39, 57, 83, 84, 93, 143
resurrection
  believers', 119, 120, 124, 126, 127, 136
  Paul's, 117, 118, 126, 127
  Jesus's, 17, 39, 53, 75, 76, 77, 108, 111, 112, 114, 115, 117, 126, 128
righteousness, 31, 37, 38, 51, 108, 111, 113, 114
Roman colony, 5, 59
Rome, 2, 3, 4, 5, 6, 8, 17, 26, 36, 37, 46, 53, 59, 62, 63, 93, 94, 116, 132, 136, 153

salvation
  completion of, 82
  end of, 82, 85
  entered into, 82
  final stage (phases) of, 124, 127
  future consummation of, 76, 122
  new covenant, 112, 115, 117, 122
  participation in, 63, 81, 107, 127

  plan of, 73, 74, 75, 77, 81, 82, 126, 127
  process, 34, 51, 52, 62, 63, 65, 70, 72, 74, 76, 81, 82, 83, 84, 85, 86, 89, 91, 95, 102, 104, 106, 107, 112, 115, 118, 121, 122, 126, 127, 150
self-sufficiency, 143, 145
semantic domain, 11, 41, 67, 120
sentence, conditional, 63, 64, 66, 79, 84, 85, 120
sequentiality, 9
servant, 24, 26, 71, 73, 74, 90
spiritual warfare, 59, 61
stative aspect, 35
subjunctive, hortative, 99, 100, 119, 120, 121, 141

textual information, 8, 9, 11
thanksgiving
  and prayer, v, 17, 23, 30, 31, 32, 33, 42, 57, 142, 152
  for the gift, 13
Thessalonica, 6, 24, 146, 148
thinking, way of, 67, 69, 70, 71, 77, 80, 108, 119, 120, 121, 124, 127
Timothy, vi, 3, 15, 16, 18, 23, 24, 26, 27, 56, 57, 87, 88, 89, 90, 91, 92, 94, 95, 96, 98, 101, 122, 123, 130, 132, 140, 141, 151, 152, 157
Triune God, 65, 67, 117, 126, 127, 128, 136

unity, of the church, 1, 19, 64, 74, 81, 85, 95, 99, 131

verbal aspect, 11, 14, 156
vocative, 132

world, 1, 6, 15, 16, 17, 27, 28, 37, 41, 59, 60, 61, 62, 63, 72, 73, 75, 76, 77, 78, 79, 82, 83, 84, 85, 86, 124, 125, 129, 135, 136, 139, 145, 149

SCRIPTURE INDEX

OLD TESTAMENT/HEBREW BIBLE

GENESIS
1:28	126
3	72, 76
17:13–14	105
18:25	38

EXODUS
19:5–6	27
19:6	27, 83
32:32	134

LEVITICUS
11:44	27
19:2	27
23:18	84

DEUTERONOMY
6:25	27, 38, 111, 113
21:22–23	73, 110
32:4	38

1 KINGS
8:38	137
8:54	137

JOBS
13:13	33
3:16	51

PSALMS
6:6	33
9:8	113
25:10	113
33:5	38
50:6	113
62:7	33
68:29	134
96:13	113
102:1	137
110:4	33
110:19	113
143:1	137

PROVERBS
15:26	139

ISAIAH
23:16	33

JEREMIAH
31:31–34	106
31:34	114

EZEKIEL
20:11	111
21:37	33
25:10	33

(Ezekiel continued)

36:27	106
37:24–28	112
37:24–26	106

DANIEL

9:3	137
12:1	134

HOSEA

2:19	38
9:4	84

MICAH

5:2	110

ZECHARIAH

13:2	33

NEW TESTAMENT

MATTHEW

5:10–12	36
6:9–10	126
6:24	124
11:12	71
22:37–40	27, 39
25:14–30	117

MARK

1:15	76
3:27	76
7:20–23	124

LUKE

10:20	134
17:32	33

JOHN

5:24	59
6:15	71
6:34	126
7:41–42	110
15:20	33
16:4	33
16:21	33
17:5	75

ACTS

8:1–3	110
8:39	71
9:1–9	112
9:1–2	110
9:15–17	116
15:35	33
16:11–40	90
16:12	59
16:13	5
16:19–23	59
16:19	132
17:2	28
18:5	6, 37, 90, 146
19:12–17	2
19:22	90
19:23–41	3
20:1–2	6
20:6	6
21:28	116
22:3	110
23:11	3
23:31–26:32	2
25:21	3
26:16–18	116
28:16	133
28:30–31	2

ROMANS

1:3	106
1:4	126

SCRIPTURE INDEX

1:8	30, 31
1:9	33
1:16—8:39	156
1:28	112
3:20	114
3:24	106
5:12	115
7:7	114
8:11	126
8:15–16	106
12:1	101
15:17–19	116
15:26	6, 37

1 CORINTHIANS

1:2	28, 81
1:4	30, 33
1:5	31
1:10	101
1:12	6
9:24	116, 117
11:25	106
13:12	53, 117
15:38	126
15:45	126

2 CORINTHIANS

1:1	28
3:18	126
8:1–2	37
9:2	6
10–13	105
10:1	101
11:8–9	146
11:9	6, 37, 90
11:27	145, 150
13:11	13, 97, 102

GALATIANS

1:1-2:10	157
3:10–11	114
6:16	106

EPHESIANS

1:4–6	77
1:5	126
1:6	139
1:10	126
1:12	139
1:14	139
4:1	101

PHILIPPIANS

1:1—2:18	3, 6, 14, 68, 156
1:1–2	v, 17, 23, 30, 57
1:1	2, 17, 24, 59, 66, 74, 83, 90, 133
1:2	17, 24, 29, 96
1:3–11	v, 15, 17, 23, 30, 31, 42, 43, 57, 142
1:3–8	17, 23, 30, 31, 32, 42
1:3–7	133
1:3–5	150
1:3–4	17
1:3	30, 31, 32, 33, 142
1:4–11	31, 136
1:4–7	17
1:4	31, 32, 33, 48, 135
1:5–8	17, 31, 32
1:5–7	25, 66
1:5–6	32, 34, 35
1:5	6, 31, 32, 33, 34, 35, 121, 147, 150
1:6	31, 32, 34, 35, 39, 46, 84, 136
1:7–8	31, 32
1:7	2, 8, 31, 32, 36, 46, 47, 52, 95, 120, 122, 142, 146
1:7a	35
1:7b-8	35
1:7b	35, 36, 37
1:8	25, 30, 31, 32, 36, 65, 66, 93, 150
1:9–11	15, 17, 23, 30, 31, 32, 37, 42, 66, 94, 97, 99, 112, 117, 118, 136, 140, 149
1:9–10	28
1:9	30, 31
1:9a	32
1:9b–10a	32
1:10b–11	32
1:10	31, 38, 39, 41, 48, 60

(Philippians continued)

1:11	30, 31, 42
1:12—4:20	v, 18, 30, 42, 56, 87, 96, 130, 141, 151
1:12-26	v, 8, 14, 18, 25, 30, 40, 42, 43, 56, 57, 87, 89, 96, 97, 98, 112, 130, 140, 141, 151
1:12-18a	v, 18, 43, 44, 49, 50, 55
1:12-14	2, 18, 43, 44, 45, 46, 47, 84
1:12	25, 42, 43, 44, 45, 128, 142
1:13-14	44, 46
1:13	4, 8, 44, 45
1:14-17	48
1:14	8, 36, 43, 44, 45, 46, 47
1:15-17	18, 44, 45, 47, 48, 132
1:15	43, 45, 47
1:16-17	45
1:16	43, 45, 47, 95, 146
1:17	2, 8, 41, 43, 45, 47, 48
1:18	43, 47, 97, 102, 135, 142, 143
1:18a	18, 43, 44, 45, 48, 51, 52
1:18b-26	v, 3, 18, 43, 49
1:18b-20	18, 49, 50, 52
1:18b	43, 48, 49, 50
1:19-20	49, 50, 53
1:19	43, 49, 51
1:20	8, 43, 52
1:21-24	18, 49, 50, 51, 53
1:21-22a	50, 53
1:21	49, 50, 112
1:22	43, 49
1:22a	49, 50, 53
1:22b	49, 50, 53
1:23-24	50
1:23	49, 50, 53
1:24	43, 49, 50, 53
1:25-26	18, 49, 50, 52, 54, 60
1:25	4, 43, 48, 50, 91, 135
1:26	43, 51
1:27—4:9	141, 142
1:27—4:1	149
1:27—2:18	v, 15, 17, 18, 42, 56, 87, 89, 96, 98, 130, 141, 151
1:27—2:17	103
1:27—2:4	112
1:27-30	v, 6, 18, 26, 27, 36, 40, 57, 63, 64, 84, 85, 93, 95, 99, 123, 136, 153
1:27-28	13
1:27	8, 14, 43, 56, 57, 60, 64, 78, 85, 97, 99, 125, 127, 133, 135, 142
1:27a	18, 57, 58, 59
1:27b-30	18, 57
1:27b-28a	57, 60
1:27b	58
1:27c	58
1:27d-28a	58
1:28-30	127
1:28-29	46
1:28b-30	57, 62
1:28b	57, 58, 62
1:29	36, 58, 62, 146
1:30	6, 26, 58, 62, 84, 98
2:1-12	6
2:1-4	v, 18, 40, 41, 57, 61, 63, 64, 68, 69, 70, 71, 74, 78, 80, 82, 85, 95, 99, 132, 153
2:1-2	18, 64
2:1	1, 64, 65, 67
2:2-3	74
2:2	48, 57, 63, 64, 68, 72, 74, 102, 120, 131, 135
2:2a	66
2:2b	66, 67
2:3-4	18, 64, 67, 80
2:3	48, 63, 64, 67, 68, 74
2:4	64, 67
2:5-11	v, 18, 40, 57, 68, 69, 77, 85, 132, 140
2:5	18, 57, 68, 69, 70, 78, 80, 120
2:6-11	1, 16, 18, 68, 69, 78, 81, 98, 99
2:6-8	68, 75, 123
2:6	68, 69, 70, 71, 73, 74, 75, 80
2:7-8	68, 69, 73, 74, 80
2:7	26, 69, 71, 73, 90, 106
2:7a	73
2:7b-8	73
2:7b	73, 74
2:8-11	114
2:8	8, 69, 73, 75, 82, 95, 106

SCRIPTURE INDEX

2:9–11	68, 69, 75, 77, 81, 126	2:30	92, 95
2:9	69, 75	3:1—4:19	99
2:10–11	69, 75, 76, 136	3:1—4:1	vi, 6, 15, 19, 87, 96, 98, 99, 100, 130, 141, 151
2:10	75	3:1–21	98, 99
2:11	75, 78	3:1–17	28
2:12–18	v, 18, 57, 69, 78, 79	3:1–14	122
2:12–13	18, 40, 78, 79, 80, 82, 86, 99	3:1–4	91
2:12	25, 57, 78, 79, 80, 81, 95, 104	3:1–3	vi, 19, 100, 101, 106
2:13	79, 82	3:1	13, 14, 19, 25, 48, 97, 99, 100, 101, 103, 104, 127, 128, 135, 142, 143
2:14–16	18, 78, 79, 82, 84, 85, 99	3:1a	102, 103
2:14–15	6, 136	3:1b	102, 103, 104
2:14	79, 82	3:2–3	19, 96, 101, 104
2:15–17	140	3:2	98, 101, 104, 109, 119
2:15	41	3:3	97, 101, 105, 107, 109
2:15a	79, 83	3:4–14	vi, 19, 100, 106, 107, 118, 120
2:15b-16	79, 83	3:4–6	19, 100, 107, 108, 109, 118
2:16	83, 84, 116	3:4	106, 108
2:17–18	18, 79, 80, 84, 85, 135, 142	3:4a	109
2:17	3, 48, 80, 84, 85, 97, 102, 103, 135	3:4b	109
2:18	48, 57, 79, 80, 85, 87, 97, 102, 103, 104, 135	3:5–14	25
2:19—4:23	102, 156	3:5–6	97, 108, 109
2:19–30	vi, 15, 18, 56, 87, 95, 96, 101, 130, 141, 151	3:5	97
2:19–24	vi, 16, 18, 26, 87, 88, 92, 140, 152	3:6	113
2:19	3, 18, 57, 87, 88, 89, 91, 94	3:7–14	100
2:20–22	18, 88, 89	3:7–11	19, 107, 108, 115, 120
2:20	88, 89, 90	3:7–9	118
2:21	88, 90, 91	3:7–8	97
2:22	88, 90	3:7	100, 108, 111, 113
2:23–24	18, 88, 91	3:8–11	113
2:23	3, 88, 89, 94	3:8	100, 114
2:24	3, 4, 88	3:8a-b	108, 113
2:25–30	vi, 3, 16, 18, 87, 91, 140, 142, 152	3:8a	108
2:25–28	18, 91, 92	3:8b	108
2:25-26	3	3:8c-11	108, 113
2:25	15, 25, 91, 92, 93, 94, 128	3:8c	108
2:26-27	92, 93	3:8d	108
2:26	93	3:9	97, 100, 107, 113
2:27	93	3:9a	108
2:28	48, 91, 92, 94, 97, 102, 135	3:9b	108
2:29–30	19, 92, 93, 95	3:10–11	108, 114, 115, 117, 118, 140
2:29	48, 92, 95, 98, 135, 141	3:10	123, 127
		3:12–14	19, 107, 109, 115, 118
		3:12	97, 100, 109, 115, 116, 124, 144

(Philippians continued)

3:13–14	109, 116
3:13	25, 100, 115, 128
3:13a	109, 116
3:13b-14	109, 116
3:13b	116
3:14	101, 107, 117
3:15—4:1	vi, 19, 100, 118, 119
3:15–21	96
3:15–17	98
3:15–16	19, 41, 100, 119, 120
3:15	96, 97, 119, 120, 121, 141
3:15a	119, 120
3:15b	1119
3:16	96, 97, 119, 120, 121, 141
3:17–21	19, 99, 119, 120
3:17	16, 25, 26, 84, 91, 96, 97, 100, 101, 118, 119, 120, 122, 123, 124, 125, 128, 140
3:18–19	28, 119, 120, 123, 125
3:18	91, 123, 125
3:19	124
3:20–21	6, 17, 53, 117, 119, 120, 124, 136
3:20	59, 96, 97, 134
3:20a	125
3:20b	125
3:21	96, 99, 100, 119, 125, 126, 136
4:1	19, 25, 48, 99, 100, 101, 119, 120, 127, 128, 135, 142
4:2–9	vi, 19, 96, 99, 130, 131, 141, 151
4:2–3	vi, 15, 19, 29, 40, 41, 48, 61, 65, 66, 99, 100, 131, 142
4:2	6, 19, 100, 101, 131, 134
4:3–9	130
4:3	6, 19, 99, 100, 130, 131, 132, 134
4:4–9	vi, 19, 131, 134, 135, 142
4:4–5	99
4:4	19, 48, 97, 134, 135, 142, 143
4:5	6, 19, 135
4:6–7	19, 134, 135, 136
4:6	136
4:7	138, 140
4:8–9	16, 19, 28, 41, 99, 134, 139, 140
4:8	13, 14, 25, 97, 129, 139
4:9	26, 99, 130, 135, 139, 140
4:10–20	vi, 13, 15, 19, 28, 130, 141, 142, 149, 150, 151
4:10–13	vi, 19, 142, 143
4:10	19, 48, 97, 130, 135, 142, 143, 144, 146
4:11–13	19, 142, 143, 144
4:11–12	143, 145
4:11	148
4:11a	144
4:11b-13	144
4:11b	144, 145
4:12–13	144, 145
4:12	145
4:12a-b	144, 145
4:12c	145
4:13	143, 145
4:14–18	vi, 19, 142, 143, 146
4:14–16	19, 142, 143, 146, 148
4:14	141, 146, 147, 148
4:15–16	25, 37, 66, 146
4:15	6, 142, 146, 147
4:16	6, 146, 147, 148
4:17–18	19, 143, 148
4:17	143, 148
4:18	6, 38, 66, 143, 148
4:19–20	vi, 19, 143, 149
4:19	99, 142, 143, 149
4:20	97, 99, 143, 149
4:21–23	vi, 19, 141, 142, 151
4:21–22	vi, 19, 151, 152
4:21	152
4:21a	152
4:21b-22	152
4:21b	152
4:22	4, 152
4:23	vi, 19, 151, 152, 13

COLOSSIANS

1:3	30
1:13	59
2:15	76
4:18	33

1 THESSALONIANS

1:2	30, 33
1:3	33
2:7	25
3:6	33
4:1	14, 97, 102
5:12–13	28

2 THESSALONIANS

1:3	30, 31
3:1	14, 97, 102
3:9	25

1 TIMOTHY

2:1	101, 137
3:2	28
3:8	139
3:11	139

2 TIMOTHY

4:6	84

TITUS

1:7	28
3:2	139

PHILEMON

4	30, 33
8–9	25

HEBREWS

12:23	134
13:7	33

1 PETER

2:9–10	83
2:9	27, 139

2 PETER

1:3	139
1:5	139

REVELATION

3:5	134
13:8	134
17:8	134
20:12	134
20:15	134
21:7	127
21:27	134

www.ingramcontent.com/pod-product-compliance
Lightning Source LLC
Chambersburg PA
CBHW050812160426
43192CB00010B/1727